Samuel Rawson Gardiner

Notes of the Debates in the House of Lords

Samuel Rawson Gardiner

Notes of the Debates in the House of Lords

ISBN/EAN: 9783337153700

Printed in Europe, USA, Canada, Australia, Japan

Cover: Foto ©ninafisch / pixelio.de

More available books at **www.hansebooks.com**

NOTES

OF THE

DEBATES IN THE HOUSE OF LORDS,

OFFICIALLY TAKEN BY

HENRY ELSING, CLERK OF THE PARLIAMENTS,

A.D. 1624 AND 1626.

EDITED,

FROM THE ORIGINAL MS. IN THE POSSESSION OF E. G. CAREW, ESQ.,

BY

SAMUEL RAWSON GARDINER.

PRINTED FOR THE CAMDEN SOCIETY.

M.DCCC.LXXIX.

PREFACE.

AFTER a long delay I am at last able to place in the hands of Members of the Society another volume of Lords' Debates from the Crowcombe Court MSS. It contains the notes of the last Parliament of James I. and of the second Parliament of Charles I. Those of the first Parliament of Charles are not preserved at Crowcombe Court, and may possibly have gone astray in the hurry of removal from Oxford. At any rate it is not likely that anything of importance took place in the Lords in that Parliament, and we may therefore put up with the loss without much repining.

What we have for 1624 gives us the Debates on the war projects of Buckingham, on the Monopoly Bill, and the impeachment of Middlesex. In 1626 we have the affair of Arundel's imprisonment, the limitation of proxies, the impeachment of Buckingham, and the charges against Bristol.

There still remains the book relating to 1628, undoubtedly the most interesting of all, as it contains the debates on the Petition of Right.

Of the official persons mentioned in this volume, the Lord Keeper was Bishop Williams in 1624, and Sir T. Coventry in 1626 ; the Lord Treasurer was the Earl of Middlesex in 1624, and the Earl of Marlborough in 1626. The President of the Council was Viscount Mandeville in 1624, who became Earl of Manchester before 1626. The Earl Marshal was the Earl of Arundel, the Lord Chamberlain the Earl of Pembroke, in both years, and the Lord Steward the first Marquis of Hamilton in 1624, and the Earl of Worcester in 1626, the latter being Lord Privy Seal in both years.

ERRATUM.

At p. 194, line 11, *for* " tare" *read* " taxe."

LORDS' DEBATES IN 1624 AND 1626.

[Parliament met on Feb. 16, and was prorogued to Feb. 19, when the King's Speech was delivered. The Speaker of the House of Commons was presented on the 21st.]

MONDAYE, 23 FEBR. 1623.

[Call of the House.—L. J. iii. 214.]

PRYNCE moved for a Conference with the Commons about the buissines, &c. Message for a Conference.

ADMYRALL. Hathe rec[eived] advertisement from Spayne that greate shipping are prepared in Spayne, with advyse to look well to the coastes.

HAUGHTON. A Comittee to viewe the Journall booke and to peruse the orders before they be presented to the House.

[Message to the Commons for a conference that they may hear Buckingham's narrative.—L. J. iii. 215.]

HAUGHTON. That the message be wrytten.

SOUTH[AMPTON]. Yea, yf the Judges mistrust their meaninges.

The Judges and Sergeants going retourned: yett went with the verball message.

*   *   *   *   *

24 FEBR. 1623.

[L. J. iii. 216.]

B

MERCURII, 25ᵗᵒ FEBRUARII, 1623.

[L. J. iii. 217.]

JOVIS, 26 FEBR. 1623.

[L. J. iii. 218.]

B[ishop of] Worcester excused.   L. Steward excused.
Hospitalls ereccion.

RUSSELL.   That noe proviso for those Hospitalls which have
ben erected synce the 20ᵗʰ yeare of Eliz. and before this acte, which
is six yeares space.

Mr. Justice Winche and Mr. Justice Chamberleyne presently
perused the bill being shorte and Mr. Sergeaunt Davis perused the
same.   Creewe and Fynche: the defecte apparent.

L. KEEPER.   A newe to be drawen, or to expecte a byll from
the Comons.   This to sleepe notwithstandinge yt past yesterday.

Agreed.   CHAMBERLEYNE.   A newe to be drawen.

Hodie 2ᵈⁿ *vice lecta billa* for continuance of Hospitalls.

BATHE AND WELLS moved for landes gyven for reparacion of
churches.

Agreed.   The Comittee to take notice of yt.

TREASURER.   That landes heretofore gyven to supersticious uses.

*   *   *   *   *

DIE VENERIS, 27 FEBR. 1623.

[Report by the Lord Keeper of Buckingham's narrative.—L. J. iii. 220.]

PEMBROKE.   Noe aspersion is layd on the K[ing] of Spaynes
person; justefyed B[uckingham] in delyvery of all.   That ᵃ he
ought to have concealed any thinge.

ᵃ i.e. Denies that he ought.

CANTERBURY. Thankes to God for cleering of theis mistes, thankes to the Prynce for the discovery, with prayers. Obligacion to B[uckingham] his paynes and hazarde to bryng theis thinges to light. God will blesse the K[ing and] P[rince], and shewe favour to the D[uke] of B[uckingham] whoe is soe threatned, etc.

PRESIDENT. We all to be suiters to the K[ing] to avowe the D[uke] of B[uckingham's] accion, and to————

WARWICK. The Lower House to knowe this; not doubteing but they wyll allso joyne with us.

SAY. A Comittee.

STEWARDE. The Commons to be acquaynted with it: bothe Houses to satesfye ᵃ the King.

SOUTHAMPTON. B[uckingham] had deserved very yll yf he had shortened his narracion, his justifecacion to be full —— by question.

Question. Whether, &c. that the D[uke] (of) B[uckingham] hathe expressed any[thing] in this relacion that was unfytting for him to doe; and, yf he hath, whether that dothe not taxe the wholl House.

Such as are of opynion that he hathe not, etc. and that yf he had yt toucheth the honour of the wholl House, saye content, they which are of another opynion saye not content. All agreed.

DURESME. And all ᵇ that he hathe deserved thanks of us.

WALLING[FORD]. Not only thanks but only to consider whence yt came, and to requyre of the Spanish Embassador howe he came to the noatice of yt.

PR[INCE]. We shall loose our labour.

B[UCKINGHAM]. I desyre only my justificacion and approbacion, noo revenge: [er]go, desyred not this,

MESSAGE.

WENTWORTH. That yt be in wrightinge. Co-comittee to be named to penn yt.

ᵃ M.S. "the satesfye the the," with a penstroke through all.

ᵇ i.e. are agreed that.

PRYNCE. By poll, for losse of tyme.

THE MESSAGE.

Whereas the D[uke] of B[uckingham] hathe ben aspersed in some informacion to his Majeste for [having] uttered something in his last² to bothe House[s] which touched the K. of Spayne in his [honour] which he coulde not satisfye but with his hed, this House grewe very sensible therof, and with an unan[imous] vote of the House hathe cleered the Duke's honour, and thoughte fytt by a selecte Comittee to the king, not only to signifye that they clere him, etc. Themselves touched yf they had suffred, ete. Thankes to the D[uke] for——

Q[uære] si to the K[ing].

And that the Lords have determyned by a Comittee of the wholl House to gyve his Ma[jes]t[y] satisfaccion herin: that they may hould good correspondeinge with them they have signifyed thus much unto them.

A Comittee of the wholl house to yntimate this to the Kinge.

The Pr[ince] intreated to intymate unto them his Ma[jes]t[y's] pleasure when the House shall attende him. The L. Keeper to delyver the Message to the King:

BUCK[INGHAM]. What you wyll resolve uppon this narrative for ordering the buissines.

PEMBROKE. To debate this amongest ourselves firste, before we meete any more with the Commons.

PR[INCE]. This afternoone at 3, the wholl house syttinge.

Agreed. The House may be adjourned befor the Messenger retourned.

Q. Whether the house to be adjourned firste or noe?

Adjournatur to 3 *post m[eridiem].*

---

² " In his last" are inserted in the MS. underneath the word "something," and may be meant to come in where I have put them, as they do not seem to fit anywhere else.

27 FEBR. 1623, POST MER.

[Answer from the House of Commons.—L. J. iii. 234.]

LORD KEEPER. To consider what you are mett about, and what you wyll propose unto yourselfes to doe.

THE L. PRESIDENT. First to state the question. Herd a true narracion. Putt to a streicte yssue upon a letter from Spayne 5to Jan. There is the aunswere to 3 proposicions. Uppon that aunswere our resolucion. Whether to advyse the King to proceede in the matche and to expecte the Palat[inate]?

MR. ATTOURNEY reade that letter agayne, accomodatinge the buissines of the Pal[atinate] 3 poyntes:

1. Good offices to the Emperor for the same.
2. A tyme lymited.
3. Yf not, to ymploy his Armes against the Emperor.

1. Promisseth the first, the Prince Palatine perfourminge the due submission, etc.

2. Content that a tyme be lymited, to agree with the Arch-duches or his Embassadors, etc.

3. Yf the mediacion take not effecte, then to ymploy his armes against the Emperour. This wyll bereave him of the power of a mediatour. Wyll gyve offence to the Emperour, but you may be confident that I wyll contynewe, etc. without drawinge my hande from yt untill your Majestes desyre be accomplished.

BUCKINGHAM. He hathe a letter from the Embassador that Spayne promissed to assiste the King against the Emperour.

19 Aug 1622. Digby to the Secretary.

19 Aug. a°. eod^m. To the Kinge. Digby.

Dec. 1622. Another letter to the Kinge. Digby.

21 Oct. 1622. Digby.

Sir Walter Ashton acquaynted with nothinge, and Digby lefte him thes instruccions (going to negociate ellswhere) to make none but generall answeres.

CANT[ERBURY]. Custome of this House to be scrupulous to

Prynce, before I came thither D[igby] and Sr W. Ashton assenred him uppon——

entor into matters of greate importance untill a proposicion be firste made to leade them therinto. Remembered the Kinges speech to be advysed by his people, etc. This buissines concernes a greate kinge that is yett in amyty with our K. Therefore that we speake nothing that may be dishonourable to that greate prynce, but to confyne them to the officers; the King is young, all is handled by the Ministers, and them only I wyll touche. Propounded, a simile of the Elephant his strengthe against horse and shott of muskett. Yf the Rinoceros creepe but under his belly he teares him and kylls him. A serpent kylled by one in the heade, endure many other. The hedd of this buissines:—Whether the K shall receave an humble advyse from us to contynewe or dis-contynewe the treaty of maryage. This is the chiefest. The Palatinate wyll followe as allso the transgressions if any of the King's ministers of State there. Whether the King shall breake of this treaty of maryage or not. We have ben deceaved.

Q. Whether sufficiently, or shall we be more deceived?

To judge of things to come by that which is past.

1. Q. Whether in the tyme of the former ministers of Spayne a maryage was not propounded betwene the elder daughter of Spayne and Prynce Henry, and continewed long and putt of with a demande of alteracion of religion.

2. Q. Whether the Spanish King with the ministers of the kingdome gave not commission to his Embassador to proceede in that matche. He protested he had, and that was afterwards dis-avowed by his m[aste]r (of Spayne).

Pr[ynce]. The treaty of this maryage was before the treaty of the Palatinate. Yett he entreates the Lordes to advyse of the Palatinate firste, and soe the King propounded yt. Consider in what way to proceede with the Commons.

Pembr[oke]. Not to advyse the King before conference with the Commons. But we to advyse therof first amongste ourselves, what to say to the Commons at the conference. The Question is touching the last conference for the Palatinate, but this must be joyned with the consideracion of their former proceeding even from the Cha[ncellor's][a] negociacion at Bruxells.

L. KEEPER. The King himselfe hathe stated the q[uestion] as the Prynce delivered yt, viz. the Palatinate firste, the rest as they are incident.

Adjournatur ad libitum.

CO[VENTRY] AND LICH[FIELD]. To collecte all the disappoyntements which the King hathe received in thes treatyes.

PRESIDENT. Touching the Palatinate, observed what was promised before the King's[b] coming, what they undertooke to perfourme and omytted.

WALLINGFORD. The Palatinate firste. Look into the former proceedings not knowen to the house. Commissions have been to the Emperour. D[igby] going thither, the Emperor answered soe that D[igby] hyred Mansfield to come downe thither with an army.

STEWARDE. A resolucion with the Commons. The Palatinate firste. The match desyred bycause she a greate Prync[e]s, but chiefly for a restitucion thereby of the Palatinate.

Q. Whether the match, or disadvantages taken in the meane tyme by the enemy. Delucions many. Advyse the King to leave this, and to take some other way to recover the Palatinate which yf yt be not, this kingdome wyll ever suffer in honor.

PEMB[ROKE]. *Idem* with Wallingford. Whylest Mansfield stayed there all proceeded well; but he retyred uppon the King of Spayne's earnest letters etc. not to contynewe the treaty, whereof soe badd effectes have followed.

PR[YNCE]. Spayne is a cloudy countrey; Germany clere, for D[igby] coulde see there; but not with spectacles in Spayne.

L. KEEPER. The restitucion of the Palatinate most propper for our resolucion either by treaty or armes, by treaty with the Emperour, but that is not probable—with the King of Spayne either for amity or alliaunce: the alliaunce not probable, for Siressa[c] sayeth the King of Spayne hathe sett asyde all treatye of the

---

[a] Weston, Chancellor of the Exchequer.   [b] ? The Prince's.   [c] Ciriza.

matche. Amitye, the former promisses effectuall. The laste gyves noe assurance; a promise only requyred by the King to assiste the recovery with armes; yf denyed absolutely not to take of his hand, &c. his agents expounde yt by a promisse of further treatye, only he knowes not how otherwyse to advyse the King then not to trust to any thing but himselfe for the restitucion of the Palatinate.

Pr[ynce]. 3 points the King not satisfyed with

1. The honour of the Pal[atine].   2. The breeding at the Emperours Courte.   3. Noe promisse to assiste in armes. The King requyred D[ghy] to satisfye him in thes 3 points &c.

Brook. The Treaty in 2 branches the maryage and the Palat[inate] joyned, nowe to the Palat[inate].

Pr[ynce]. The Palatinate first, not only—

Brook. To the Palat[inate]. What yt hathe suffered by ytselfe. Lett fall our armyes, discouraged the parties, forced[a] lost many importunitye[b] and shall yf wee doe not take heed loose thys sprynge. The first proposicion: tolleracion, Pope's supremacy. 2 proposicion: the educacion of the Kinges grandchillde, yt is not a treaty betwecn England and Spayne only, but many others, and wyll take up much tyme. The Pope the Emp[crour] Catholique Pr[ynces], the treaty not safe by many reasons, especially for that the war is for religion, &c.

Duresme. Concurres with the rest, we shalbe delyed and abused by a treaty. Nowe the Palat[inate] must leade the maryage. This toucheth the Catholique League, their prynted bookes avowe the cath[olics] to be ingaged in this buissiness: never aunswered whether the King's army myght have leave to passe thoroughe his countrey. Hartes and meanes in Englande to goe to the Palatinate whether the King of Spayne wyll or noe.

London. Wyll spende himselfe to the uttmost fartheing all his estate and God had blessed him &c. had he his feete as a harte he woulde be in the hedd of the troupe. The Spa[nish] Embas-

---

ᵃ Blank in MS.   ᵇ Sic.

sadour in daunger. To send unto him peremptorily of yt, and yf he wyll he shall have a garde.

SAYE. The advyse from bothe Houses. A conference first, to be prepared in some particulers.

2. Whether you wyll lymitt yourselfes to this only, or the matche allso? And to come prepared and resolved in them bothe.

CAMB[RIDGE]. The Palat[inate] first. Whether by freindship with Spayne or by force? One of theis to be resolved of.

EP[ISCOP]US BRISTOL. To treate further is to loose tyme. Unworthy of this kingdome to receave assistaunce soe often, when they able to doe yt of themselves.

L. KEEPER. The lower house hathe taken tyme till Monday next, noe opynion nowe, the partes of the buissines only opened, the resolucion to be deferred till Monday.

PEMBR[OKE]. *E contrario*, not to come to them unprepared, lest they be jealous of us though without cause. Either we must gett the Palat[inate] by a treaty or by force; either advyse the maryage, or to breake of the matche.

SHEFFIELD. *Ad idem*, either to wynn the Pal[atinate] by the sworde or by treaty. Not by sending forces into the Palatinate, but by way of diversion.

PEMBR[OKE]. Resume the House and adjourne the House.

STEWARD. At our next either to advyse the K[ing] to proceed by waye of matche or by force.

SOUTH[AMP]TON. To leave yt nowe unresolved, to treate of the maryage and Palatinate together at our next meetinge.

PRESIDENT. Bothe together, the Palatinate firste, the Q. whether &c.

PR[YNCE]. The Question howe to regayne the Palatinate. To treate of both together.

The L. Keeper retourned.

* * * * *

DIE SABATHI, 28 FEBR. 1623.

[L. J. iii. 236.]

*   *   *   *   *

L. VISC^{r.} ROCHFORD. Whether to begynn where they left last nyght, or to other buissines?

Agreed. With the last nyght's buissines.

He to treate of the matche first, notwithstanding yt was otherwyse thought last nyght.

SHEFFIELDE. Bothe together.

SPENCER. They are twynns: fytt to gyve the K[ing] councell not to trust to any treaty and to drawe home his owne ministers. A president of H. 7 of longe treatyes. Called a parlement: delivered his owne opynion: they supplyde him: then he raysed an army of 25,000 men and 2,000 horse; went himselfe in person, and had his owne condicion[s]. Advyse the K[ing] to doe the lyke.

DURESM. Treatyes to be accompted as desperate thinges, and to be layde asleepe &c. in a negative supposicion. The Amonytes would have peace with Israell &c. but woulde pull out their right eye firste. They abuse the name and worde Catholique. Comended H. 7. The sworde &c. to drawe them to reasonable condicons.

CANTERBURY. Howe to fytt ourselves for a conference with the Commons, the Pal[atinate] and matche to goe together. Propounded:—Whether to advyse the Kinge to proceede noe further in the treatye, neither for the matche nor Palat[inate]?

Pr[YNCE] approves, but to consider next what you wyll doe after; for Spayne wyll loose noe tyme.

PEMBR[OKE]. The advyse is to come from bothe houses, not conclude yt without a conference firste: which was well allowed of by many.

c contra.   SAYE. They are twynns. The warrs. Differ from Pembroke, for fytt to come to a resolucion and passe by vote what we wyll delyver at the conference to the Commons.

CAMBR[IDGE]. Instruccions to be delivered to the Comittees that shall be appoynted to conferr, not to passe by vote first.

SHEFFIELD. Our voate only what we shall move them to doe.

BUCK[INGHAM]. To gyve our reasons at the conference, match and Palatinate to goe together. This bnissines of the match was propounded to make their owne endes. The matche and Palat[inate] bothe together. The buissines of the matche is the hedd of yt.

Adjournatur ad libitum.

L. KEEPER. The state of the question well putt by Buck[ing-ham].

Consultacion *non est finis sed &c.* The treatyes 2. of maryage and amity 1. restitution 2.

To be considered of and our advyse delivered joyntly to the K[ing] Q. *de modo.* Whether to delyver any vote before we meete with the Commons? Not to vote, but to agree at this Comittee here, but not to brynge with a leadinge opynion.

PEMBR[OKE]. This meaninge not to voate of the advyse to the King, but what shal be sayd to the Commons at the Conference. To cease the treaty drawes on the warr.

L. KEEPER. The House to make the proposicions first and then he wyll putt yt to the question. The Commons not to be drawen to the

COVENTRY AND LICHFIELD. This mocion presented as his fancye 1 where an ympossibillity of repose, a breache, thanks to God that he hathe gyven that judgment to his Highnes to discerne, to the D. of Buckingham to discover. The firste mover of the Palatinate and matche is the Pope; for the Palatinate is under the Catholique league. Catholique a worde of religion. Rome, Catho-lique Roman church, hereticall against the article of the Christian feithe published before any Romane churche. supply of a warr until they are ac-quaynted with yt, and, &c.

The Matche, the Pope the first mover. Ympossible to thinke that the Bishop of Rome wyll yielde to any good. Without the Pope impossible. Edictes and promisses not observed by the Em-perour in the case of J. Hus. because without consent of the Pope. Believes noe certeinty in treatyes. Concludes, rayse armes.

DURESME. To state the questions.

BATHE AND WELLS. Proposicions 3. 1. Amity. 2. Maryage.
3. Force.

ROCHEFORD. The Questions 2.

1. Whether to cease from further treaty for the matche and
Palatinate. 2. To a speedy resolucion to the warres.

SAY. The question.

SHEFFIELD. We have conceaved this, but have not resolved on
yt absolutly untill we knowe their opynions.

PEMBR[OKE]. 2 questions. 1. Whether to declare to the
Comons that we holde yt fytt to treate of theis 2 buissinesses bothe
together?

The House resumed.

2. Question. Whether of necessitye in this advyse of ours to the
K[ing] by his direccions we are to take into our consideracions of —

1. Whether in this conference the Lords intend to have with the
Comons touching the advyse you are to gyve to the K[ing] your
Lordshipes doo conceave there is a necessitye to treate of this
match and the Palat[inate] together?

Agreed *nemine dissentiente.*

2. Whether the Comittee that are to —— shall propounde unto
them, not as a resolucion, but as an opynion or inclinacion[a] of
theirs, to depende noe more uppon the treatyses.

Cambr[idge].   Havinge taken into our consideracion all the matters opened unto
us, we are opynion, with a reservacion to heare better reason, to
advyse the King to truste noe more to treatyses for the recovery of
the matche, or to treate of the maryage.

Yf we ——

2. Q. Whether the Lords that shalbe of the Comittee to confer
with the Commons shall delyver unto them that your Lordships are
of opinyon that His Majeste relye not uppon any further treatises,
except their Lordships shall heare from them better reasons at the
conference.

---

[a] " a proposicion " was originally written. The " a " has been changed to " au,"
but the writer forgot to draw his pen through " proposicion."

PEMBROKE. To consider what reasons we shall gyve to strengthen our opynion, and whoe shall delyver the same at the conference.

ARUNDELL. A comittee to serche into former presidents, howe the King hathe ben used in former tymes, &c.

*   *   *   *   *

DIE LUNE 1ᵐᵒ MARCH 1623.

[L. J. iii. 237.]

*   *   *   *   *

SAYE. Daunger in delaye. A message touching Buck[ingham]. Not well undertood by them &c. To lett them knowe that ye have not done this alone. Greate comend[acion] of Buck[ingham]. The misch[ief] of the Sp[anish] emb[assadour] greatest honour to him.

RUSSELL. An omyssion to the Commons. Message by Grymes of the staye conceyved of the Pr[ince] in Spayne; to be opened to the Comons.

BUCKINGHAM. 2 lettres allso omytted.

PR[YNCE]. The Comittee have prepared the matter committed to them. A message for a meetinge with them for conference.

PRESIDENT. The lettres there omytted to be sent unto them.

SOUTHAMPTON. The message touchinge Buck[ingham] firste. Then as the Pr[ince] moved.

Message sente by Sergeant Crewe.

Wheras their LL. sent a message to them for their cleeringe of B[uckingham], they doubte whether they understoode the meaninge of the Lords in this that the Lords sayd they woulde signifye the cleering and justifying.

SOUTHAMPTON. We think yt most propper that as the warr[ant] was d[clivere]d to both Houses, soo bothe Howses should signifye this to the King, yf they shall soc thynke fiytt.

BUCK[INGHAM]. They of the Comittee 28 Febr. doe fynde the Sp[aniards] ever ment to juggle with us. To take into your consideracion &c. Tyme is precious: cannot be recovered: losse of the sprynge.

1. Comittees to oversee the strength for municions, and to provyde, if any wante.

2. Whether as Admyrall to staye shippinge. Many of great burthen to the Easte Indyes, well furnished: they generally well allowed of the staye.

OXON. Addes for our safety at armes : the Papistes have prepared armes, &c. to disarme them.

CANTERBURY. To confyne them allso.

SHEFFIELD. Municion.

NORTHAMPTON. Can accompt of the papistes armes from tyme to tyme.

STEWARDE. To this after our advyse to the King.

SOUTHAMPTON. Survey of municion. Staye of shippinge agreed. Moved for survey of municion allso, wherof there is but one megazin, vizt. in the tower, all other places have but their proporcions. The L. Carewe Mr. of the Ordinances to gyve an accompt^a what store is there.

THE L. CAREWE promised to doe this tomorrowe.

BUCK[INGHAM]. A Comittee to be appoynted.

SHEFFIELDE. Many Magazins; shoulde by every Lieutennaunt of the Shire. That they may certifye howe they are furnished.

MARSHALL. That Comittees may peruse how theis Magazins are stoared and the fortes.

*   *   *   *

This Committee to viewe the Magazines stoares and the fortes.

---

^a The words "gyve an accompt" are an interlineation. The words "satisfye us" are left uncrased, a line being drawn under them instead of through them.

To consider of the weaknes of the lande either at home, or in Irelande ; and to present their opynions to the House.

RUSSELL.   To suppresse all licenses for transportacion of Ordinaunces.

STEWARDE.   Yf the invencion be founde abrode [?] yt wyll hynder the sale of ours, and the Enemy be provyded ellswher. The Comittee to consider of this, for that hath ben often moved at the Councell table and undecyded there.

Aunswere to the Message retourned by Mr. Sergeaunt Crewe Mr. Attorney.   Consideracion.   Thanks for your correspondency. This mourning wyll retourne aunswere by messengers of their owne. Message to the Commons for a conference of this greate buissiness to morrowe in the afternoone. yf they can, at Whitehall, by the Master of the Rolles and Lord Chief Baron.

This greate buissines, &c. advyse greate haste for exped[ition] &c.   Conference with the wholl house to morrowe at 2 in the P[ainted] Chamber ; and sooner, yf they conveniently can, for the weighte of the buissines is urgent and requyres haste.

The L. Keeper to reporte yt.

PR[YNCE].   Whoe shall open the buissines to the Commons ?

CANTERBURY.   To digest them firste into order.

STEWARDE.   Many to be named to open the buissines.

CHAMBERLEYN.   A reporte of this to be first.

Reporte by Buckingham.   They have gyven time to the Clerks of the papers for abstracts therof.

PR[YNCE].   In one of D[igby's] papers, a cosenage herefore. Cotton,[a] the firste ryse of this buissines ; Chancellor [b] cosenage allso, Bellfast,[c] the lyke.

STEWARD.   That all moved first from the Span[iarde].

---

[a] Sir R. Cotton, who acted as messenger between Somerset and the Spanish Ambassador.

[b] Sir R. Weston, Chancellor of the Exchequer, sent to Brussels in 1622.

[c] Lord Chichester of Belfast, sent to Germany in 1622.

MARSHALL.. The Comittee to acquaynte such as shall speake at the conference with their colleccions.

Agreed. BUCK[INGHAM]. Cotton to make his owne reporte to the Commons.

WARWICK. The Comittee to reporte the same firste here.

BUCK[INGHAM] reported the effecte of Cotton's speeche at the Comittee.

PRESIDENT. Yt is alledged first from hence. Jan. 1614. The first proposicion came from thence. A distribution of partes. Eache to be assigned what to alledge, and their allegations to be first knowen to the House.

Agreed. BUCK[INGHAM]
CANT[ERBURY] } to open the buissines to the
L. KEEPER Commons at their Conference.
SOUTHAMPTON

*   *   *   *   *

[A conference appointed with the Commons.]

At this conference with the Commons presently touchinge Buck-[ingham], Canterbury to open the clering of Buck[ingham] here. and this wholl house appoynted to satisfye the Kinge therof, when the Pr[ynce] hathe intimated his Maᵗˢ pleasure.

BANGOR. The dissarminge of the papistes to be presently executed. Millforde haven to be blocked upp. Commended.

MENEVEN[SIS]. *Ad idem pro* dissarming of papistes, and Millford haven.

*   *   *   *   *

MARTIS 2ᵈᵒ MARCII 1623.

[L. J. iii. 239.]

*   *   *   *   *

CANT[ERBURY]. The Conference this afternoone. To prepare the heddes therof against they meete the house to be a Committee.

L. Keeper removed.

SAYE. At this conference what the Comittee hathe observed. Adjourned. A colleccion of those allso which were omytted and not de- *ad* —— ? clared.

1. One, the resolucion by his hyghnes, yf he had ben restreyned: their intent to restreyne.

2. That Spayne dyd undertake to joyne with the King for the recovery of the Palat[inate] by armes, which is nowe soe much denyed.

PRESIDENT. Whoe shall make the induccion?

Named the L. Keeper.

CANT[ERBURY]. Whether the induccion out of some generallitye propounded by the K[eeper]. Then to fall in to the matter and relate what Sr. Robt. Cotton, &c.

KEEPER. The house to be acquainted what they knewe not of allready. A preparacion out of some generallityes, &c. he understands that the Commons have undertaken a resolucion to breake the treaties for alliance and the Palat[inate], and soe declare without any reasons. Whether we shall gyve any reasons?

PRESIDENT. Prepare the reasons: not to offer, that makes other men judges: we owe noe accompt but to the Kinge.

CANT[ERBURY]. The principall reasons not knowen to this House; the same to be reduced into hedd and related.

1. A former treaty sought by them frustrated.

Urged, 2. They dissavowed their Embassadour : resolute not unlesse a papist, yf soe resolute then ——.[a] And the same minister D[igby] sett this on foote agayne. To heare Sir Robt. Cotton relate his knowledge therof here.

SAY. This cannot be denyed, the Comittee ought to doe yt.

---

[a] Meaning, I suppose, that the former treaty for Prince Henry's marriage, which had been opened by the Spanish Ambassador, came to nothing. When it was pressed by Digby in 1611 it was broken off, and the Ambassador disavowed, on the ground that the marriage could not take place unless the Prince were converted. But, if they were so resolute then, how could they be less resolute at a later time?

Approved. PR[INCE]. Not against the mocion. Eyther herafter for a manifesto; a declar[ac]ion. For we grounde not our opynions uppon any thinge done heretofore, but only upon what hath happened synce my journey thither, &c.

[Letters read.—L. J. iii. 239.]

SOUTHAMPTON. What to doe nowe? What at the conference? The omission (*ut per* Say) to be such other lettres as reade here, and not with the Comons. To lett them knowe that uppon the relacion to bothe Houses. And what synce, &c. We are of opynion that the wholl proceeding hathe beene to delude. We fynd noe grounde by the last to think that herafter they wyll proceede with more integrytye. Therefor of opynion not to rely uppon any further treatises, &c. Yf the Lower house agree with us in their opynion, then a resolucion. Then not amysse that a Comittee of both Houses may conferr and sett downe reasons of this opynion. Yf his Majeste shoulde demande any, they may be ready to satisfye him. A course to be taken to delyver this to the King with all expedicion. The haste. Delay dangerous. To nyght, if possible : that impossible, but to morrowe or as soone as yt is possible.

SHEFFIELD. To add that the King cannot holde on this treaty any longer, neither with his honour nor safety of the state, nor relligion.

PR[INCE]. Yf Comittees of bothe Houses *pro ut per* Southampton, to name them nowe.

The House resumed.

A Comittee to conferr with the Commons, &c. to drawe up reasons to fortifye the opynion of the House touching this, &c. *ut per* South[amp]ton.

[Names of Committee.—L. J. iii.]

PEMBR[OKE]. Yf the Commons sende us anon, as I thynke they ought, then we to tell them of the Committee.

•   •   •   •   •

L. KEEPER. That he myght open the hedds of what he is to delyver to the Comons at their conference.

1. Induccion out of the narrative.

2. A further — —

3. Lettres.

We are of opynion, *super totam materiam prout* the King re- Added. quyred, that his Ma^t cannott proceede :   matche nor Palatinate, our opyt they do with the safety of his honour, relligion, and state, &c. curre w or not.

1. Add the heroicall aunswere of the Pr[ince] when

2. A promise made from Spayne in a lettre to Bristoll, and in a lettre from him to the King, that Spayne woulde assiste with armes.

3. The effecte of thes last lettres, viz. : that yt was propounded Agreed. firste by Lerma to D]igby].

CRUMWELL. D[igby], his harshe speeche to the Pr[ince] that his mocions were precipitate, and this was a chylde of his owne, and he woulde proceede.

CANT[ERBURY]. Buck[ingham] and South[amp]ton to gyve this only, that they advysing *super totam materiam*, and doe fynde, &c.

The Comittee named before to be yntimated by Cant[erbury].

*   *   *   *   •

MERCURII, 3 MARCII, 1623.

[L. J. iii. 243.]

*   *   •   *   •

DIE JOVIS, 4 MARCII, 1623.

[L. J. iii. 244.]

*   •   *   *   •

[Report of the Conference to the Archbishop of Canterbury.—L. J. iii.]

SOUTHAMPTON. What was moved is nowe growen to a resolucion of bothe Houses. This the King may appoynte to be delivered unto his Ma^t.

Moved. His Majeste wyll rec[eive] yt graciously, but consider of yt, and yt may be he wyll say, you knowe what depends uppon yt. Hoape of the Palatinate gon, the care^a rest to be recovered by warre. Your assistaunce in yt.

Moved. Yf such an occasion be offred, then those that delyver this advyse may have power to add, that yf this breakes of the treaty, &c. his Ma^t need not doubte but wee wylbe ready with our persons and our estates to be assistant, and with the uttmost of, &c.

SAY. Yf this be imbraced, then to acquaint the Comons with it.

PEMBROKE. *Ad idem*, that the Sub-committee may have authoritye to signifye soo much unto their sub-comittee.

[Message from the Commons answered, that the Lords have appointed a sub-committee to meet them.—L. J. iii. 245.]

Agreed.   MARSHALL. That the sub-comittee doe yntimate the mocion of South[amp]ton at the Conference.

*   *   *   *   *

DIE VENERIS, 5to MARCII, 1623.

[Report from the Conference, L. J. iii. 246.]

*   *   *   *   *

---

* The care of the rest.

DIE SABATHI, 6 MARCII, 1623.

[L. J. iii. 248.]

*   *   *   *   *

KEEPER. Yf to reade any bylls? Answered : noe.

MARSHALL. Whether to reade bylls, or adjourne the house?

NORTHAMPTON. To reade bylls.

Question. Whether you wylbe pleased to proceede in the readinge of bylls, or adjourne the House?

SAYE. Noe question.

Question. Whether your Lordshipps wyll proceed in hearinge of bills, or staye untill this greate matter be reported?

Such as wyll have bylls reade saye, content ; the others, not contente.

Content per pluries.

*   *   *   *   *

NORTHAMPTON. The Comittees of bothe Houses to meete, &c. Agreed. toucheinge the reporte.

MARSHALL. Not untill, &c. But the Comittees that went yesterday to the King to have power to conferr with those of the Commons, yf they shall soe desyre yt, about the reporte therof.

SAY. A message to the Comons, that the reporte is not yett made in this house. Yf they have not made reporte in their house, then (yf they please) the Comittees of bothe howses to meete, and agree what reporte to make.

SHEFFIELD. *Ad idem.* To-sende to the Commons, and not to expecte to heare from them.

[Message sent. Answer accepting the proposal.—L. J. iii. 249.]

*   *   *   *   *

DIE LUNÆ, 8 DIE MARCII, 1623.

*   *   *   *   *

[Report by the Archbishop of Canterbury of the King's reception of the address.— L. J. iii. 250.]

CANT[ERBURY]. The Tre[asure]r to knowe the K[ing]'s plea- sure, and then to let us knowe, &c.

TRE[ASURE]R. The K[ing] hathe named him to gyve him an accompt. But not ready at this instant. That which shalbe gyven to the K[ing] to be severed from that for the warres. Conferr with the Chan[cellor] of the Exchequer, and then be ready to performe this charge.

*   *   *   *   *

9 MARCII, 1623.

[L. J. iii. 252.]

*   *   *   *   *

Report. CANT[ERBURY]. Bill of Sonday; yt past bothe howses last parlement, firste mocion [?] with the Commons. *idem* ———? that past beforre fytt to passe.

MARSHALL. Double exercise of armes one of the instruccions to be used on Sondayes after dynner; to knowe of the Judges, &c.

SOUTHAMPTON. We were carefull not to hynder the bodylye exercyse of the country people after evening prayer, and Mr. Justice Chamberleyne that they myght, notwithstandinge this Acte.

CANTERBURY. None but unlawfull exercyses forbydden.

KEEPER. The exercyse of armes practised in Geneva, &c.

*   *   *   *   *

2da vice l[ec]ta the Erle of Oxon's Bill.
Comittee.

SUFFOLK. Against the Bill. Chauncellor of the Universitye : founder of Magdalen Colledg in Cambridge in his owne right and his auncestors. Yt past longe agoe from an unworthy Master of that House, and lytle profitt he feares to the E. of Oxon.

PRESYDENT. A byll of greate justice.

SOUTHAMPTON. None against the bill to be Committee.

KEEPER. In comendacions of the decree by Ellsmere in favour of the Colledge of his knowledge.

*   *   *   *   *

---

10 MARCH, 1623.

[L. J. iii. 254.]

*   *   *   *

L. KEEPER. Whether the fyne of £1,000 by him layde on Sir Fr. Inglefield shalbe raysed to the use of the Lady St. John ?

Sir Fra. Englefielde and the Lady St. John are to have notice to attende.

*   *   *   *   *

JOVIS, 11 MARCH, 1623.

[L. J. iii. 255.]

*   *   *   *   *

L. TRE[ASURE]R. Amongest the weighty poynts one charge to me to informe you truly of the K[ing]'s estate faithefully and plainly according to the King's commande.

The last ballance of the K[ing]'s estate was at Mich[aelmas]: the receiptes to more then the yssues by 32,000^{li}. Synce the yssues

more then the receipts. A greate debte. That nor the generallytye
not to trouble you at this tyme. Those receipts and payements
only received and yssued since Mich[aelmas] was 2 yeares, when
the buissines of the Palat[inate] first began :

	li.
Certificatte under Sir R. Pye and Sir Ed. W[ardour] .	145,675
Extraordinary ambassador's extra enterteynement here.	6,786
Shippes Algers	64,837
Shipps to Spayne	52,256
Money taken up by the Prynce . . .	46,668
Embassador from Spayne in guyfts . . .	16,138
Defense of the Palat[inate]	172,888
Householde expenses of the King and Queen of Bohemia	30,300
besydes entrest to Denmark	5,000
Denmark borrowed of him	80,000
Burlemachi and Jacobson . . .	18,319
Frankendale red° [?]	7,918
Postage of lres	14,826

661,670[a]

besydes expenses of powder
besydes entrest of 30,000[li] of Sir Bapt. Hicks Cockyn   •
    and P. Vandlore

Received synce that tyme all bye rentes	.	.	7,100
Impostes . . .	.	.	3,4 ..
2 Subsidyes . . .		.	22,021
			72,847 . 10
			158 . 2

Ymposte on wynes . . . . .
        hopps . . .

371,740
29,030

besydes powder and entrest.

<hr>

[a] The sum should be 661,611.

This is charged on the King's estate thus:

to Denmarke . . . . .

to Hicks . . . . .

Anticipated on the rent . . .

To B[urlamachi] and J[acobson]

To Frankendale . . . . .

The rest owing to dyvers noblemen, gentlemen, and others
This the rest sequestred from this present buissines.
Ympayringe of his Ma^ts Customes.
Noe certificate as yett, which he expected.

The trade into Spayne nowe amountes unto ———— not to me
to speake of the other heddes in the Kinges speeche, but they are
well prepared, as that for Irelande. The Navy, never soe greate by
4,000 tunns, never so good, never in such a redines, this imposicion
of 20^s uppon a tunne of wyne coming to ———— is allowed wholly
to the Kinges chilldren, but a probacion till this parlement. Yf yt
be taken awaye then somewhat, &c. For the mayne, yf you proceede, &c. you may perceave, &c. that yt is not impossible but
very fesible.

SPENCER. Howe this may be fesible?

PR[INCE]. The meening is that the King cannot without your
helpes; but yf, &c. then, &c.: but your supplye for the mayne to
have prioritye to this.

CANT[ERBURY]. The last Declaracion by a lettre soe terrible
that we knewe not which waye to turne ourselfes. Nowe fesible
and possible yf we putt to our helping handes.

SOUTHAMPTON. Comendes that of the Pr[ince]. Greate satisfaccion bothe here, and wylbe to the Comons. A stande long;
nowe to proceed. The mayne buissines, nowe we see that his Ma^ts
owne estate wyll beare his ————, howe to thinke that that which
is extra and desyred by bothe howses shalbe supported. Most
propper to be entred into by the comons yf we, &c. by experience

hurte.* To putt this into a course for expedicion. Yf some thinges were cleered which may be impediments in the House of Commons. Yf to leave yt wholly to them, yt wyll ask much tyme in debate. Q. Whether at this tyme your Lordshipps ———— that we doe somwhat to stirr upp them, &c. without offence, &c. and soe I desyre. Ours with theirs; but this is soe propper to them, &c. A meetinge with them.

To be removed some jealousies at this meeting, viz.: that by the Pr[ince], for men have ben in feare of this relacion. That what shalbe sayd to this purposse may be spoaken by him that may move most. Humbly to move that the Pr[ince] be pleased to speake yt himselfe.

SHEFFIELD. For the message to be sent to the Commons accordingly.

L. KEEPER. At the E[arl's] bench. Necessary to quycken this which is most in expedicion. That the Prince be pleased to be presente, but the manner howe to propounde yt.

Q. Yf the message be not to be this that nowe you have received the reporte by Tre[asure]r, and the lyke in their house. Therefore you propounde, yf they thynke yt fytt, a meeting to be ———— and at the meeting the Prynce, &c.

WALLINGFORD. Expedicion, but the message not yet; first to lett them digest yt amongest themselves and then to sende.

SAY. That this message wyll rather take away jealousies, especially the Pr[ince] being to speake.

The message to be, that we havinge————

Yf we deferr yt till they have debated and discoursed, then many jealousyes may be raysed, &c.

STEWARDE. 1. reason for a conference, opynion jointly, counsell jointly: a meeting, or ells we are at a *non plus*, but leave the tyme to themselves.

---

* Meaning, I suppose, if we meddle with it, we know by experience that we shall do hurt.

MOUNTAGU. Yf a meeting they wyll be but hearers. Against the speedy message, not to be yett.

CANT[ERBURY] with leave. With Southampton : expedicion, and the Prynce to speake; but to putt this of till to morrowe. 1. firste we shall heare howe yt is taken. 2. every pryvate man may move his frend that expedicion is fytt.

BRIDGEWATER. The message may be soe moulded as yt may be sente nowe, *prout per* Stewarde.

BUCK[INGHAM]. The present tyme the best, for the Prynce hathe authority from the King, yf any thing be mistaken, to explaine the same. This wyll take away jealousies, yf any.

PRESIDENT. The reporte here, there the lyke as we hoape. A meeting desyred, to avoyd all misstakings that aryse; and the Prynce wylbe, &c. To day rather than to morrowe.

Q. Whether a message shalbe sente to daye, or to morrowe? Content *per pluries*.

KEEPER. Howe ——? first the Prynce.

PR[INCE]. Present relief in the Kinges estate is not expected by the Kinge.

KEEPER. Relacion made here by the Treasurer: the lyke to them as we conceave. A meeting desyred to avoyde all mistakinges that may aryse. The Pr[ince] wylbe there, &c.

MOUNTAGU. That 3 or 4 may sett yt downe in wrightinge.

[The message drawn up by a Committee.—L. J. iii. 256.]

Canterbury reported the Prynce stood up at the reporte. The L[ord] Archb[isho]p first reade the wordes; then Mr. Att[orney] read yt.

To be reade to the Commons, they to take a copye of yt; but Agreed. not to leave yt.

TR[EASUR]ER. To knowe wherin he mistooke Pr[ince], that he mistooke not, but Spencer doubted.

SPENCER, *ad idem.*

TR[EASUR]ER. This debte to be thought on, but the buissines nowe in hand to have prioritye.

PR[INCE]. *Ad idem.*

BUCK[INGHAM]. The Kinge hathe sayde as much to him.

Mr. Attorney reade the message agayne, and the worde mistaking altered and made doubtes.

* * * * *

--

DIE VENERIS, 12 MARCH, 1623.

[L. J. iii. 257.]

* * * * *

[Message from the Commons that gold has been exported "as they conceave by papists," and asking for redress.—L. J. iii.]

CANT[ERBURY.] 1. Thanks. 2. Warrant to the gouldsmith[s.] TR[EASUR]ER. 3. Wayes to knowe. 1. Whoe brought to the mynt. 2. To knowe. 3. Lay way them.

[Answer that they will redress the evil.—L. J. iii.]

MARSHALL. To prevent the transportacion.

The Treasurer and Secretary and others to take some order therin.

DURESM. Newcastle: care thereof comended, whereby much money is transported by papistes beyonde seas.

SAY. A comittee of this House only, to prevent all inconveniences with them, and to sende worde therof to the Comons.

MARSHALL. A Comittee of this House advysing with the Secretary, Chauncellor of the Exchequer, &c. and such other of the Commons as they shall please; but not to sende to the Commons.

[Committee appointed to take measures against the exportation.—L. J. iii. 258.]

CANT[ERBURY]. *Prout per* Tr[easur]er.

PR[INCE]. Sende to the serchers of the portes, &c.

This Committee withdrew themselves p[rese]ntly into the lytle committee chamber.

[Conference appointed for the afternoon on the assistance to be given to His Majesty.—L. J. iii.]

DIE VENERIS, POST MERIDIEM, 12 MARCH, 1623.

[Report of conference. The Commons lay before the Lords their address to His Majesty.—L. J. iii. 259]

CANTERBURY. The Comittees remayne untill aunswere be retourned. A Committee of 2 of a bench to consider, peruse this; either to add or, &c. as they shall thynke good.

DURESM. They expecte, howe you like of this, howe you wyll ioyne with them to his Majesty.

SOUTHAMPTON. The Sollicitor, that they have submitted to us any alteracion in the induccion, but noe further.

NORTHAMPTON, repeated their wholl proceedinge in their advyse to the Kinge and the Kinges aunswere. The Commons have considered therof and promisse to assist his Majesty, yf he breake the treatyes ; we to joyne with them in this offer.

STEWARDE. Dismisse theis, and sende them an aunswere by message.

SHEFFIELD. By Conference rather.

SAY. Ad idem, an aunswere to be carryed by the Comittee.

KEEPER. Noe power but in the introduccion, [er]go to leave it to them.

SAY.

BUCK[INGHAM]. Whether they wyll debate with us ? The concurrence with them not to be denyed.

Tooke excepcions to the induccion. For the generall aunsweres not punctuall ; what.[a]

STEWARDE. Not to distruste them, though wyshe that offer be particuler ; but not gyve occasion to breake the correspondency.

[a] The general answer does not go sufficiently into details, or say exactly what they will do.

BUCK[INGHAM.] The intent is to engage the King. They have engaged themselves allready by their advyse as farr as this.

TR[EASUR]ER. Correspondency wyll make this a happy parlement ; best yf the priviledge be kept. We advyse in the one, shall we be left out of the other ? To looke uppon the Kinges speech how that directes. The Comittee to tell them that we wyll debate this buissiness, and sende them an aunswere assoone as we maye — presently.

MARSHALL. At the aunswere, to knowe of them howe farr ——

PR[INCE]. Either to joyne in this, or propound a newe thing to them. Alter either in the form or substance. Yf we propound for the substance, yt wyll (as by experience we fynde) distaste them. To aunswere that, for the substaunce, we wyll joyne with them in this : a small alteracion in the preamble.

BUCK[INGHAM]. The Parliamentary waye: a latitude; to be expounded.

TREASURER. Have we vote to the guifte, not to the forme?

PR[INCE.] They may grant subsidyes without the House, or grant impostes without the House.

STEWARD. Sith we cannot mende yt all, joyne with them.

PR[INCE.] Power to dispute for the fourme ; the Comittee to aske them what Parlamentary way they meane.

SOUTH[AMP]TON. To proceed without colour of distaste to the Comons, yf to alter the substaunce, yll taken, and loose tyme. Joyne in the fourmer. They meane the induccion only which may be altered ; they have no power to proceede further ; wyshed, &c. Sufficient to joyne with them for the presente, and proceede after, as His Ma^ts aunswere shalbe thereuppon. Lesse tyme lost.

BUCK[INGHAM]. Ad idem with South[amp]ton. Uppon consideracion, not to declare further than they have—

PRESIDENT. The Parlamentary waye, a greate engagement for them, to joyne with them, in this. The Kinge more propper to gyve them cause to alter the substaunce then wee.

PR[INCE]. To joyne in the induccion thus far, as wheras this speakes of the house of Comons, this to be in the name of the Lords and Comons.

CANT[ERBURY]. We have read, considered; thought fytt that this be made for bothe Houses to joyne.

SOUTH[AMP]TON. This past by a question with them: [er]go to be paste here.

Q. Such of your Lordships as are of opynion to consent with this demonstrance of the Comons in the substaunce say content; the others not content.

Agreed by all *nemine dissentiente*.

The Comittees of bothe Houses to alter the fourme nowe.

The Comittees went into the Privy Chamber.

The Comittees beinge retourned :—

CANT[ERBURY] reported that they have done according to their direccion. To be read, and this Comittee of ours and theirs to present this to the Kinge.

Mr. Attourney reade the same as was altered viz. in the name of the Lords and Commons.

PR[INCE]. That the Arch[bishop] of Canterbury present this to the K[ing].

Mr. Attourney generall delyvered the wryghtinge to the Pr[ince] himselfe.

I received yt againe of Mr. Attourney 13 March, 1623.

Adjourned to 9 to morrow morninge.

DIE SABATHI, 13 MARCH, 1623.

[L. J. iii. 260.]

*　　*　　*　　*　　*

CANT[ERBURY]. In ret[?] the aunswers agreed on yesterday. His grace appoynted to delyver the same tomorrowe at 2 appoynted. His duety to be advertysed to what purposse to speake. Propounded

1. The declared[a] to be d[elivere]d in that wrighting here de-

---

[a] *i.e.* declaration.

lyvered. To be fayer written. 2. A lytle preface of ceremony and duetye firste to his Matie. To knowe whether to this purposse. — We are come again the 2 tyme from his faithefull sub[jects] the LL and Comons. Acknowledge ourselves bound to God for such a king over us that wyll heare us speake in matters of this moment, and an argument.—Thanks to his Mat: so sensible of the indignityes to his daughter, &^c. in consideracion wherof we humbly present a speech in wrightinge, for that yt myght otherwyse miscarry, and desyre leave to reade the same.

KEEPER. Himselfe touched for speaking that the Palatinate was taken away by their armes. Whether his Grace shall omitt this or noe ?

PR[INCE]. It wyll not be denyed but by their armes.

SHEFFIELDE. The Comons to be acquainted with yt by a message for the preamble to be used by Cant[erbury].

PR[INCE]. Needlesse being a preamble only which they leave to their owne messengers. That yt was agreed on before was bycause that was matter, and not fourme, viz.:—the Archbyshop of Canterbury's speech to the K[ing] 5 Marcii.

Agreed the Archbyshop to use such a preamble as he spake of

*　　　*　　　*　　　*　　　*

Q. Whether to sende to the Commons for a Comittee of bothe Houses to agree on a preamble to be used by the L. Archb[ishop] of Cant[erbury] to the K[ing] tomorrowe in the afternoone in name of bothe Houses, at such tyme as his Grace delyvers a speeche unto his Ma^t in wrightinge from bothe Houses.

Such of your LL^p as are opynion that this preface of the L. Archb[ishop] of Cant[erbury] shall be made knowen to the Comittee of the Commons, saye, Content, the others: Pr[ince^a]: not content.

[Message to the Commons to ask that the committees of both Houses may meet to consider the preamble. The offer accepted and the preamble approved by the Commons, L. J. iii. 261.]

- - -

^a The word Prince is written over " not," showing that he voted alone against the motion.

DIE LUNÆ, 15 MARCII, 1623.

[L. J. iii. 262.]

BUCK[INGHAM]. For a conference with the Commons about the K[ing]s aunswere yesterday. For that there be some mistakeing, which the K[ing] hathe gyven the Pr[ince] leave to explayne.

* * * * *

DIE MERCURII, 17 MARCII, 1623.

* * * * *

[Conference on the King's answer.—L. J. iii. 265.]

* * * * *

DIE JOVIS, 18 MARCII, 1623.

[L. J. iii. 267.]

* * * * *

DIE VENERIS, DECIMO NONO MARCII, 1623.

[L. J. iii. 269.]

* * * * *

Hodie 3 *vice lecta billa per* L. Visc. Mountagu, and beinge putt to the question:

CANT[ERBURY] remembred the care of this bill the last parlement and at this and the alter[ation] of some parte &c. Nowe Sir Fr. Englefield presents a memoriall to some Committees. 1. Fyned for his contempt ; to be remitted uppon his submission.

CAMD. SOC.   F

fynes. Q. { 1. extreated and converted to the L. use.
{ 2. not extreated but in the King's power.

2. Sir G. More, &c. Dyvers copyholdes lett uppon valuable consideracions ; theis to be decreed by the L. Keeper with power from your Lordships.

DURESME. Noe favour to Englefield, bycause of contempt, &c., and his proceedings nowe in parlement with the Commons. Noe favour untill Englefield hathe made the accompte. As for the copiholdes ——

L. KEEPER. That Sir Fr. Englefield hathe withdrawen his bill with the Commons, and wyll submitt to your Lordships. Moved for mittigacion of the fynes. 1. For those payd. 2. For those not payde.

ARUNDELL, the L. Keeper to decree for the copyholdes, to mittigate the fynes allso. But not till accompte be made by him accordinge to this acte.

not agreed.

SHEFFIELD, ad idem, in a manner.

SAY. Not to countenaunce fynes imposed in the Chauncery.

L. KEEPER. They were ever imposed, and that courte, &c.

Question for the bill.

Past, *nemine dissentiente.*

*   *   *   *   *

Morley.

CANTERBURY. To suppresse the begynning of things creepinge in, &c. remembred the peticions printed by Sr. Fr. Englefield.

1 peticion prynted by the prisoners of the K[ing]'s bench. 1 other prynted (scandalous) by Morley.

Moved that noe more peticions shalbe printed and the printers to be punished.

MARSHALL. The Stationers to be forwarned, &c. printing of scandalous peticions punnishable.

L. KEEPER. Remembred the Order in Starchamber against libells, &c. and the ——

Lecta ordine in Cur. Cam[er]e stellar. conc[er]nen' Morley et al., and a peticion red[a] being printed. Morleys scandalous prynted peticion reade.

Morley to be sent for, to be here tomorrowe at 9., and the prynter. The Committees for peticions to take order to prevent the printing of peticions and briefs herafter.

Lecta prima vice bill Brewhouses

PR[INCE]. That the King desyres yt.

Lecta 2 vice eadem Billa.

*   *   *   *   *

---

20 M[ARCH].

*   *   *   *   *

[Message by the Prince that the two Houses are to come to the King to-morrow afternoon to cleare the Duke of Buckingham.—L. J. iii. 271.]

*   *   *   *   *

Morley at the barre.

L. KEEPER delivered the charge, for spreadinge a printed paper made against himselfe in particuler, but against the Lords of the Starr chamber, not as a peticion but as a libell.

M[ORLEY]. He delivered none but to the members of the House.

L. KEEPER. The Speaker never herde of yt nor Sir Rob. Ph[elips] who received peticions never herde of yt.

OXON EP[ISCOPU]s. That he d[elivere]d one to him, but that yt shoulde be d[elivere]d to the House, for he had d[elivere]d one already to the Commons.

M[ORLEY]. That he d[elivere]d none but to the Commons. That the L. Keeper may declare whoe accused him in the Starr chamber, and averred that the L. Keeper accused him, &c. and wyll make good his peticion, &c. He delivered the peticion Wensday was sennight to Sir Petre Haymond, and yt is reade in the house of Comons.

---

[a] This perhaps stands for "received."

Withdrawen.   L. KEEPER. Not till after he was comitted to the Sergeaunt; for he sent to knowe, beinge indifferent wher yt had ben delyvered.

WALDEN. To the buissines.

BANGOR. Very sensible of this high indignity of libels, &c. example.

DENNY. Forwarde to censure. To consider of his delyvery of the peticion to the Lower House, and whether we shall nowe meddle with yt.

BRISTOL.[a] To knowe who penned yt, and whoe prynted yt.

Co[VENTRY] & L.[ICHFIELD]. Not to be referred to the Commons; he is convented here: to the Comittees for peticions.

PAGETT. Noe necessity to examyne yt, but whether for the delyverye, &c. To conceave matters of such hyghe nature and in such fowle termes ——

DURESM. The peticion is directed to the Lords and Commons [er]go we to determyne it.

CHAMBERLEYNE. Whether we be possest of this peticion as d[elivere]d to us. Howe to take noatyce of yt?

PAGETT. Yt is delyvered to one of the Comittees for peticions, to Oxon Ep[iscopu]s.

OXON Ep[ISCOPU]s. That M[orley] sayd he d[elyvere]d not to be delyvered to this house, for that he had d[elivere]d yt as a peticion to the Commons allready.

STEWARD. A message to the Commons about yt.

MARSHALL. 1. Equitye of the cause. 2. Proceeding in this manner.

1. Leave the equity: not tyme as yett. 2. Censure him for the 2.

BRIDGWATER. A fortnight synce yt wos d[elyvere]d to the Commons and delyed.[b] Yf we suffer yt, much disherten the chief officer of justice. Correspondency, &c. and yet to be sensible of the wrongs of our owne members.

---

[a] The Bishop of Bristol.   [b] Probably "delayed."

Message. To knowe howe farre they have proceeded. Punnishe him for the libells. A member of our——

Pr[ince]. Noe member nor officer to suffer long under this burthen of sclaunder.

An order that noe peticion be herafter printed.

Buck[ingham]. Whether d[elivere]d to the Commons or noe? (yea). No jealousie to the Commons. The person whom yt concernes so carefull of the greate buissines. Suffer rather. But we to shewe ourselves, &c.; and sende a message to them to enter presently into this cause (for that yt was d[elivere]d to them), or cells to turne yt to us. Example good to deterr others.

Stewarde. The prynter to be punnished.

L. Keeper. This peticion not of the forme of peticions, &c. yet scattered, not d[elivere]d till yesterday afternoone being prisoner to this House, and their House never possessed therof till nowe. Indifferent where to be tryed: expecte to be cleered and justifyed howsoever, having a good conscience, a goode Kinge, &c.

Marshall. The petition not d[elivere]d to the Commons till prisoner here: to consider therof.

Say. Not to take yt into our handes as yett. Defer yt till Monday and then, &c. They are nowe in a greate buissines.

Buck[ingham]. The peticion not d[elivere]d to the Lower House untill a prisoner here, whereby he hathe aggravated his offence, yt may be to doe yll offices betwixt us. Not to deferr this till Monday, but to sytt so long as we may knowe that the Commons have digested the buissines they are nowe in.

Pr[ince]. To be put off till Monday.

Spencer. } To be under arrest, but with libertye to goe
Marshall. } abroade, &c.

Sheffield. M[orley] refuseth to lett knowe the printer. Imprison him for that.

Morley at the barre agayne.   At the barr.

L. Keeper. Whoe prynted this peticion?

M[orley]. I know not his name, he dwelles by Fishe streete

in Distaffe lane, he wyll bryng the Sergeant to him. Mr. Davyd Waterhouse dyd penn ytt, he prynted 500, dispersed but 4 or 5. Sir Peter Haymon, &c.

He is appoynted to attende on Wensday next in the House of Commons.

PR[INCE]. Morley to be in the Sergeant's handes as before, but soo at libertye as he may followe his buissines in the Lower House, and to fynde out the prynter.

MARSHALL. To be examined in the meane tyme who penned and prynted yt.

SAY. Morley to be at libertye, for that he is to attende the house of Commons; he wyll not starte. Yt wyll take away all distaste of jealousye.

BUCK[INGHAM]. To be restreyned with libertye to attende the Commons suffycient.

The printer to be sent for and Waterhouse allso, on Monday next.

L. KEEPER. The truthe is—he offred his peticion yesterday. They aunswered, yf he woulde delyver his peticion, he must attend on Wensday next, and no otherwyse.

L. PRESIDENT reported the bill of Informacions of intrusion: a conference, about the amendment.

Message to the Commons.

The clerke to remember this on Monday morninge.

Ad. to Monday, 9.

— — —

DIE LUNÆ, 22 MARCH, 1623.

[L. J. iii. 273.]

*   *   *   *   *

CO[VENTRY] AND LICH[FIELD] moved touching Morley's libell.

PLURES. That the Lower Howse is not possest with yt.

SUFFOLK. To proceede against Morley presently.

L. CRUMWELL. Warninge to be gyven to the wardens of the Brewers, to be here to-morrowe mourninge at 8, and the lyke warning to such as brewe about Westm[inste]r.

[Message to the Commons for information about Morley. The Commons reply that on Friday he presented a complaint to the Committee of Grievances against Sergeant Richardson, which was rejected as frivolous.—L. J. iii. 273.]

*   *   *   *   *

[Message from the Commons for a conference on the offer which they will make to his Majesty. The Lords answer that they have appointed the former Committee to meet them presently.—L. J. iii. 273.]

SUFF[OLK]. Not to loose tyme. To meete this afternoone touching Morley.

STEWARDE. A reporte to be made of the Comittees of bothe howses goinge to the K[ing] yesterday concerning the D[uke] of B[uckingham].

Archb[ishop] of Cant[erbury] to reporte this conference with the Commons. *Agreed.*

*   *   *   *   *

[Report of the conference. The Lords express their approbation of the offer of the Commons.—L. J. iii. 273.]

And being retourned,

CANT[ERBURY]. Those of the Comittee of the Comons expecte y[ou]r aunswere. Whether in this—

One L. gyves his vote the other waye. Whether to saye, but one only dissassenting, not namynge the Lorde, or to saye, by the consent of the LL. of the Upper House, as yt is nowe for the generall consent of the Comons :—and for the LL. (and with the full assent of the LL)——

} *Q[uaer]si.*

With a cherefull consent, noe one——

With a cheerefull consent of the house of Commons, noe one man dissassenting, and with a full and cheerefull consent of us the LL.

} *Agreed.*

BUCK[INGHAM]. To meete agayne in the afternoone and sytt,
&c. yf his Matie wyll that——
South[amp]ton to intimate soe much to the Commons.
Agayne into the p[ainted] ch[amber]. Retourned.
CANT[ERBURY]. d[elivere]d the paper we altered. They to
wryte yt fayre: to sytt this afternoone.
WALLDEN. Morley and the prynter to att[end] this mourn-
inge.
STEWARDE. The D[uke of B[uckingham] to move his Ma^t
when we shall attende him with this, &c.

Ad. to 3 post m[eridiem].

DIE LUNÆ, 22 MARTII, 1623, POST M[ERIDIEM].

*   *   *   *   *

BUCK[INGHAM]. His Majestes pleasure is to attende him tomorrowe at 8.
PR[INCE]. That we firste conferr with the Commons for the
alteracion of one matter, viz : the cause of Religion to be omitted
in the proposicion which is to be delyvered unto his Ma^t from bothe
Houses.
Message by Mr. Attorney and Sergeant Crook.
That Buck[ingham] aunswereth from the King, and the Lords
desyre a conference presently.
BUCK[INGHAM]. For the alteracion :—that his Grace explayned;
and the offer of the parlement, and that yf the King acceptes therof,
the parlement wyll afterwardes take care of his Majesty.
The Clerke reade that parte which is desyred to be amended.
Then, as yt is, leavinge out theis words (the trewe Relligion of All-
mightye God) which is conteyned in effecte in the rest, and therefore thought good to be omytted (as yt was omytted in that of
5 Marcii) leaste his allies thynke this a warre for Relligion.

Aunswered.

They wyll meete presently.

[The Commons asked to agree to the omission.—L. J. iii. 274.]

Buckingham. Some resolucion touchinge Morley in the meane tyme.

[The Commons agree to the omission.]

Morley at the barre.

L. KEEPER. For scandalizing in his person the court of Star chamber.

MORLEY. The aspersion which he hathe layde is for an informacion, whereby my indictement founde trewe by a jury was stayed. Upon your L^{ps} suggestion this order was made. Your L^p being my judge and my accuser, and pleading ag[ains]t me. For seeking, &c. after the — —

Being demaunded yf herd the L. Keeper, &c. Aunswered noe, but coulde prove yt by wyttnesses, he doubted not.

KEEPER. The order to be read. The p[rese]nce of the Judges of that Court observed.

MORLEY. Yt was uppon your L^{ps} undewe informacion. You sayd it was untrew, but the jury founde yt to be a trewe indicte· ment. Yf your L^{ps} had not stoppt the indictement, and had the serjeante ben arraigned, adjudged, &c. what fyne had come to the K[ing] by Serg[ean]t Richardson? At leaste 10,000^{li}.

The prisoner withdrawen.

The L. Ch. Justice satisfyed the LL. the ordinary course of theis indictement the — — who receaves the Bill made saye [?]ᵃ of yt before yt came to the Jury: which he dyd in open Court. We coulde not by the rules of the lawe deny the delyvery therof to the Jury, but dyd agree to acquaint the L. Keeper the next day, being Star-chamber day, with yt, which procured this order.

We herde councell. We all delyvered our opynions to be voyd

ᵃ Perhaps this should be "might say."

in lawe. As he was delyvering of his opynion Morley interrupted him. The other Judges comitted him for 4 days, untill he made his submission.

Cant[erbury] and Arundell *ad idem, et* Wallingford (as I remember).

L. PRESIDENT. The L. Keeper d[elivere]d openly in the courte what the L. Ch. Justice had tolld him, he moved me, as Morley sayeth.

The LL.s all then p[rese]nt, thought yt very straunge that such an inditement shoulde be.

It was the order of the Courte pronounced by the L. Keeper, all their LL.s agreeing.

Q. of my Lord President.

His reasons for the order, vizt.:—

SAY. To heare his councell for the matter; but, yf you wyll, punishe him for his insolent words here.

MARSHALL. To punish him for the matter also, considering what is related by the Judges nowe unto us.

CANT[ERBURY]. The matter is sufficiently apparent synce his delyvery of the peticions synce his restreynte. When this is published in the countrey, what wyll they thynke of the L. Keeper?

SHEFFIELD. For the matter: yt is a lawe in force, though ancient. For the manner, yt is very yll.

PAGETT. For the manner of the facte.

L. CHAMB[ER]LEYN. The matter is not in question: but the question is whether, the Judges proceedinge as they infourmed us, and the L. Keeper theruppon acquainting the Courte of Starchamber with that indictment; (wheruppon that Court conceaved that order for which Morley hathe thus scandalized the L. Keeper, and thus insolently behaved himselfe) deserves not to be hyghly punished?

DURESM *Ad idem.* To include in your censure the matter allso. What can his councell say? What his wyttnesses?

STEWARDE. To heare his councell for the matter. Punnishe him for the manner. Enough to induce us to yt.

L. PRESIDENT. Punishe him now for the manner only rather then this to rest, being on the L. Keeper.

Suff[olk]. Gyve him noe lib[er]ty for the matter. Either you must disprove the acte of the Starrch[amber] or dissallowe of the matter. To punishe him now for the matter and manner.

Pr[ince]. Punnishe him for the scandall layd on the L. Keeper and for his false informacion of us that [?] ª this was in the Lower House.

L. Keeper. The matter was not entred into by the Starr-chamber. The manner only was there spoaken of, and the matter was not entred into by the Starr chamber, the manner only was there spoaken of, and the matter left to be examined by the Judges and Attorney. His quarrell ag[ains]t his Lᵖ for perswading the K[ing] to reject Morley his suite to be the generall promoater of England: for he was never punnished by the order of the Starr-chamber.

[Sentence on Morley. Imprisonment in the Fleet during pleasure of the House: fine of £1.000: to stand in the pillory with his petition on his head: to make sub-mission to the House, to the Star Chamber, and to the Lord Keeper.—L. J. iii. 276.]

*   *   *   *   *

Die Martis, 23 Marcii, 1623.

[L. J. iii. 277.]

*   *   *   *   *

Russell. To prepare the charge against Waterhouse, that he penned the peticion and was of councell with Morley therin.

Waterhouse at the barre, questioned: Whether he penned the peticion of Morley shewed unto him; and he, perusinge the same aunswered:—He penned the firste draughte of that peticion; Morley tooke that draught from him and added some violent wordes.

ª Perhaps this should be "false information to us," namely that his grivance had been listened to by the Commons.

Denyed the outbravinge and over toppinge of the public courtes of Justice, &c. But he acknowledged the generall scorne of that peticion to be his owne.

Q. Whether he sawe yt after yt was printed, and allowed of yt?

R°. He sawe yt but reade yt not.

Q. Whether he coulde conceave the L. Keeper dyd comitt such an offence in moving the Courte of Starrchamber, &c. as the breache of his Oathe?

R°. His instruccions were, that the L. Keeper dyd informe the Courte and ordered, &c.

Q. Whether he sawe the order of Starrch [amber]?

R°. He dyd see yt.

L. Pr[esident]. This Order was made after the indictment was declared to be voyde.

Duresme. That the Lord Chief Justice enfourmed the L. Keeper of yt.

Chamb[er]l[ain]. *Ad idem,* at the request of the wholl Courte of Kinges Benche.

Waterhouse. He hathe drawen dyvers other peticions concerning the L. Keeper, some of a farre higher nature then this.

Moved what he shall doe in this case, he beinge a lawyer, and his clyent requyringe him to doe yt?

L. President aunswered him. Yt is noe parte of a lawyer to drawe peticions.

L. Keeper. He desyres noe favor for matters of corrupcion neither of God nor man.

Northampton. This man hathe as much cause to be punnished as Morley.

Rocheford. His lodginge to be seirched for papers of this nature.

Mountagu. This man to be punished; more worthy than Morley.

Morley at the Barre.

Q°. Whether Waterhouse dyd drawe the peticion.

R°.   Himselfe added some fewe wordes viz.:ᵃ that Mr. Attorney denyed to examine him, viz. the nature of an injunccion—invitacion of evill doers. Confessed many sharpe wordes. Withdrawen.

Waterhouse at the barre agayne.

Confessed the wholl scoape to be his owne, only a fewe wordes added here and there by Morley. Protested his griefe for the same.

L. Keeper. Whether Waterhouse deserves any censure. Agreed generally.

Northampton. An exemplary punishment.

L. President. The man is of more daunger and more scandalous, countenancing the same with his—

1. Closse prisoner. 2. Fyne 500*l.* 3. Stande in the pyllory with one of the peticions as Morley. 4. Submission and acknowledgment of his faulte.

Marshall. *Ad idem.*

Buck[ingham]. *Ad idem;* worse than Morley, having noe intrest—a gentleman ; *ergo* fyne and imprisonment only—noe pyllory.

Chamb[er]leyne. The pyllory to be spared—ymprisonment and fyne.

Co[ventry] and Lich[field]. The fourme of the subsubmission to be sett downe. 1. Closse prisoner in the fleete, and to be debarred from ynk and paper during the pleasure. 2. fyne—500*l.* 3. Submission as for Morley. 4. To be debarred the use of penn and ynke and paper.

Pr[ince]. To take order that he make noe more peticions.

Meneven[sis]. To be censured for the pyllory, and that to be spared.

Rookeford. Renewed his former mocion that Waterhouse his chamber be serched for papers of the lyke nature.

Marshall. To be barred penn and ynke, and some exemplary punnishement.

ᵃ The words from "vizt." to "examine him" are underlined. It is possible that the writer may have intended to draw the line through them.

SAY. Sensible of traducing any man of place and honor; but moderacion. Noe perpetuall blemish on his posteritye.

PR[INCE]. Not crewell, yett sensible of any L[ord's] honour. To take away use of penn, ynke, and paper, which we may myttigate.

Commended, not ordered. LONDON. Waterhouse to drawe the submission, the prynter to prynte yt. Morley to brynge the peticion into the house.

Question 1.

{ 1. Waterhouse to be prisoner in the fleete.

Agreed generally. 2. To undergoe the fyne of 500*l*.

3. To make his submission and acknowledgment here and in the Starrchamber and to the L Keeper and in the King's Bench.

Question 2.

Agreed per pluries. 4. To be debarred of penn and ynke and paper during the pleasure of the House.

Question 3.

The L. of Loudon's mocion. That Waterhouse shall penn this submission and ackn[owledgement] to be made.

It was not putt.

The prynter.

Q. By what authoritye he prynted Morley's peticion ?

R⁰. Confessed he prynted yt, and Sir A. Thomas his peticion.

Q. What became of the copye?

R⁰. Morley had yt awaye; he had but 15*s*. of Morley for yt.

Withdrawen.

His fees to be payd out of Morley's fine. { ROCHEFORD. That Morley paye his fees.

MARSHALL. The prynter to be committed and Morley to pay his fees.

CANTERBURY. To be ymprisoned for example, for that he prynted without licence, and the reasons why yt is forbydden soe generally.

The censure against the prynter.

1. To be ymprisoned duringe the pleasure of the House.

2. Submission *prout* Morley and Waterhouse.

Pr[ince.] To be admonyshed not to prynte any more without lycence, and to be severely punnished yf he dothe.

Question.

1. That the printer shalbe ymprisoned duringe pleasure.

Ordered, that all the fees of the prynter's ymprisonment for his attachement by the Sergeant shalbe herafter payde out of Morley's fyne. In the mean tyme to paye noe fees. } Agreed.

Question was then putt.

1. To be ymprisoned during the pleasure of the House.

2. To be admonished, &c.

3. To make his submission and ack[nowledgment], &c.

The L.L. in their roabes.

Morley at the barr and kneeling.

The L. Keeper pronounced the sentence. He besought mercy, &c.

Withdrawen.

David Waterhouse at the barre.

The L. Keeper pronounced the censure.

He acknowledged the censure to be most just holl [?][a] and favourable.

Withdrawen.

Bernard Alsop at the barr.

The L. Keeper pronounced the censure.

Withdrawen.

Ordered to be brought hither to-morrowe mourninge to make his acknowledgement.

L. Keeper touching the bason and ewer which Waterhouse spake of which he supposeth to be the same that Sir Fr. Englefield ——. And the scandalous peticion, &c. besought comisseration, rather the meanest place, yf not &c.

Ad: to 9 to-morrowe.

---

[a] "Honorable" [?].

Die Mercurii, 24 Marcii, 1623.

[L. J. iii. 278.]

*   *   *   *   *

Not agreed on, Erle Marshall had this awaye from me, yt being written all with his L.ps haud.

An order conceaved by the Subcomittees for mitigacion of fynes, &c.

lecta 1ᵃ vice.

Pr[ynce]. Not at this tyme, leaste yt encourage offendors

Canterbury. Reporte of the Bill for Popish Recusants.

3ᵃ vice *lecta.*

Putt to the Question, past.

Expedit.

exped.   Petre,[a] St. John of Ba., D[omin]us.

Rocheford. 2 reportes.

1. Of Buck[ingham's] Justific[ation].

2. Of the K[inge]s aunswere yesterday.

Buck[ingham]. The K[ing] intendes to sende a presente dispatche into Spayre that the Parlement requyres him to breake of the treaties, &c. with the reasons therof.

Agreed.

Agreed to be declared to the Commons.

[Message to the Commons for a conference about the King's answer. Conference held and reported.—L. J. iii. 278.]

Die Jovis, 25 Marcii, 1624.

[Message to the Commons for a conference.—L. 7. iii. 282.]

Agreed.

This to be intimated to the Comons, & the reasons

Pr[ynce]. To gyve power to the Comittee to tell the Commons when the House shalbe adjourned, and to what day, on Thursday next yf the Comons shall lyke of yt.

[a] Apparently the names of those who voted " not content."

BUCK[INGHAM]. To resolve of 2 of each House to assiste the *why on this day, yf they* Kinges Secretary this vacancy, for drawinge up a manifesto of this *woulde have a longer tyme.* buissines, yf occasion shalbe to use any.

L. Chamberleyne.

E. of South[amp]ton. } Named by the LL.

Agreed. To be intimated to the

The LL. went to the Conference, beinge retourned.

THE L. PRESIDENT. That the L. Archbyshop delyvered unto his Ma^te on Tuesdaye last a —— from Comittees of bothe Houses of [Parliament]^a his Ma^tes declaracion, as yt was agreed on and perfected, &c. read by the L. President himselfe, and then by Mr. Attourney.

Comons at this conference. Reporte.

CANT[ERBURY]. After the delyvery of this, his Ma^tes declaracion, he kneeled downe and shoulde not rest on his Ma^tes declaracion herin. His Ma^te aunswered that ——, and that he woulde despatche a Messenger presently into Spayne, &c.

MARSHALL signifyed to the Comons the tyme of our Adjournment, &c.

Ad. to Thursday next, at 9.

DIE JOVIS, PRIMO APRILIS, 1624.

*   *   *   *   *

The accesse to Parlement after Easter.

[Conference demanded on Buckingham's motion for considering the employment of the subsidies to be voted. Buckingham announces that the treaties had been broken off. The Commons reply that their attendance is too small as yet for them to be able to give an immediate answer.—L. J. iii. 284.]

DIE VENERIS, 2DO APRILIS, 1624.

*   *   *   *   *

CANT[ERBURY]. Municions mett yesterday, to meete agayne *Q. si.* this afternoone; to appoynt a Subcomittee to prepare some buisines.

^a " Comons" in MS.

PRYNCE.   Somewhat yesterday that touched a [Lord]s honor, &c. The Subcomittee to have power to take oathe.

MARSHALL. Take the oathe in the house, and examyne them after.

TR[EASUR]ER. The oathe to be taken presently, for an aspersion is layde, &c. To be examined.

[Committee named. L. J. iii. 286.]

SOUTH[AMP]TON. To consider whoe are to be enquyred of that they may be sente for p[rese]ntly.

*   *   *   *   *

DIE SABATHI, 3 APR., 1624.

[L. J. iii. 287.]

*   *   *   *   *

Canterbury reported bill of Monopolies, 2 things consid[erable]. 1. The main body. 2. The reservacions. Many thinges in the first worthy to have a conference. Touching the reservacions many petic[ions]. Not to meddle with them untill the conference, and oe order yett then the peticions to be reade, &c., a conference in the begynning ade, and yett of the weeke. was not nyed·

*   *   *   *   *

ROCHEFORD. Noe greater daunger then securitye. Seconded the mocion of Buck[ingham].[a] 1º Apr. Wee sent to the Commons then, &c., which they enterteyned, but woulde not proceed to gyve aunswer untill their house were fuller; nowe to take some course amongest ourselfes for the raysing of some greate summe of money for the speedy supply of this greate buissines.

*   *   *   *   *

[a] For a conference on the use to be made of the subsidies.

BUCK[INGHAM]. Renewed his mocion on Thursday last, and the message to the Comons. Theyr resolucion they woulde gyve us an answere. This contynewes the corresp[ondence]. We to preserve yt, to sende to the Commons for an aunswere and to further the buissiness ourselves.

L. STEWARD. Yt hathe been yntimated to the Commons. Sende to them agayne. Not to presse them before their owne tyme for an aunswere, but to pray a newe conference.

L. KEEPER. Their aunswere, not able to make a speedy aunswere in respecte of the thynnes of their house, and the importaunce of the buissiness, considerable nowe, what to do to quycken the same.

DURESME. They have appoynted Monday.

CANT[ERBURY]. A message to putt them in mynde of yt.

CHAMBERLEYN. Not to press them till Monday.

KEEPER. Yf you here not on Monday, then to sende.

  * * * * *

[Message from the Commons for a conference on Recusants.—Agreed to.—
L. J. iii. 257.]

HAUGHTON. Remembred a mocion and appoynted to be ordered, for Comittees to gyve you accompt, and to take their first places at Comittees.

MARSHALL. Yt is generally observed. Comittees for Municions to meete in the afternoone.

PR[INCE]. The Order is, none of the Comittee of the Commons are to come in untill the Comittees of this House are sett.

HAUGHTON. To adde, and noe Lord to goe untill the Comittees are firste gone.

SAYE. Orders made the laste parlement once reviewed nowe the Comittees for priviledge to sytt agayne on Monday mourninge and peruse them, and then to be reade openly in the House. } *de hoc, si.*

  * * * * *

SAY. The LL. that are gone before hande into the P[ainted] Ch[amber] to be sente for backe agayne. Agreed.

MARSHALL. Remembred the Order propounded before the recesse touchinge fynes.

[Order that fines imposed are to be reported to the House before the end of the Session for mitigation if it be thought fit]

CANT[ERBURY]. The Comons presented to this purpose 1. thankes for expedicion. 2. They have taken into their consideracon warr lykely to fall uppon the dissolucion of the treaties. Daungers at home. A peticion in wrightinge, against Jesuites priestes and popishe recusantes. Yt is with a blanke for your LL^{ps} to joyne, yf you please.

MR. ATTOURNEY read the peticion.

CANT[ERBURY]. They expecte aunswere.

The Comittees retourned and answered them that their Lordships wyll take this into their consideracion, and when they are resolved, which is nowe to late,^a they wyll gyve their aunswere.

Ad. to Monday morning 9.

DIE LUNÆ, 5to DIE APRILIS, 1624.

[L. J. iii. 288.]

*   *   *   *   *

L. Keeper putt their Lordships in mynde of the mocion of Buck-[ingham] on Satterday touching money to be provyded.

THE PRINCE moved to stay sending to Lower howse concerning borowing moneys, because they have it in agitacion but to advise of the peticion from the Comons concerning Recusants

The peticion read against Recusants.

CHAMB[ER]LEYNE. The House to be putt into a Comittee.

Ad. ad libitum.

PR[INCE]. 2 partes of this peticion, 1 the preface, 2 peticion.

^a i.e. for which it is now too late.

Somwhat in the preface considerable as to sharpe in the preface: fytt to be amended.

Mr. Attourney read the preface.

CANT[ERBURY]. The mocion of the Spiritt of God to put this into the mynde of the Comons, and yt dothe concur with the wysedom of the State and Assembly nowe gathered; for yf Religion be neglected, noe blessing to be expected. *A Jove principium:* next, we are to provyde ourselves &c.

1. The insolency of the adverse parties cause this—

The B[ishop] of Calcedon is come hither pyttifull to relate what he hathe done: publique going in London; in Staffordshire with crosses; confirmed many, contrary to the jurisdiccion of the Crowne.

Many seminaryes of late builte beyonde seas: dreyned great summes of money; many boyes and girles stollen thither: the King loste the hartes.

2. There is not at this daye a man of any worthe that hathe remayned longe beyond seas, but is nowe in Englande: Worthington, Leander, Champneis, Kellison and 200 persons of choice men of that relligion, to make a partie, and to recary money with them.

3. They goe by 1000 to masse, and to the greate offence of the people.

Theis are the motyves; but as touching the poynt his highnes moved touching the preface, whether any or noe: nowe considerable.

L. KEEPER. Nothing to be amended. 1. The generallity. 2. The particulers. For the 1, all uppon matters of state, not uppon relligion. For the 2, the presente insolences of the papistes; not to quallify. Next, yt supposeth the priestes and Jesuites to be incendiaryes. Their owne booke shewe yt: their owne religion confesse the Jesuites to be so. Next, a partie here at home againste us. This cannott be denyed, yf we observe the affeccions of the papistes in their joy in anything concerning Sp[ayne]. Next, they conceave a hedd abroade. I remember very well that at his highnes being in Sp[ayne] firste, a booke written by one of their owne wytts: reasons whye sent his owne son, for that our K[inge] knewe that all the Catholiques of Englande depende on Spayne, and therefore the Kinge sent his sonn thither. Concluded, not one syllable to be amended.

SAYE, agreed that (as his hyghnes meved) the preface may be dyvyded from the peticion, whether any necessitye to use such wordes as may be inconvenyent, when we may have our effecte without the same. Noe conclusion here, without conference with the Comons, and noe conveniency at this tyme to use bytter wordes, &c.

PR[INCE]. The preamble to be taken of, or mitigated. Other reasons may be given, yf yt were fytt to gyve any.

CHAMB[ER]LEYNE. The preface only to be moved to the Comons for mitigacion. We speake of a matter of Sp[ayne] as yf we feare an invasion from Sp[ayne]. The Treaties of the Pal[atinate] and Match are dissolved, not of Amitye: to provyde agaynste invasion, but not to putt this in our pericion at this tyme.

PRESIDENT, ad idem.

STEWARDE. At conference with the Commons the peticion to be d[elivere]d without a preamble, or a very shorte one, as we dyd our advyse 5 Marcii and to provyd our reasons (as then) yf the K[inge] demaundes any; and there are more reasons to be added then theis (as the Prynce moved) as fytt or fytter to be added.

HAUGHTON. A preamble, but not in theis wordes; to be omytted, the papistes the engines of Spayne; to be omytted, nothinge ells.

PR[INCE]. Those wordes to be left out; but the Comons wyll not happily yielde unto yt. [Er]go (as Stewarde) to leave out the preamble altogether, and have reasons by themselves.

STEWARDE. At short introduccion only, for we peticion only for execucion of lawes allready made.

CANT[ERBURY] acknowledged that we may agree to alter (uppon Conference with the Comons) as is moved touchinge the preface. The preface to be shorte. This to lye by us yf demaunded by the K[inge].

BUCK[INGHAM]. This question is soe well handled that he wyll not speake much. The zeale of some, and the affeccions of others; contrary desyres, some to add, some to take away. Daunger in clogging a bill: the example of 5 *Martii*. Desyre the thing without reasons, unlesse called for; and soe I thynke we shall obteyne our desyre. Peticion for the lawes in force, and avoid the objeccion of a warr of relligion.

BROOKE. Noe over earnestnes of wordes; for the Kinge knows the dangers himselfe. A conference; the preamble shortened; the peticion to be graunted.

L. KEEPER. Noe reason to retracte his opynion; yett the conveniency he ever lefte to be considered of: only he justifyed the zeale of the Commons herin.

L. TR[EASUR]ER. The matter not to be lost for the manner. The preamble all true and much more. The truthe not questioned, but the conveniency only considerable. We shall prejudice ourselves, gyving a colour of occasion that this shalbe a warr of religion. Putt the matter as home as we cann.

PRYNCE. Yea. Are all resolved the preamble to be altered; the way to alter yt. 1. by leaving yt out and an induccion only. 2. by mitigacion.

PEMBR[OKE]. Propounde that unto the Commons which wylbe most pleasant, as Cant[erbury].

BUCK[INGHAM]. Q. Whether any thing in the body of the peticion that is an addicion to the lawes in force?

PR[YNCE]. Yt is not their intention not to make any newe lawe, which is concluded in the last clause.

SAY. The peticion hathe one thynge more. A day prefixed for the Jhesuites to be banished by a day, or ells by the lawe they are to be hanged.

BUCK[INGHAM]. *Ad idem.* Gyve them a day to be gone.

PEMBR[OKE]. The K[inge] carefull not to gyve occasion to

make this a warr of relligion, we to be carefull not to move him to doe any such acte. Moderate nowe, for I knowe we shall have another Session at Michælmas, and then, yf neede be, we may re-newe our peticion in a more sharpe manner.

Mr. ATTOURNEY reade the peticion, the 1 poynte.

SOUTHAMPTON.   As that is placed, yt is a punnishement to be placed afterwardes.

6. reade: then the 1 reade agayne.

PR[YNCE].   The wordes—viperous brood—to be taken away, and to expresse that we gyve them warning uppon favour to be gon by a daye.   All lawes against priestes, Jhesuites and Popishe Recusants to be put into execucion, and this particuler against priestes and Jhesuites being sharpe, to have a daye to be gone..

Dissarme Recusantes legally convicted and vehemently suspected.

PR[YNCE].   Not to make new lawes.   I am perswaded and have some cause to knowe yt, that the King wyll doe yt himselfe (dissarme them), but we not to urge him at this tyme, and he will doe yt the sooner.

ROCHESTER.   Defecte in the lawes, thoughe executed to the full.

The 3 article to confyne them and discharge all by paste lycences.

SOUTH[AMP]TON.   Not as yt is sytt downe here least yt be noysed we wyll begynn a persecucion.

Doe yt without clamour, *tacite*, in puttinge the lawes in exe-cucion; they are confyned by lawe.

PRESIDENT.   Many of the Recusantes of quallity have lycences.

PR[INCE].   Very fewe have lycences, and those but for a tyme.

PEMBR[OKE].   This to be remedyed by the Councell of State, and not by this publique peticion.   At Mich[ael]mas we may peticion yt, yf we see cause.

DENNY.   The execucion of the lawes wyll make a noyse of this matter, and therefore yf we wyll respecte that, we cann doe nothinge.

PEMBR[OKE].   Our meaninge is to make noo noyse of newe

lawes, or addicions; but not for executing the olde lawes. Lett them talke of yt.

PR[YNCE]. I have some grounde that you shall have good satisfaccion here very shortly, only not to peticion any addicions at this tyme.

The 4 clause not to resorte to Embassadors to masse.

5. To discharge the popishe Recusantes from being Lieutennants of the Shires, &c. convicted and non communicants.

7. Beinge delyvered from the daunger of the Treaties, to secure us that uppon noe occasion herafter the Kinge wyll diminishe or slaken the lawes against Popishe Recusantes.

PR[INCE] approved yt well. All to be conteyned in the 6 clause. Then the 1 clause and this 7 clause: well debated yt nowe, to put yt in fourme tomorrowe morninge, and then to move for a conference.

*   *   *   *   *

L. KEEPER. Moved touching conferences for the Bills, not to slipp it over to longe.

PRYNCE. Comittees to meete for municions : to meete to mor- Agreed. rowe at 2 in the ——

TR[EASUR]ER. To hasten any thing that concernes him. He desyres noe favour, but expedicion, and when they have done, wyll shewe a dangerous conspiracy and combinacion against him.

PR[INCE]. The Subcomittee to meet this afternoon touching Agreed. municions.

PRESIDENT. To be examined howe he founde the treasure, howe he ordered yt, and how he left yt.

Ad. to 9 to morrowe.

DIE MARTIS, 6th APRIL, 1624.

[L. J. iii. 291]

*   *   *   *

CANT[ERBURY]. Reporte.

Subcomittees attended the Pr[ince] touching this peticion have drawen up a shorte peticion against recusantes with a briefe introduccion. Preamble left out. Large reasons to be drawen and to be delyvered to his Ma^t yf requyred.

Mr. ATTOURNEY reade the peticion.

P[RINCE]. The worde—may departe—to be altered and made —must departe. Agreed to be—shall departe. 2da vice lecta per Mr. Attorney.

CAN[TERBURY]. Remembered the message sent yesterday that the Commons shall have an aunswere to daye.

L. KEEPER. To be paste here firste.

Firste to be agreed on by the Comittees of bothe Houses.

This is allowed of the House to be proffered to the Comittees of the Commons.

Message by Mr. Sergeant Crewe and Mr. Sergeant Fynche.

That wheras they sent worde yesterday that they woulde provyde themselves for a conference this day touching the peticion to be delyvered to his Ma^t: And nowe they are ready for the conference, and desyre the same to be presently in the p[ainted] ch[amber], yf their leasure wyll permitt.

CAN[TERBURY]. That a^s this Comittee they may firste shewe the desyre of this House to contynewe correspondency, and then their reasons whyc they have not alltered this peticion from theirs, though they have contracted the same: but that yt conteynes in yt the wholl effecte of that they sente. Though they leave out the reasons in the preamble of this peticion, yett they thynke fytt to have reasons ready to be d[elivere]d to his Ma^t yf he shall please to call for the same: and for that purpose your Lordships have gyven authority to us to appoynte a Subcomittee for the same, &c.

SAY. Yf the Comons allowe to contracte this peticion; to lett them knowe that our Comittee hathe power &c. *ut per* Cant-[erbury].

*   *   *   *   *

CANT[ERBURY]. Signifyed that we thought fytt, yf their House Reporte. shall concurre, to abridge the peticion against Recusantes. Reasons, that fewest wordes wylbe best wellcome. The asperity of some wordes avoyded in ymmitacion of that 5 *Marcii*. Delyvered the draught. They are retourned to their House, and wyll acquaint them with yt, &c. Subcomittee to be appoynted.

*   *   *   *   *

DIE MERCURII, 1624.   7 APRIL.

[L. J. iii. 293].

*   *   *   *   *

CAN[TERBURY]. Remembred the conference for the Bill of Monopolies touchinge the body of the Bill, not touchinge the provisoes or exceptions.

The Comittees reade.

PRESIDENT. The Bill of intrusion. The Amendem[en]ts may Reporte. stande with the Bill, and soe reported the Bill fytt to passe.

DURESME. To quicken the proposicion to the Commons.

L. KEEPER. Not till the peticion be perfected against Recusantes.

[Message to the Commons for a conference on the Monopoly Bill.— L. J. iii. 293.]

*   *   *   *   *

Peticion of Morley reade.

PR[INCE.] Yt is a skorne. Noe favour.

HAUGHTON. Yt acknowledges a fault in manner, not in matter.

STEWARDE. Peticion to the Lord Keeper. He hath peticioned to me, but a mere skornefull peticion.

DURHAM. To be rejected.

PR[INCE]. We dyd condemn him for the matter, viz': That he falsely sayd, that the L. Keeper stayed the indictement.

DENNY. To be rejected.

ALL.

* * * * *

DIE JOVIS, 8ᵛᵒ APRILIS, 1624.

[L. J. iii. 296].

* * * * *

[The Commons asked to defer the Conference on Monopolies on account of the weighty cause on which they are engaged.—L. J. iii.].

* * * * *

DIE VENERIS, 9 APR. 1624.

[L. J. iii. 296.]

* * * * *

ESSEX. A nobleman of this House[a] some five days synce, that such a conspiracy in this House as, &c. daungerous—none safe, &c.

[a] The Lord Treasurer. See p. 57.

TREASURER. I sayd practises and conspiracyes against me, such as I must—to this House and the other for justice: that none shalbe safe: I think soe still: and I desyre some may be examined and to doe me justice. Expedicion for municions. All that he desyres is justice, &c.

SAYE. Touching the conspiracy, such as never were knowen, and nowe Sr Myles Fleetwood hathe brought me in in the Lower House.[a] Examinacions in this House touching municions which myght concerne him. Fytt therefore the L either names the parties or cleere the Houses.

ROCHEFORD. Ad idem, either the members of bothe Houses to appeare spottlesse or the faulte punnished.

DENNY. To clere the doubte which the House conceaves.

MARSHALL. Being his Lordship was moved in passion, the matter in facte to be first handled.

STEWARDE. Cleere that the L. Treasurer ment neither of the Houses, for he desyred expedicion: yett yf he meant any particuler Member, his Lp to name them.

CANT[ERBURY]. A tyme to reporte the matter of municions.

L. KEEPER. Yt concernes every man to be very sensible of his honor, out of which his Lordp fell into that passionate speeche: yett to name whome he meant in particuler, although he hathe cleered the House in generall.

Q. Whether he shall name them presently, or shall have tyme gyven hym?

DURESME. Not to name them presently.

TR[EASUR]ER. I am questioned here by Informacion of Sir Roberte Pye in the other House by Mr. Cooke in a buissines concernes neither of themselves. As honest and as feithefull to the K[inge] and Kingdome as any subject whosoever. Wronges done: but yt wyll light upon another man or other men (I wyll accuse none). Lett the matter fynde the man, yt wyll not light upon me, I knowe.

Enter this speech at large.

[a] This seems to be a continuation of the speech of Middlesex.

He cleered bothe Houses. Just proceedings in bothe, craved pardon not to name the parties as yett, and to stande right in their LL^ps opynion untill be proved faultie.

HAUGHTON. The Sub-comittee to make their reporte to the Grand comittee. The Lords to name afterwardes.

SOUTH[HAMP]T[ON]. The buissines of the Sub-committee concernes not this. A generall cleeringe of the 2 houses, noe cleeringe; for yt never entred in to the harte of man that the 2 Houses coulde be conspirators.

L. TR[EASUR]ER. That he named no member, nor ment any at that tyme: that at that tyme he did not intend any member of this House.

TR[EASUR]ER. The Sub-comitee to meet $p[os]t$ $m[eridiem]$ to report to the Comittee, and they to the House, concerning municions.

* * * * *

DIE SABATHI, 10no DIE APRILIS, 1624.

[The Commons desire a conference on the petition concerning Recusants, and are now ready to confer on the Monopoly Bill.—L. J. iii. 297.]

PR[INCE]. Monopolies not till Monday, the peticion presently.

L. KEEPER. Monopolies not till Monday at 2 in the p[ainted] chamber. Peticion presently in the p[ainted chamber] with the former Comittee.

* * * * *

The Lords retourned from the Conference touching the modell of the Peticion against Recusantes, &c.

CANT[ERBURY] reported—

They have taken into consideracion some few worde of explanacion: but 4 in number.

His grace read the modell.

1. By some such course as your Ma[t] shall thynke fytt. They desyre yt by proclamacion to take away excuse from the adversary; to encourage our own Relligion: the justices may take noatice: done formerly by proclamacion.

2. The lawes in execucion, against all Seminarye priestes and all popishe Recusantes. To be added, all justly suspected popishe Recusantes.

3. A day certeyne to avoyd: desyre a speedy daye.

4. Engagement from the K[inge] not to slacken execucion &c. which were their owne wordes. To be added against Jhesuites, priests, and popishe Recusantes.

1. Pr[ince]. An inconvenience to appoint the K[inge] to doe yt by proclamacion. Considerable, and to be left out.

L. Keeper. The K[inge] hathe but 2 wayes, by lawes, by proclamacion. Noe proclamacion nowe, for he never gave any conivence by proclamacion. What hathe ben projected to be done was only by a letter from his Ministers, and yett not done. His Ma[t] to gyve charge to the Judges and Justices to putt the lawes in execucion.

Lo[rd] Chamb[er]le[yne.] To be left to the Kinge.

Pr[ince]. *Idem.*

Lo[rd] President. Noe auc[tori]tee to dispense, therefore no need of proclamacion.

Lo[rd] Keeper. To be left to the Kinge.   Agreed.

L. Dunelm.[a] Noe lawe extinguished, therefore his Maj[t] may declare himselfe as pleaseth him.

Lo[rd] Say.[b] *Idem* Lord Keeper, to leave it to the Kinge.

Archb[ishop]. Justly suspected Recusantes to be disarmed.

Prince. Fitt to be done, I thinke the K[inge] will doe yt, but not to be mencioned to the Kinge to do yt, but leave it unto him.

Lo[rd] President. The word suspected, to leave it to the K[ing], for noe man can determyne legally who they be.

---

[a] The Bishop of Durham.   [b] Zay MS.

Pr[INCE].   And for disarming Recusantes, we entreat your Ma' to do as you have formerly done, being an Act of State.

Archb[ishop].   The same cause may be taken for disarming them as formerly hath ben.

3. A speedy day yelded unto.

4. The addicion against Jes[ui]tes and Rec[usants] agred unto.

Reasons to be given to the Comons why the first is not yelded unto.

3 Reasons, 1 no proclamacion for the connivency, and therefore a proclamacion needles.

2 It will appeare to postery hereafter that the papistes had a publique connivance.

3

Agreed Pembr[oke.]

4 to be left onely to the Kinge, and to give no reasons.

L. Sheff[ield].   To be left onely to the Kinge without reasons.

Pr[INCE].   To put the Commons in mynd that we be not nowe slacke, and not forward to proceed about subsidies.

Lo[rd] Steward.   To remember them of it after the pe[ticion] and the prynce to do yt.

Lo[rd] Sheffield.   Not fitt at this time.

L. Duke.   It may breed a jelouzy in the Kinge of our slacknes in yt, and therefore to be nowe remembred to the Comons.

Lo. Haughton.   That the Prince or some other may put them in remembrance of yt, when the business for the peticion is ended.

Agreed.   Lo[rd] Chamb[er]lei[n].   When they have exprest their consente to the peticion, then to move yt to the Commons.

The Lo[rds] Comittees returned from the conference.

Lo[rd] South[amp]t[on].   You meane to put them in remembrance of the subsidies; if you think fitt the prince to do yt of himselfe, not from the howse.

Pri[nce].   That it wilbe a good ground for him to moove the Kinge for the peticion.

The Comittees go to the Comittees of the Comons againe about the petition.

Comittees retorned.

Can[terbury]. 4 thinges in proposicion.

The 3 yielded unto : the 4 the proclamacion not to be yntimated to the King.

They have agreed unto yt.

Cant[erbury]. The Comittees for municions mett. Have Reporte. drawen up the facte. Noe judgement of ours. That we leave to to your LL^ps.

Moved that yt may be handled on Monday next, and fynished Agreed. before wee ryse.

Ad. to Mondy at 8.

Die Lunæ, 12 Aprilis, 1624.

[The Commons ask for further postponement of the conference on monopolies, the Lord Treasurer having asked to be heard by counsel. Conference fixed for to-morrow at 2.—L. J. iii. 299.]

Rochefordе. Much trencht into the priviledge of this House for any Nobleman of this House to sende into the House of Commons without consent of the House.

L. Keeper. Yt may concerne him as a member and a Judge ellswhere, and he hearinge of matters moved against him with the Commons, his cause was satisfyed by the parties councell.

President. A Member of this House ought not to sende his aunswere to an accusacion in the House of Commons, without con- sent of this House.

Haughton, Ad idem. Every member of this House to aunswere those only whoe are his Judges.

Marshall. Noe member of this House can make his aunswere to the Comons as beinge called or cyted, but whether he may aunswere voluntaryly or noe, he doubtes.

Duresm. Against this distinccion.

KEEPER. Every cause that concernes a Judge hathe two parties. The plaintiff or defendant may complayne. Q. whether the parties councell may not enfourme that House of anything concerning the Judge? Agreed he mayo doe yt.

BUCK[INGHAM]. The Lord not to be blamed. He that moved yt not to be blamed, the Commons not to be blamed.

An order to be made that, uppon leave, any member may aunswere.

L. TR[EASURER]. They sente me a charge on Fryday night laste, and requyred my aunswere the next mourning. Such a charge, order for such an aunswere, at such a tyme. I sente for a longer tyme, which was much debated amongest them, and at last they yielded to this daye in the afternoone. Moved that he myght have leave.

SAY. Yf the Comons sent the charge and requyred to aunswere. Uppon the matter, he is questioned.

SOUTH[AMP]TON. Yt was desyred of the Commons, the L. Treasurer myght have a copye. Aunswered he shoulde, and liberty to aunswere how he pleased.

MARSHALL. Yt was only agitated in that House, and moved by some of the Lord Treasurer's friends, that his L^p might have a copye.

L. KEEPER. That House had a greate respecte to the priviledge of this House.

THE LORD TR[EASUR]ER craved leave to aunswere to the Comons by wrighting.

CANT[ERBURY]. Care beinge had for the stoares of municions, &c. uppon consideracion therof somwhat happened which concerned the Lord Treasurer's honor, his Lordship desyred yt myght be examined. Men sworne: a subcommittee appoynted whoe signifyed that which they founde to the Prynce &c. and nowe they have brought the same into the House. Desyred to have yt reade.

Peticion of Tho. Dalyson reade concerninge the sale of his lande to the L. Treasurer. The L. Treasurer explayned the manner of the purchace and yf any man wyll buy yt agayne he shall for £1,000 or £2,000 lesse.

Moved. Whether the L. Treasurer may be present when this Reporte is reade.

Agreed, he may to heare yt, but not when yt is debated.

MR. ATTOURNEY reade the Reporte.

CANT[ERBURY]. The fact is drawen upp by the Comittees, the judgement is lefte to the House. We have examinacions of all parties to justify and explaine anything.

L. TREASURER. Remembred the accusacion of Sir Roberte Pye touching Dalison's buissines, which he desyres to [be] well examined and to satisfy your Lordships therin, which he hoapes he hathe fully done; for any other matter concerning the order, &c. they never came into his thoughts. He desyres his charge in wrightinge, and libertie to examine his wyttnesses and he wyll aunswere yt fully in wrighting.

Touching municions : more done for the advauncement of the office of ordinaunce synce his tyme, then in 7 yeares before. That the Officers of the Ordnance ever against the booke of —

Besydes the debte of Dallisons cleered by him, he hathe yssued out in money above £28,000. Take not my accions in peeces, but the totall together: his care and honor wyll appere.   *Exiit.*

CHAMB[ER]L[AIN]. Whether the Comittee dyd not gyve the Subcomittee power to examine the stoare of Municions, asswell as the matter of Dallison (wherof only the L. Treasurer sayeth he was accused).

PRYNCE Cleered yt that all was referred to be examined by the Subcomittee.

All the others agreed to yt, and they were appoynted by the House.

L. KEEPER Stated the cause : double deccipt to the Lord Treasurers charge.

1. Dallison's buissines.

Q. whether he hathe paid the mony and howe.

2. the matter of charge, herof he expectes not to make aunswer at this tyme, for he hathe made noe defense.

CANT[ERBURY] declared the cause why this Comittee was appoynted. Chiefly for the stoare of municions which they founde emptye, and that is the mayne matter referred.

Mr. ATTOURNEY reade the reporte agayne.

Pryvy Scale of £3000 yearely, payment of £13,000 odd money which was rejected by the Officers of the Navy, as contrary to their proposicion.

1. The cause wherefore none of the 3 contractes sett downe were observed?

PRESIDENT. Seven observable poincts out of the two charges.

1. Ordinaunce, the first charge wherin 3. 2. the bargaining for Dallison's lande, and therein 4. 7 in all.

Three establishments made, none kept in 2 yeares and 6 months wherin Middlesex was Treasurer.

1. In which tyme all Christendome was in warres, and noe powder at all provyded.

2. In this tyme £10,000 myght have been retrenched and saved to the Kinge and a supply [?] made.

3. The Kinge lost £4000 by the omitting sale of the powder at 10d. being served at 7d.

4. Observacions in the bargayne. In June, 1620, he agrees to buye this debte of £13,000, and in consideracion of this agrees to paye £8000 of an olde arrere due, 15 yeares synce. He payes this debte of £13,000 by £1000 per annum, the lande being worth £12,000 per annum and soe the rente paid for the purchas. But he agrees allso to paye this arere, which moved the officers to departe with their debte of £13,000 to hedge in that arere.

5. In Nov. 1621, he is Treasurer, procures noe Pryvy Scale, but uppon a Pryvy Scale dormant payes.

Noate. There is a payement of £9000 without any warrant, for the Pryvye Seale dormant was discharged by the newe establishe-ment. But the King can have noe losse, he may be called to an accompt for it. This he payde in 6 moneths.

6. He posted the King's debte uppon the King's ferme for wynes; losse the fermes;ᵃ but that losse repayed out of the King's purse.

7. The bargayne with Sir Thos. Dallyson, money ; baronetts. The King's tennants to be enfranchised.

Sale of Honour, of 6 Baronetts, worthe —— enfraunchising the King's copyholde tennants.

PEMBR[OKE]. The Treasurer to have his charge in wrightinge.

Q. Whether this day or noe; or to be deferred untill you heare further from the Commons, as he may have his charge of all together. The L. President to drawe up the heddes of this charge.

L. KEEPER. Whether of all or of the municions only, for he desyred not that of Dallison's.

STEWARD. Not a copye of this report to be delivered, but a shorte charge, that by his neglect the stoare of municions is unfur-nished, &c.

DURESME. The charge from the Comons, and the charge here, severall, and therefore to be severally delyvered; for he wyll make severall aunsweres. The heddes of the charge to be drawen by the Attorney, &c., and not by any member of the House.

Denyed. This maye drawe in a gappe her-after, that the King's Coun-cell shall con-sider with what to charge a member of this house. Denyed.

SHEFFIELDE and SAY. Ad idem with Pembroke.

HAUGHTON cum Duresme, for we shall loose tyme, and knowe not whether yt wyll come or not.

MARSHALL. This is in the House solely to be nowe d[eliverc]d.

PR[INCE]. Yt may be that before the charge be drawen into fourme the commons wyll sende up their charge.

STEWARD. A Comittee attendant with the K[ing]s learned councell to drawe up this charge, and Dallison to be herde touching his peticion.

Agreed.

CAN[TERBURY]. Dallison to have copy of that which in the

ᵃ i.e. It was a loss to the farmers.

reporte concernes him. The L. President is added to the former Subcomittee touching municions, &c., and they to drawe up the heddes of the charge against the L. Treasurer, out of the briefe and examinacions reported by the Comittees this mourning.

Ad. to 9 tomorrowe.

DIE MARTIS, 13 APRILIS, 1624.

[L. J. iii. 301.]

*   *   *   *   *

Hodie 1ª *vice lecta est billa.* An acte for confirmacion of the sale of the landes of Sʳ Henry James, Kᵗ att[ainted] of a Premunire.

*   *   *   *   *

XIIII APRILIS, DIE MERCURII, 1624.

[L. J. iii. 303.]

*   *   *   *   *

DIE JOVIS, XVTH DIE APRILIS, 1624.

[L. J. iii. 304.]

*   *   *   *

2ᵈᵃ vice *lecta.* Billa concerninge the lands of Sir Henry James, Knᵗ unto Martine Lumley and others.

CANT[ERBURY]. To be herde, not against the body nor intencion of the Bill, for the forme only. A stricte exccucion of the oathe of allcigeaunce. Many complaints against Sir H. James. Receaved many priestes into his house: had a library of bookes for them: perverted his Lady to Popery, and then woulde have her reconverted for savinge of charge. His chilldren ready to begge. His Majesty informed. I sent for Sir H. James, but founde him most obstinate. He was convicted of a Premunire for denying the oathe of allegeaunce. Noatice to me that this lande was escheated to me by Patent, being within my fee, which much troubled me, for that I had pressed justice against him; remembred the example of Dunbarr, and desyred the lyke himselfe. He acquainted the King with yt and gave yt to his Majeste, who accepted yt. Bestowed yt. By office founde, which cost me £50, the lande is founde to be within my fee. And Emerson presente at the Office. The lande bestowed on Holdernes with Emerson's pryvitye. To be hollden of the K[ing] as of East Grenwich by Socage. Prejudiciall to his Sea and Successor. Mr. Emerson in all the blame, desyred his tenure to be preserved, which cannot be done by the generall savinge, as Sir Edw. Cooke lately delyvered the other day at the Conference touching Monopolies.

*   *   . *   *   *

[Conference appointed for the afternoon on the complaints against the Lord Treasurer.—L. J. iii. 306.]

DIE VENERIS, 16 APR[ILIS], 1624, POST MERIDIEM.

*   *   *   *   *

[Report on the Conference.—L. J. iii. 307-310 —The sheet containing the debates from the 17th of April is missing. The next sheet begins in the middle of Serjeant Crewe's charge against the Lord Treasurer.—L. J. iii. 344.]

DIE SABATHI, 8vo MAII, 1624.

*   *   *   *   *

LUNÆ, 10 MAII, 1624.

[Continuation of the charge against the Lord Treasurer.—L. J. iii. 364-370.]

DIE MARTIS, 11ᵐᵒ MAII, 1624.

[The Lord Treasurer asks to be excused attendance on account of business. A committee sent to visit him. Report by Southampton of his answer.—L. J. iii. 371.]

We founde him a bedd but stronge: his spirittes well. Such a course as never against any to be here 8 houres to stande, weakened: knewe not what would become of this buissines, yt was unchristian-lyke.

SAYE. Such a course to prosequete him in this manner: to stande 8 houres together. 2 lawyers against him, and none one his parte, yt was such unchristian dealinge, and without example, &c. that he knewe not what woulde become of yt.

SOUTH[AMP]TON. The Phisician, that he spake strongly and well. His Lordship pretended noe sicknes.

CANT[ERBURY].⎫ A memoriall of this message and aunswere
STEWARDE.　⎭ to be entred in the Journall booke. He desyred penn and ynke: his helpe of his Secretary: and graunted him: a stoole gyven him: nothinge denyed him but councell.

ROCHEFORD. He had Satterday last gyven him for further respitt.

MOUNTAGU. The LL. who were sent to him, to sett yt downe in wrighting.

KEEPER. He pressed all matters for him of his selfe, as his copyes to be read; his secretary: respitt for Satterday last: a stoole. His speech (Treasurer's) not long together, &c.: Treasurer hathe noe cause of aspersion on the House: he owes thankes.

＊　　　＊　　　＊　　　＊

SOUTH[AMP]TON. The Message commended by the House. Reporte. The aunswere besydes the aunswere to the House, theis wordes: A L[ord], to be thus followed &c.: reade per Mr. Attourney 1ª et 2ᵈᵃ vice, and signed by all the Lords.

STEWART. The speeches uncivill; many other uncivill speeches heretofore: all to be objected against him after the ende of his charge.

MOUNTAGU. To proceed against him for this first.

CHAMB[ER]LEYN. Yt wyll deferr the other proceedinges.

KEEPER. An Order to be entred for the cleering of the House.

SHEFFIELD. His man stood behynde him and prompted him: connived at, and he had a stoole to sytt when he woulde.

PR[INCE]. Not to proceed in this nowe. The Treasurer takes a course to be comitted to the Tower, &c.

Ad. to 2 post meridiem.

DIE MARTIS, 11ᵐᵒ MAII, 1624, POST MERIDIEM.

[Continuation of the Charge against the Lord Treasurer—L.J. iii. 373.]

DIE MERCURII, 12ᵐᵒ MAII, 1624.

[The Lord Treasurer's Defence—L.J. iii. 378.]

PRESIDENT. To cleere the House; touching the weake estate you founde the Tresure in.

[TREASURER.] I lefte yt not worse then I founde yt. I yssued £160,000, and yett left yt £10,000 better than I founde yt.

Treasurer withdrawen.

LINCOLN. That he explayne the words used by him touchinge the conspiracy, &c.

KEEPER. Those particulars to be putt of, till theis great buissines be first ended.

The House adjourned *ad libitum.*

CAMD. SOC.   L

SOUTH[AMP]TON, propounded. Whether he be guilty, and how farre? Take his partes asunder. Begynn with the first, and soe conclude by the vote of the House, of which he is guilty, and of which not, not; and howe farre.

Mr. ATTOURNEY reade the charge.

arderoabe. 1. Warderoabe, *prout* the charge delivered to the Treasurer.

PRESIDENT. The settlement of that great office altogether broaken, and nothing accompted for. The institucion of the K[ing] of Englands house more glorious (next to that of Solomon's) then of any king in the worlde. This to be broaken, a great fault.

CHAMBERLEYNE. The certeinty of the fees not above £4000 or £5000 per ann: the assignements come from the Chamb[er]-leyne, the Master of the Horse, and Groome of the stoale. What they are wee knowe not: he hath not cleered himselfe herin.

KEEPER. 5 faultes touching the Warderoabe; for 3 first, they are small, not to censure him: for the 4 and 5 vizt noe accompts and the K[ing]s bounty destroyed. For the service the Kinge expected from this Master of the Wardes, was the accompt, whereby a ——^a myght be made for direccions herafter. He destroyed the K[ing]s bounty, gott much: many exceeding greate summes. Noe bounty, yf he knowes not what he gyves.

SPENCER. Tr[easur]er hathe turned the course of the right way, making noe accompts.

SAY, *ad idem,* touching the accompts: faulty allso for not serving the warrants, though but 8 appere; 60 may be unserved, for he entred none. Pressed to serve some for the Kinges owne bedd; and yett he neglected yt for his owne gaynes sake.

STEWARDE. He pleades his greate service. Yf the L. Tr[easur]er had discovered the missusing of the place and shewed him yt myght be reformed by another, he had deserved well. But, as he caryed the matter, to procure a certeine assignement, to buy at the lest, and to his owne profitt. But he hathe not accompted, not putt thinges in such order as the K[ing] myght see howe the missorders myght

^a Blank in MS.

be redressed herafter: [er]go, noe deserte, and yett very large gaynes.

CANT[ERBURY]. Treasurer noe way to be excused. Neglect of what belonged to the K[ing]s owne. Therefore in other matters of lesse moment. He was to accompte, and had his patent ben with-out accompt, his fault, having sought yt, and complained of miss-orders in others. *Honestant bonos viros,* &c. Simile of Herods destroying the books of genealogies of the Jewes, he beinge an Edomite, &c. Noe accompt, such a confusion into that office.

MARSHALL. Treasurer, that the Kinge wylled him to keep noe accompt. A cryme to keep noe accomt.

PR[INCE]. Carlile right. He offered when the Queen, my brother, my sister, and I were all supplyed out of the Warderobe, he offred to discharge the same for £24,000 per ann: soe he myght have yt imprest as the Treasurer had. The Treasurer knewe (by his owne wordes) that £14,000 per ann: woulde discharge yt: and yett he demanded £20,000 per ann.

STEWARD. Carlile demanded allso the arere to be paid, being a gentleman borne, coulde not see the olde officers put of, &c. unpayde; which this neglected.

SOUTH[AMP]TON. The not accompt, a mayne faulte and a will-full. He stood uppon yt that he was not to accompt by his patent: and yett his patent being reade, he was bounde to yt, and he knewe yt, as I suppose. Wyllfully done. This not the only faulte: a pre-cedent faulte. He came in to doe the Kinge greate service in reducing and reforming that office: a destruccion only apperes. Uppon this pretence, his Majesty confident: contracted, the Trea-surer the better bargaynes for his owne gayne. For consider, whoe were to be served when Carlile had the office, and whoe when he undertooke yt, and yt wyll appere playnly he ment not soe much service to his Mat as himselfe. He gayned, as he sayes himselfe, £8000 per ann; and yett negligent in serving the warrants, though graunted warely and uppon greate advyse, not to graunte any thing unnecessaryly, but he sayes 300 asswell for none apperes entred.

He vallued his service as a greate and extraordinary meritt. Yf noe good service, then a greate demeritt. Nay it is in his patent, for which he is created an Erle. Conclude him faulty in the trust, in the service and all.

HAUGHTON. His not accompting, and not serving the warrants, his two faultes; for which to be censured.

DURESM. By patente to accompt, his *Quietum est* is without accompt. That is without accompt as a debtour, but not without accompte for direccion herafter what may be done by way of restoracion.

Moved, that the accomptes may be made up (as he offred) for a president for the office.

SHEFFIELD, *ad idem*, touching the accompt, &c.

SAY. The generall accompt, which he sayes he made to the Kinge, not sufficient. Touchinge the gaynes, when he was to leave this place, he vallued the gayne very hyghe, and sayd yf yt were taken from him, his lyfe blood was taken from him, and lefte yt not but with £4000 *per annum* taken from the Crowne.

NORTHAMPTON. Whether a faulte, beinge not called to accompte?

CHAMB[ER]LEYNE. The accompt is only his entring the warrants and empcions in his booke, which he ought to have done, and dyd not.

BRIDGEWATER. To be satisfyed touching the pardon.

PR[INCE] and ALII. The pardon is touching the surplusage, and not a pardon for not accomptinge. The debte is pardoned, and not the cryme.

MOUNTAGU. The Treasurer for his gayne tooke away the honour and state of the King and Kingdome in the Warderoabe, a greater faulte then not accompteing.

CHAMBERLEYNE. To judge him, *super totam materiam*, and not uppon any one faulte.

The House resumed.

Question. Whether the Lord Treasurer hathe offended?

Mr. ATTOURNEY satisfyed the House touching the Lord Treasurer's pardon, vizt, touching the civill parte only, not the criminall parte; the inducement of the pardon is his greate service.

Co[VENTRY] and LICH[FIELD]. The pardon to be seen.

PR[INCE]. Passe the vote whether he hath offended or noe? Respit the censure till you see the pardon.

KEEPER. Noe pardon, a *Quietus est* only.

DENNY. Procured from his Ma^t uppon an opinion that he was free from accompte.

DANVERS. He had his patent first *ad placitum*, and when he founde the proffitt of yt, he surrendred that and tooke another for his lyfe.

Q. Whether the Lord Treasurer for his caryage in the office of the Wardroabe is censurable or noe? See many of your LL. as are of opynion that he is censurable, saye, content. They that are of another opynion say, not content.

Agreed *per omnes.*

Ad. to 2 *post meridiem.*

DIE MERCURII, 12 MAII, 1624, POST MERIDIEM.

[L.J. iii. 380.]

Prayers.

The *Quietus est* to Lionell L. Cranfield to discharge him of the surplusage of the £20,000 per ann: assigned him for the Warderoabe was reade.

PRESIDENT. The K[ing] greatcly abused, to enfourme his Ma^t that the M[aster] of the Wardes^a needed not to accompte.

The House is adjourned *ad libitum.*

Mr. ATTOURNEY reade the charge touchinge the 3 Bribes of the 2. Brybes. Fermors of the Customes to the Lord Treasurer.

---

^{a} *i.e.* Wardrobe. Middlesex having held both offices, the mistake was easy.

PRESIDENT. 3 disguysed Bribes. 3 crymes in one. 1 Bribery. 2 Extorcion. 3 Deceipte for an officer of trust is a taker of the K[ing]s customes. The money is not denyed. Q: howe gyven? howe taken? To be clered whether the L. Treasurer had any partes or noe? Observe the tyme. At the first, he myght have had partes; but the fermors beinge suitors that they myght dispose of the same, promissinge a thankefullnes, his Lordship was contented, and the Lord Treasurers neweyeares guifte theruppon encreased from 1000 markes to £1000. Distribucion of the proffitts and noe demaunde made by the Lord Treasurer of any partes: and soe made a recapitulacion of all *prout per* Mr. Attorney. Yf gyven for the warrants, a Bribe. Yf taken against their wills, as wronge from them, extorcion. Yf for his partes, as he pretendeth, deceipte, &c.

CHAMB[ER]LEYNE *ad idem.* When those gentlemen fell of (whoe the Treasurer sayeth were to have his partes) they came to Merchants, not to the Lord Treasurer, and soe shewed that his Lordship had noe color to any partes of the ferme. Yf he wyll keepe the 2 warrants and delaye them justice therin, a bribe: yf to enforce them to gyve him £1000 for his partes, extorcion. The antedating of the letter and acquitt[ance] as foule as any other.

L. KEEPER. The smallest (and I woulde to God they were all soe) is the Neweyeares guifte. This noe bribe nor corrupcion: a sordide receavinge of yt by his Lordship. The other twoe: the one but a rewarde (yf naked of yt selfe) for his warrant for the securitye to be taken of the 4 Merchants: this noe bribe, but a rewarde, yf yt had ben naked of yt selfe, the 2 a mere Bribe and extortion, coloured with an entrest in partes of the Customes, wheras he had none. Theis the very showes of bribes, the antedate of the lettre and of the acquitt[ance], which his Lordship aunswered noe other-wyse, but that he feared Jacob his deathe.

STEWARD. The Neweyeare guift, nowe due by custome; but in the Treasurer, having such power in his place with the King, and forcing yt in that manner, extorcion, ungentlemanlyke, &c. The other two are Bribes, or much worse. The King referred the complaints of the Merchaunts unto him, soe he was their Judge; and then he extorted from them this money under pretence of a bargayne. Yf not a bribe, a worse, viz', deceipt of trust reposed in him by the King.

CANT[ERBURY]. Noe rewarde proved, to execute justice as a judge. But as a merchaunt (as he hathe ben) fyndinge theis men to have need of his helpe and favour, he palliated a bribe with a bargaine. And soe his Grace shewed howe the Lord Treasurer had nothinge in the partes, which he pretended afterwardes right unto. The antedate of the lettre and acquit[tance] remembred. A fowle cryme and a heavy censure.

SPENCER. Touchinge the Newyeares guyft; lawfull, yf meate or drynke. The Treasurer refused the wyne, and receaved the money. The bargaine: he the first Treasurer that dyd barter. Simile of a servant trusted to make a Lease of 100 acres, and reserves 40 acres to himselfe.

BATHE AND WELLS. The Treasurer tooke excepcion to the deposicions for the incongruity of tyme.

L. KEEPER. Garrawayes exam[inacion] cleered this. The order for Jacob to pay my Lord was taken in June, and after in July for Hyde his man to repaye Jacob agayne.

The House resumed.

Q. Whether the Lord Treasurer in this charge that lyes uppon him concerning theis 3 guiftes be censurable or noe?

STEWARDE. ⎰ The Newyeare guift taken in this manner a mere
SAY. ⎱ extorcion.

2ᵈⁿ Questio. Whether uppon this wholl charge the L. Treasurer be censurable or noe?

Agreed *per omnes, nemine dissentiente.*

The House *ad libitum.*

Mr. ATTOURNEY reade the charge touching the lease of Sugars, 3. Sugars. and the explanacion therof.

L. Keeper. I begyn, bycause I have a Message from his Mat touching this charge, vizt: The King gave him freely £4000 per ann: out of the Lease of Sugars to begyn presently from the date of the Lease, which quyttes the L. Treasurer touchinge this charge and the transferringe of the £7000 to the Tobaccho ferme. Touchinge the denying of repayement of customes uppon exportacion of Sugars by the Merchaunts; this the King quittes him not of. But I fynde noe legall demand made by the Merchaunt, and for that the L. Treasurer affirmes the Fermors are lyable to the repayment yf due, I cannot fynde the Lord Treasurer guilty of any thing here.

President. The Kinge deceaved herein, for not enfourmed aright, that the lease was charged with the debte layd on yt to Heryott. Yf he had, then the transacting of the £7000 to the Tobaccho noe cryme, yett he must have had a Privye Seale for yt. The warderoabe for lyfe. Sugars for 21 yeares ratable to 3 lyves.

South[amp]ton. Treasurer faulty in a proporcion in this charge. He came to the lease uppon false informacion of good service done in the Wardcroabe. The assignacion of £7000 uppon the Tobaccho, to the ende he myght putt himselfe in presente possession, he hathe ever protested against the lyke in all other mens cases; yea, when the King hathe signifyed his pleasure therin only in his owne case he wyll doe yt; to[a] blame, and soe for the denyall of the Customes uppon the exportacion of Sugars.

Stewarde, ad idem, touchinge the consideracion uppon a wronge grounde, in cheating the Kinge in that point, but Q whether a cryme, for that the King is pleased to saye he gave yt freely. But this shewes the disposicion of a ravenous man, in the tyme of this scarcety of money, to procure this greate guifte. Not to judge him for this, nor the exportacion; but to have yt in memory when we judge him for the other matters.

Chamb[er]leyn, ad idem.

Pr[ince], agreeth not to censure any man for a guift gyven by the K[ing]; but I may say he played the extorcioner uppon the

a "Too" MS.

K[ing], and soe shewed howe—not to judge him, but to remember what man he is.

SAY. Reserve yt for an aggravacion in all, for he hathe used false pretences of good service in all. Noe satisfaccion touching the exportacion of sugars.

The House resumed.

3ª Question, Whether the Lord Treasurer shalbe freed from any censure in this particuler charge or noe?

Agreed to be freed, *per omnes nemine dissentiente.*

Adj. *ad libitum.*

Mr. ATTOURNEY that parte of the charge.

SERG[EAN]T CREWE. That the Lord Tr[easur]er called to him this morning touching this point, by Barrett's booke brought him this morning. Copy of a letter wrytten by the Tr[easur]er to Bristoll 1610, agreeth with the lettre written by this L[ord] Tr[easur]er. Many papers shewed allso, of some of Bristoll, whoe had payd some composicions for Grocery, and other papers concerning Exceter, &c., amongest which some saye—dyvers paye; others denye to paye, being encouraged for that they of Bristol wyll not paye.

STEWARTE. Herin the Tr[easur]er, carefull for the Kinges service, peradventure done somwhat to much in writting to stay the merchandise, &c.

CHAMB[ER]LEYN. ⎱ Yf any grounde for a composicion as in
SAYE.   ⎰ this?

L. KEEPER, *ad idem,* and the Treasurer noe way to be censured.

PR[INCE]. True, for in this only he gott nothing to himselfe.

SPENCER. This complaint by the Commons for an imposicion, layd by the Lord Treasurer, his Lordship therefore assuming Regall authorytye: to be satisfyed?

SOUTHAMPTON, *ad idem.*

PR[INCE]. To respect what the Commons sayd, but to judge soe, yf we fynde yt otherwyse.

CAMD. SOC.   M

(margin note: 1. Groacery and Composicions.)

SOUTH[AMP]TON. As yt wylbe published we have freed him, soe to be published allso uppon what grounde we freed him.

PRESIDENT. The sense of the Commons is for that.

Resumed.

4ᵗⁿ. Question. Whether the Lord Treasurer shalbe free of censure in that charge of groacery or noe.

Agreed to be freed.

Adj. *ad libitum* agayne.

Municions, &c. and Dallison's landes.

5ᵗᵃ. Mr. ATTOURNEY reade the next charge touching the establishement for the stoares and municions, &c. and Dallison's lands.

L. KEEPER. Tr[easur]er faultie in all the three bargains for Dallison's landes. I wyll not speake of them as yf I were to reliefe them in the Chauncery. Extracted them all. As to the misdemeanors to be judged in parlement, he made the payement of the K[ing]s money to be a colour for his bargaynes, the greater offence for that he hathe herde the Tr[easur]er presse the lyke farr against others.

2. Baronetts estimated: coppyholdes of Wakefield; with losse to the Kinge. The Tr[easur]ers excuse worse then his faulte. His excuse is, he dyd yt not for the bargain, but knowing the King to pytty Mounson, he moved the K[ing] for him. This most sordide for the Treasurer to make use of this pyttye of the K[inge] to gett a bargayne from Mounson, a man then in miserye, once of good accompt in his countrey; to be nowe pytied, for he fell with his friende.

3. As touching Dallison's lease, his wrighting to the Judges, &c. To be censured in all theis 3 pointes.

CANT[ERBURY] *ad idem*, and remembred 4ᵗʰ, vizᵗ, Neglecte of the stoare of municions which concerne the K[ing] and kingedome very highly.

PRESIDENT *ad idem* for them all 4.

PR[INCE]. For his particuler proffitt he coulde paye arere; but would paye noe money to furnishe the K[inge]s stoare of municions.

Resumed.

5 Question. Whether the Lord Treasurer be worthy of a censure in regarde of this wholl charge, bothe for the 3 bargaynes, and for not supplying the office of the Ordinaunce?

Viz. [?] with Armor and Powder.

Agred to be censured per o[mn]es *nemine dissentiente*.

6. Mr. ATTOURNEY reade the 6 parte of the charge, viz[t], touchinge the Courte of Wardes.

L. KEEPER. 1. Noe fee imposed on the Secretary, but one proofe that he demaunded a fee: the rest, that he tooke what was gyven him. Freed the Lord Tr[easur]er of this. 2, and freed his Lordship touching the tyme of concealment for wards, reduced from 3 yeares to one. 3. Touching the fee doubled for contynuances, to be censured. 4. And soe touching the stampe, a hygh offence that a man *plebeius*, creeping into soe many offices, where there are soe many worthy and learned noblemen; and shall he not spare soe much tyme as to signe his owne name, but comitt the trust to his man by a stampe? For this to be highly censured.

PRESIDENT. 1. The Secretaryes taking, &c., a faulte. 2. Concealment may be prejudiciall to the Subjecte and a Judge to be charged with a May be. 3. Stampe a greate faulte. 4. Double fee lykewyse.

STEWARDE. As to the double fees, in this, as in other thinges, he was tyrannous to the subjecte, and covetous. Stampe, the Secretary dyd what the Master of the Wardes myght doe. Nay by leaving out ynke from the lower parte of the stampe: only he myght fetche the Kinges money as Treasurer: and shewed many enormityes by putting this greate power into his servaunt. He left this to his Secretary as he myght intende other buissines of more mischeefe, &c. To be censured.

CANT[ERBURY]. When many and some of greate place and birthe have come to speake with the L. Tr[easur]er, they were ever shortly aunswered, My Lord is at bedd; unmannerly and lazilye: and yett used a Stampe. To be punished for all.

DURESM.   Much in commendacion of worthy olde Burleighe, whoe was Lord Treasurer and Master of the Wards.

SAY.   Double fees uppon contynuances, the L. Tr[easur]ers aunswere—Yt was the Kinges grace to the People, lett them paye for yt.   Yf his Secretary tooke greate fees, &c., the L. Tr[easur]er aunswered, Then he is a knave: and shall soe greate a truste be committed to a knave?

SHEFFIELD.   *Ad o[mn]ia.   Quære tamen.*

MARSHALL.   For the Stampe, and double fees only.

The House resumed.

6. Question.   Whether the L. Tr[easur]er deserves a censure uppon this wholl charge, or no?

Agreed *per omnes, nemine dissentiente;* to be censured.

CHAMB[ER]LEYN.   Restate how farre you wyll agree in your censure.   Deferred to tomorrowe.

Adj. unto tomorrowe, 8.

DIE JOVIS, 13° MAY, 1624.

[L. J. iii. 382.]

*   *   *   *   *   .

L. KEEPER.   Yf your LL^ps entende to sentence the L. Tr[easur]er this mournyng, then to sende a message to the Commons not to ryse to soone for that they shall have occasion to sende unto them.

Sent by Mr. Sergeant Davos, Sir Ed. Salter.

Aunswered they wyll.

Ordered, the Gent[leman] Usher and the Serg[ean]t at Armes to somon the [Lord] Tr[easur]er to appere before their LL^rs presently. Signed by the L. Keeper and d[elivere]d to the Gentleman Usher.

Adj. *ad libitum.*

The heddes of the 6 charges, and the questions theruppon, were reade.

LORDS' DEBATES IN 1624. 85

PRESIDENT. 1. Warderoabe. 2. Bribes. 3. Bargaines with officers. 4. Wardes. 1 shewed the presidents of the L. Latimer 50 E. 3, to be fyned, ransomed, putt from his offices and councell. 2. Wickham's case, and pardon: fyrst fyned and imprisoned. 3. Lions 50 E. 3, for gayninge 10,000ˡⁱ of the K[ing] by p[a]y[emen]t of 20,000ˡⁱ. 4. For estorted guiftes. 5. Segrave for pryses, H. 3. 6. Accusacion against Hugh Spencer for compassinge the lande of Damory. 7. Langton, the Bishop of Hereford, for compassinge the mannor of Newbottle from de Ferrers by payement of the arere of a debte due by the Kinge to be paid Ferrers. 8. De la Pole, censured for not executinge the orders of ——. 9. Wm. de la Pole, H. 6, censured for getting the Honor of Erledom of Pembr[oke] by false pretences to the King.

SOUTH[AMP]TON. Consideracion of the L. Tr[easur]ers punishement. Whether his meritts overweighe his faultes? Yesterday, he reckoned up the services for which he deserved well. 1. Warderoabe. 2. Houschould. 3. Irelande, 4. Navye. To consider his demeritts herin, there be that are able to gyve satisfaccion herin. Steward for the houschould: Grandison and Chichester for Irelande; others for the Navye.

STEWART. As far as I cann, considering the shorte tyme I have ben there, I have learned there were comissioners to settle better orders, and to refourme abuses of the Household. The groundes for governement of the Houscholde as good as any can be devysed. The Comissioners to amende the abuses crept in, and to make a savinge of some thinges. The Treasurer one, but noe more then any of the reste. Synce, a doore beinge opened to a projecte of more savinge, hathe putt the House out of order: much wantes, and noe credditt to the Household. His Maᵗ had sometymes wanted parte of his dynner, had not I gyven credytt. £10,000 by the projecte stroaken of by the L. Treasurer brought into the exchequer. Want of money. This savinge rather a robbery: for the King, wanting for provision for his owne mouthe at this tyme, the Lord Treasurer gott many guiftes to himselfe in the meane whylle.

Cant[erbury]. This reformacion of the householde begann by
Vavasour. Comissioners appoynted, his Grace one. Under comissioners appoynted; he the Treasurer one of them. Mervayll that
his Lordship woulde assume unto himselfe the reformacion. Shewed
the proceeding of the Comissioners saved com[mun]ibus annis
17,000ˡⁱ per annum, but this propounded by the others and examined
by us. Noe man had allowance of one bytt the lesse by this reformacion. Bolldnes in the Treasurer to assume the reformacion to
himselfe.

Keeper. The Treasurer resumed to himselfe the reformacion
of the Warderoabe, Houschould, Ireland, and Navy, and saving the
Kinges exchaunge to Germany. Warderoabe: he saved 10,000ˡⁱ
per annum, but to himselfe. Saved, dyett from many, as from the
Deane of Westminster, butt sett up another for himselfe. Navy, he
not pryvye to those imployments havinge ben otherwise bredd, used
the helpe of others, namely of Mr. Cooke, and at last assumed the
wholl glory to himselte. Irelande, to make yt stande of yt selfe, but
howe, by appoyntinge the arere to be paid out of olde debtes not to
be levyed, and the nowe establishement out of the revennues, which
are lesse then the establishement. Germany; how saved he money
in Germany? The warres raysed the coyne there, and he caused
the Kinges money to be payde accordingly, which caused Count
Mansfield's souldiers to runn away when they shoulde fyght, and
the Englishe to starve with great miserye.

Pr[ince] added he bragged much what he saved the King in
Germany, but he neglected to paye the poore men in Frankendale,
whoe are yett unpayde.

Chichester. Contracte to paye eache souldier 4ˢ 6ᵈ the weeke
for 8000 souldiers establishement. When we came into Germany the
floryns were there much enhaunsed and the Treasurer sayde he must
pay accordingly. The rates extreame dere. A floryn but 14ᵈ; we
brought yt to 2ˢ 2ᵈ. The Lord Treasurer thought we had ben too
hygh. The merytt (yf any for savinge the Kinges money) is from
4ˢ 6ᵈ the weeke to 2ˢ 2ᵈ, which was done by us, beinge comanded to

be as sparing as we might. We borrowed much to paye this, and he thought we payd too much. 100,000ˡⁱ Irelande. 100,000ˡⁱ debtes to souldiers in Irelande. 2.3 partes ᵃ agreed to be payde readily, wheras we had payd our companyes fully. Then his Lordship appoynted us to be payd herafter according to the establishment, which 66,000ˡⁱ *per annum* out of the revennues, and all the revennues not 50,000ˡⁱ *per annum,* and yett he hathe ordered the 66,000ˡⁱ *per annum* to be payd out of yt.

GRANDISON affirmed that of Irelande, and shewed their good husbandry therof for the K[ing]. Comissioners founde 100,000ˡⁱ due by the King. Tr[easur]er ordered this to be paid out of olde debtes due to the King. Allthough we had tryed *usque ad carcera* to levye yt, and coulde not gett above 2 or 3000ˡⁱ. Accompte tendred, and a warrant founde with Auditor Gofton for abatement of one thirde parte due to all men. Nowe noe possibillitye but to runn in arere again, for 66,000ˡⁱ per annum cannot be payd out of 50,000ˡⁱ revennue, the K[ing]s beinge noe more. As touchinge the offer which the Lord Tr[easur]er spake of to be made him out of Irelande, he cleered the same, and denyed any such offer to be made.

CHICHESTER, *ad idem.*

MOUNTAGU. The patent of his honor to be seen.

LINCOLN. One thinge omitted, the not aunswering of lettres out of Irelande.

L. KEEPER. Touching the censure, to consider therof.

CANT[ERBURY]. Consider his faulte, his punishment: greate offence. Whether to loose his offices?

MARSHALL. And so to the rest.

Resumed.

1. Question. Whether the Lord Treasurer in regarde of theis missdemeanors proved againste him shall loose all his offices which he holdes in this kingedome, or noe? Generally agreed, to loose all his offices.

ᵃ *i.e.,* two-thirds.

2. Q. Touching uncapable of office herafter.

Pr[ince]. This offence symply of yt selfe not soe greate, but considering howe he came in uppon reformacion and proved a sharke for himselfe &c., to loose them.

South[amp]ton. The Tr[easur]er's faults farr greater than the Lord St. Alban's. For unfeithfull to the K[ing]: extorcion and tyranny, and a wolfe to all the kingedom. St. Alban's but a fewe.

L. Keeper. The L. St. Alban's faulte as greate as any. For bribery; yea, by contracte, which destroyed the formallitye of his place. Noe such proved against the Treasurer for his judicature. Faulty for extorcion, whereby he destroyed allso the formallitye of his place. Noe faulte can be greater then a Judge to be corrupt.

Co[ventry] & Lich[field]. Nabuchad[nezzar] fell and restoured ; his sonn contynued in his fathers sins, and punnished, for he tooke noe warninge.

P[rince]. I made noe comparison. The——

2. Q. Whether to be for ever after uncaple of any office, place, or ymployment in the State or comonwelthe, or noe ?

Agreed to be uncapable &c.

3. Q. Whether the L. Treasurer shalbe ymprisoned in the Tower duringe the K[ing]s pleasure, or noe ?

Agreed to be committed to the Tower.

4. Q.: Whether the L. Treasurer for theis offences shall paye a fine to the K[ing], or noe ?

Agreed.   Ad. ad libitum.

Duresm. To cancel the lease of sugars.

L. Keeper. Yt is morgaged for a greate summe. His intrest to be reserved.

Marshall. Fyne : not his goodes.[a]

Keeper. Yf a fyne, to be suitor to his Maj[t] howsoever he shall disspose of the matter not of the manner : prout against Vic[t] St.

---

[a] i.e. Fine him, but do not confiscate his goods, as you would if you cancelled the lease of the sugar duties.

Alban, this fyne begged, and all his landes protected thereby against his creditors.

SPENCER. His fyne to be transacted into Irelande for the service of that countrey.

ALII. This to be lefte to the Kinge.

BANGOR. Dyvyde the fyne into 2 partes: 1. To the Kinge, the other to the warrs.

STEWARD. The quantity of the fine only in question. To the K[ing] alone. The fyne to be accordinge to his faultes and abillitye, and to peticion the K[ing]e afterwardes that some parte may be ymployed for restitucion. But firste for a question, What he hathe gotten from the Kinge?

SOUTH[AMP]TON. The q[uestion] allso what the K[ing]e hathe loste, as 20,000^{li} gyven to Carlile for the warderoab.

DANVERS. Touchinge 20,000^{li} gyven to Carlile, his Lordship never received but 3,000^{li} though recompensed otherwyse from his Ma^t.

SAYE. A proporcion betwene the Tr[easur]ers gettings and fyne.

PR[INCE]. Tyme to noe purpose, for yt is impossible to knowe what he hathe gotten.

L. KEEPER. Stayed the Sugars, 1 parke and 2 l[ordshi]ps, and the parsonage of Cranfield ; the office of Surveyor in the Custom house ; olde debtes uppon his owne lands ; the areres of wynes. The Kinge a bounteous master—he noe carefull servaunt.

SOUTH[AMP]TON. Presidents that dyvers have had in their censures, all the landes and guiftes gyven them by the Kinge taken from them. Moved the lyke nowe.

STEWARD. He came in corruptly &c.; grewe riche ; yf he keepe theis at his goinge oute, yt will be an encouragement to others. Leave him welthy, and you punnishe him not, he wyll laughe at us all.

MARSHALL. 50,000^{il}.

Pr[ince] agreeth to the fyne, and to ransome allso, yf he had noe other punnishment.

CAMD. SOC.   N

L. KEEPER. Shewed howe this fyne myght equall his gettinges.

PRESIDENT. To be putt to the question, whether 50 or 60,000^{li} fyne. His lande cannot be taken away without an acte.

DENNY. 60,00^{li}.

CANT[ERBURY]. Looke uppon his faulte, the complaint against him, and what you wyll leave him, an Erle of highe honor and riche. What punnishement. 50,000^{li} ?

SAY. Lande may be taken away by this House *prout* in the case of Lions & de la Pole. His gaynes greate and vaste. 60,000^{li} fyne.

SPENCER. The Treasurer is a Peere of the Realme.

Resumed.

L. KEEPER. The summes are 50, 60, or 80,000^{li}.

ROCHESTER. Other fynes afterwards.

5 Question. Whether a fyne of 50,000^{li} be a sufficient fyne to be ymposed on the L. Treasurer for his offence, or noe ?

Agreed to be a sufficieut fyne.

SOUTHAMPTON. The L. Tr[easur]ers house at Chelsey a greate vexacion to the subject, being enforced [?].

6. Question. Whether the L. Treasurer shall never sytt in parlement ?

Agreed generally never to sytt in parlement.

7. Q. Whether the Lord Treasurer shall never come within the verge of the courte ?

Agreed never to come within the verge of the courte.

OXON. That the preamble of his patentes of honor may be altered.

CHAMB[ER]LEYNE. Some other matter on recorde to alter the preamble of his patent.

PRESIDENT. To be expressed in our sentence.

SHEFFIELD. This preamble to rest as yt is.

CHAMB[ER]LAIN. An acte to make his landes lyable, lest he hathe conveyed yt over afore hande.

Ordered a shorte acte to be drawen to make the Lord Tr[ea-sur]er's landes lyable to such fyne as shalbe ymposed on him.

The L. Keeper redd the sentence.

Putt to the Question.

ROCHEFORD. Parte of his sentence to make restitucion.

SHEFFIELD. *Ad idem*.

PR[INCE]. Not satisfyed; whether restitucion ?

MARSHALL. *Ad idem*.

ROCHEFORD. Proved uppon oathe before the Committees.

PRESIDENT. The Comittees to make reporte herafter, and the parties to be relieved accordingly.

L. KEEPER. *Ad idem*, and not to be myngled with this sentence.

HAUGHTON. Ellys fyned, and damage yielded in the same sentence.

STEWART. The L. Treasurer not herd as yett.

The Lord Keeper reade the sentence.

Question. Whether this shalbe pronounced as their Lordships sentence, or noe?

Agreed generally, *per omnes nemine dissentiente.*

The Sentence. That Lionel Erle of Middlesex, nowe Lorde Treasurer of England, shall loose all his offices which he hollds in this Kingedom, and shalbe made for ever hereafter uncapable of any office, Place or ymployment in this State and Commonwelthe; and that he shalbe ymprisonned in the Tower of London duringe the Kinges pleasure: And that he shall paye unto our Sovereigne Lorde the Kynge the fyne of 50,000li: And that he shall never sytt in Parliament any more: And that he shall never come within the verge of the K[ing]s Courte.

Message to the Commons by Serg[t] Crewe and Mr. Attorney generall.

That the Lords are ready to gyve judgement yf they with their Speaker wyll come and demande. Answered.

They wyll attende presently as the manner is.

The Lords beinge all in their roabes, the Lord Treasurer was brought to the barre by Gentl[eman] Uusher and Serg[ean]t at Armes. His Lordship came with lowe obeysaunces, and kneeled all in blacke, and then stood betweene the Usher and the Sergeant.

The Speaker (with his Sergeant) and Commons came in, the Sergeant putting downe his Mace.

The Speaker came to the barre. K[nights], cit[izen]s, and b[u]rg[esses] heretofore transmitted severall offences against Lionell &c. the particulers formerly related, bribery, extorcion, oppression and other grievous misdemeanors, and nowe the Commons, by me their Speaker, demaunde judgment.

Middlesex began to speake: denyed; may by peticion afterwards.

L. KEEPER. The highe Courte of Parlement dothe adjudge. This is the Judgment of this highe Courte.

The Lord Treasurer was withdrawen by the Sergeant.

STEWARD ｝to name a Committee to acquaint the K[ing] with
PRESIDENT ｝ this sentence, and to take away the staffe.

Canterbury, President, Stewarde, Marshall, Duresme; to goe to the Kinge accordingly. A warrant to the Gentleman Usher to carrye the Lord Tr[easur]er forthwith prisoner to the Tower.

SAY. The Treasurer to have leave to go to his house firste, and to the Tower afterwards this daye, but not to be out of the Officers' custodye.

DURESM. A tyme for the buissines concerning the officers of the Ordinaunce.

DIE VENERIS, 14 MAY. 1624.

[L. J. iii. 384.]

Prayers.

Lecta 2 vice bill Yorkehowse to the Kinge, &c. and Brighton Acomb to the Archb. of Yorke, &c. Committed.

BANGOR. Against the Bill, for a Bishops house.

L. KEEPER. He had comission from his Maj^t touching this exchaunge, and that yt myght be beneficiall to the Archbishop of Yorke. The Archbishop departes with an olde house for a mannor of about 100ᵘ per annum olde rent.

*   *   *   *   *

Haughton, touchinge the arrest of the E[arl] of North[amp]ton's servant, the partie sent for and attended longe since to be dispatched. North[amp]ton sent for at my complaint: submitted himself; his stay sufficient punishment. His name is Flemynge. Flemynge at the barr.

The Lord Keeper told him of his fault: pardoned at the E[arl's] entreaty uppon his submission. Discharged.

Pugett, above 40 bylls dependings, dyvers pryvate, to be comise- South[amp]-rated, havinge past 2 broaken parlements before. To be considered ton. of. Ad idem.

*   *   *   *   *

SPENCER. That a Bill be drawen by the Kinges Councell to Ordered. make the E[arl] of Midelsex landes and estate to be lyable unto his owne creditors, his fyne to the K[ing] to accompt unto the King herafter, and to restitucion to such whom he wronged.

SAY. The Message touching Midd[lesex]. Comittees to meet on Concealments presently.

CANT[ERBURY]. Reporte the Bill for York house. His harte goeth not with that Bill, the firste example against the K[ing]s provident care by Acte to prevent the decay of Bishopricks. The exchange beneficiall to the Bishop. But the consent of the Deane and Chapter of York is to be had, as his Grace supposeth; though some presidents otherwyse. Bonum to be bene, and their consent to be had. Charges of the olde foundacion of one quallity contrary to those of the newe ereccion. In the vacancy of the olde, the rents belong to the Deane and Chapter; in the vacancy of the newe, they belonge to the Kinges exchequer. His con-science. Bishopp endowed ever since the Primitive Church. Anathemas on Abbeyes, &c. of latter tymes. Lett those the Abbeyes goe. Butt some, not on other.

the Howses of Bishopricks dedicated and perchaunce with severe menaces, &c. Not blessed. And his Grace notwithstanding retourned the Bill reported by the Comittees as fitt to passe with amendements and one proviso, but not with his harte.

CHAMB[ER]LAIN. Noe prejudice to the Deane and Chapter to departe with this House to the K[ing]. They never had use of yt. Exchanges without their consent, usuall by parlement, as by the presidents shewen. The exchaunge very advantageous to the Bishop.

L. KEEPER. Protested his care that this exchaunge myght not be prejudiciall to the Bishop. Not acquainted with it untill within this fortnight. But 4[li] per annum payd to the Sea of Yorke since Archbishop Heathes tyme. Noe Archbishop ever dwelt in since. The House ruinous; ready to fall. Noe way necessary for the Deane and Chapter's assente sede plena. Yt is usuall, but not necessary. The rent but 4[li] per ann. out of the House and 7[li] out of the tenements, whear out of this lands may be shortly (the lease expyred) 700[li] per ann.

Touching the Anathema. Yt was not ever the auncient house and seate of the Archbp. of York, but lately annexed to that Sea, enjoyed by dyvers. That noble Lord to whom yt is meant, ever loved well B. B[a].; and doubted not but shoulde long enjoye the same. The Kinge hathe gyven more to this Bishoprick then ever K[ing] dyd synce the first of H. 8.

MOUNTAGU. ⎤ Not to debate the body of the Bill uppon the
PRESIDENT. ⎦ reporte with amendement, before the amende-ments are reade. Gave his reason for the conveniency of the exchaunge. For the Deane and Chapters not assent: not necessary, for that this is not a conveyance from them, but an Acte of parle-ment: and presidents according. The proviso to restreyne that noe more houses passe then belong to that house; another proviso, that the Deane and Chapter may resorte in the Vacancie to the lands gyven in exchaunge to the Archb[isho]p.

<hr>

n i.e. the Bishops.

The amendements and proviso reade.

DURESME.   A farther consideracion of some other matters.

MARSHALL aunswered all the objeccions of Duresme and Canterbury, especially touching the jurisdiccion which the Archbishop of
Yorke may have in that house when he dwells there.

BATHE AND WELLS.   Touching dispensacions when a B[isho]p
is in another diocese.

NORWICH.   Arch[bishop] Canterbury gyves us our grace to
exercise jurisdiccion, &c.

DAVIDS gave his reasons for the Bill.

The Bill for Yorke House reported with amendments and proviso, and reade.

Putt to the question: whether to be engrossed with the sayd
amendments and proviso.

Agreed *per pluries* to be engrossed.

SAY.   To sett this afternoone to dispatche publique and pryvatt
bills.   Ad. to 8 tomorrowe mourninge.

DIE SABATHI, 15 MAY, 1624.

*   *   *   *   *

[Message from the Commons to renew the Conference on Monopolies.—
L. J. iii. 385.]

*   *   *   *   *

Hodie 3ⁿ *vice lecta est billa* for Yorke House.

ST. DAVIDS vissited Buck[ingham] at his Graces com[mand].
1. To make his protestacion, that he never dyd, nor wyll endeavor
any hurte to the Churche.   Yf yt be not very advantageous, he
desyres yt not.   2. At the first he intended to provyde for a house
for the Archbishop of Yorke, when he shall attende here.   And
nowe he wyll provyde one to be gyven that sea in fee symple.
Desyred his honour to be preserved, that he never intended any
hinderaunce to the Church.

The Bill was putt to the question.

Past *nemine dissentiente.*

*   *   *   *   *

DIE MERCURII, 19ᵐᵒ MAII.

*   *   *   *   *

[Report of Conference touching the Bishop of Norwich.—L. J. iii. 388.]

*   *   *   *   *

Peticion of the Bishop of Norwich reade concerninge Thomas Stokes.

Thos. Stokes to be sente for.

Wylliam Neve and Chr. Ponder to come to justifye the truthe of this, &c.

Certificate of the Expositors reade.

Certificate of the Maior of Norwich read.

SAY. A comittee to examine this buissines.

PR[INCE]. Leave the 4 first poyntes to the highe Comission. Examine the other 2.

CO[VENTRY] AND LICH[FIELD]. In comendacion of Norwich.

KEEPER, the Pr[ince]. That the four first partes be referred to the Highe Comissioners. I that the latter two allso, for the one concernes fees, which must be judged by the table made by Whitgyft, and in the custody of Archb. of Canterbury.

PRESIDENT. With the Prynce, that the 4 first be referred to the hyghe Comission and the 2 latter to be here examined.

ARUNDELL. | The Archbishop of Canterbury may satisfye CANT[ERBURY].| the House to morrowe mourning touching the fees, &c.

SPENCER. To examine all 6 partes.

STEWARDE. To referr yt to the Comissioners, and they to reporte, otherwyse we shall wrong our priviledges by putting yt quyte from us.

PR[INCE]. Yt is assmuch against our pryviledges yf we may not referr yt.

SH[EFFIELD]. Yt agreeth with auncyent orders to referr buissinesses complained on here to be fynally determined in other Courtes.

SAY. Dyvyde yt not: but referr the wholl to be reported to the House and then the House to be judge.

PR[INCE]. My meaning was to refer yt to them, the Com-[missione]rs, to examin, and they to reporte to us, and we to judge.

* * * * *

[Reference to the Commissioners ordered. But the House to judge on their Report.—L. J. iii. 390.]

MERCURII, 19 MAII, POST MERIDIEM.

[Report on the Bill of Continuance and Repeal of Statutes.—L. J. iii. 391.]

* * * * *

DIE JOVIS, 20 MAII, 1624.

[L. J. iii. 393.]

* * * * *

PRESIDENT reported the Bill of monopolies with amendements and proviso. They are once reade 1ᵃ vice.

PRESIDENT. For the L. Dudleyes Patent of makinge iron with sea coales.

Ordered the same to be inserted in the Proviso.

L. KEEPER. A snare on his Maᵗˢ servants. Yf they write a letter, &c., a Premunire by this Lawe. Some Lordes may be enforced to wryte, as yf yt passe by question at the Councell-table that such a letter be wrytten.

PR[INCE]. A proviso for this; otherwyse doubtes the Kinges assent.

ARUNDELL. Ad idem; a letter may be written at unawares, the Commons confesse the premunire in such cases.

CANT[ERBURY]. The Commons sayd, theire maine ayme is that such letters be subjecte to a premunire.

CAMD. SOC.   O

Reporte.
Monopolies.

SAYE. Thinkes noe snare in yt. Noe Premunire unlesse letters be wrytten to staye execucion after judgment, which every man may take noatice of, and the letters neede not ; yf convenyent, a mocion in Courte wyll doe yt.

PRESIDENT. To add only in that clause—Noe person and persons (Prosequutinge)—and then yt wyll not touche the Councell.

SOUTHAMPTON. The greate expectacion of this Bill, and the benifytt. Feares yt wyll not passe yf that clause be altered, or taken awaye. That the penalty may remayne greate and severe, or else yt wyll not restreyne our nation's naturall inclinacion to monopolies: [er]go to rest as yt is, lest yt passe not.

STEWARDE. Yt must be made passable in 3 places, with the Commons, with us the Lords, and with the Kinge. Not to passe with this daunger to the Councell: to be altered *prout* President.

SHEFFIELD. The prosequntor only to be subjecte to the Præmunire.

SAY. The prosequutor cannot be subjecte to a præmunire before a judgment.

Q. Whether the Judges ought to staye judgment uppon letters, &c. *prout antea*, &c.?

PRESIDENT. *Prout antea.*

2da *vice lecta sunt* the sayd amendments and proviso. Recomitted to the former Committee.

[Conference on recusants. L. J. iii. 304.]

*   *   *   *   *

DIE VENERIS, 21 MAII, 1624.

[L. J. iii. 397.]

*   *   *   *   *

Monopolies, amendements & proviso, reade 1^a *et* 2da.

*   *   *   *   *

L. KEEPER. Monopolies against those amendments touchinge

letters to be writt by the Councell to staye proceedings, &c., as not sufficient. Moved to be eased therof altogether. Shewed the first begyn[ning] of a præmunire.

MOUNTAGUE. Not to speake against amendments till they be redd.

Amendments on the Bill for Monopolies.

     *   *   *   *   *

SHEFFIELD. To remember their L^{ps} of the petition exhibited by the Commons concerning Recusants.

Pet[ition] read.

Adj. ad libitum.

CANT[ERBURY]. The matter desyred that Recusants and justly suspected Popish, &c. may not exercise places of authoritye, &c. herin I assent with them. The K[ing] and Pr[ince] gyve example to all men to hear and receive the communion. An encouragement to us all, yf they in office would encourage their inferiours.

The manner to be considered whether, 1. We to joyne with them? 2. Howe to present yt to his Ma^t? Whether by a Committee of both houses, as heretofore, or by the Pr[ince] alone?

Altum silencium.

PRESIDENT. The Pr[ince] to present the peticion & names.

STEWARD. *Ad idem* for the matter with Canterbury; not to joyne with the Commons, to present the names of the justly suspected, &c., for that many of them are but uppon fame, or for kynred sake.

L. KEEPER. The Justices of the Peace are in commission by my knowledge. My only apology is, I never placed any one but by the immediate commendacion of the Kinge, of the Judges, or of four at the least of the other Justices nere adjoyninge. They may be putt out agayne by me, uppon certificate of any Justices that they are justly suspected Recusants. Wyshes noe Papist or suspected for such myght beare office, &c.: but not to displace theis persons by a judicious sentence, uppon surmises only. His Lordship remembred, whether any inquisicon may be made of any that are Members of this House, but here only. His Lordship lyked the matter, but not the manner of this Peticion.

Pr[INCE]. We have demaunded this same thinge of the K[ing] allready and granted. The King wyll take yt unkyndly yf he be misdoubted. Refuse not the Lower House correspondency. The K[ing] to be acquainted with yt by some Member of this House by way of yntimacion; but not to passe as an Acte of this House, nor publique peticion ; and to acquaynt the Lower House with this course first.

South[amp]ton. The Commons are inquisitors; we procecde (not concluded by them): we examine, &c. The Commons have proceeded herin according to their wonted manner. We to procced according to our manner, which we cannott fynnishe in such short time. Moved to gyve the Commons reasonable satisfaccion.

A meeting to deliver the reasons and streightnes of tyme to be shewed them.

The Pr[ince] to acquaint the K[ing] with this.

Steward. This not to be the deede of the House. There be many Privy Councillors with the Commons: they (noe doubte) wyll shew the King their names. We not to move the Prynce to doe yt. But yf we doe nothing, the Commons wyll proceede alone.

Sheffield. ⎫
L. Chamberlain. ⎬ Ad idem.

Pr[INCE]. I intende to doe yt privately, not as a Committee. A conference with the Commons presently.

Resumed. Message to the Commons by Mr. Serg[ean]t Crewe and Mr. Attorney.

Aunswered theym. A presente conference with them about the Peticion they re-c[eived] yesterday, with the same Committee, 24.

Say. That Cant[erbury], Steward, Chamb[erlain], South-[amp]ton and Sheffield may sett downe the heddes of what they wyll ymparte to the Commons. Soe they dyd.

Haughton added.
And is to be added to the Committee for this Conference.
CAN[TERBURY]. Reported what his Grace and Steward, &c.
had concluded to intimate to the Commons at this Conference.
Approved of.

*　　　*　　　*　　　*　　　*

SABATHI, 22 MAII, 1624.

[L. J. iii. 400.]

*　　　*　　　*　　　*　　　*

Hodie 3ᵃ *vice lecta* Bill monopolies, with amendmentes and provisoes.

Dyvers of the Lords *pro et con.*, in respect of the notice given
that the accion depending is grounded uppon this statute.

Some thought this caution enough to forwarne any Lords not to
runn into the Præmunire. Others thought yt not caution enough,
and that yt is not yett determyned what a Monopolie is, and un-
equall therefore to incur a Præmunire, which some runn into
unawares.

PR[INCE]. I was wylling to have had a larger caution but am
nowe fully satisfyed that there is caution enough.

HOUGHTON. By the lawe of E. 3, whosoever shall wryte
letters —— shall incurre fyne and ransome, without any caution at
all that noatice shalbe gyven him. By this Bill, he is to have
noatice, &c.

PRESIDENT. As touchinge the noatice, &c. yt is not incerteyne
as some thynke, but certeine. For the noatice is to be gyven by
the partie interressed viz': the plaintiff or defendant, and by none
ells.

Putt to the question and assented unto.

*　　　*　　　*　　　*　　　*

[Message for a conference on the Bill for continnance of Statutes.—L. J. iii. 401.]

*　　　*　　　*　　　*　　　*

ADHUC DE 22 MAII, 1624, POST M[ERIDIEM].

[L. J. iii. 402.]

*   *   *   *   *

S' E. Cooke.   PRESIDENT. At the conference with the Commons this mournyng, the Commons desyred to present to the Lords their reasons
against the amendementes of the Bill for cont[inuance] and repeale
of Statt[utes], touching the repeale of the Stattute of 7 E. 6 for
sale of wynes, and related their reasons whye that Stattute shoulde
be repealed.

1. The inconveniencye in, 1. the impossibillitye; 2. the dispensacion; 3. the uses.

2. The Kinges aunswere in parliament *Anno* 7 *Jacobi* to the
peticion of the Commons touchinge the licences of wynes, that after
the deathe of the E. of Nott[ingham] noe such lycences shoulde be
longer used.

Then Mr. Attourneys aunswere to them all 3, and to the
K[ing]es aunswere, not to graunt the power of the dispensacion to
any subjecte, but not that the Kinge himselfe woulde not take any
I herde him   benefytt of the said dispensacions. Then touching the amende-
not.   ments, &c.

Mr. NOY. The ende of the lawe is tourned to another ende then
was intended : [*er*]*go* fitt to be taken awaye.

PRESIDENT concluded. The Earl is yett lyvinge ; not tyme to
request yt before the Earl's death. Noe tyme to take away a
revenue from the crowne: provyded by the Bill of Monopolies to
contynue noe longer then the proffitt comes to the Crowne, &c.

CHAMB[ER]L[AI]N. What shalbe sayd to the Commons in this
buissines ? To make what wee have done, by as sweete meanes as
may be. Not to bynde the Kinge to his promisse by Acte of
Parlement. Nott[ingham] is nott yett dead.

PR[INCE]. In the begynning of the Parlement they propounded
to take away nothing of the K[ing]es revennues, untill they had
gyven him as much another waye.

STEWARD.

SHEFFIELD. To putt them in hoape of the K[inge]s promisse to be performed in due tyme, when Nottingham is deade.

L. KEEPER. Yf this Acte passe not, yt is much to the prejudice of the subjecte, for whose good yt only is.

SAY. To alter nothing, but to sweeten yt. That noe conference. Aunswere, we then knewe not but that the session woulde have ended on this day.

P[RINCE]. They yielded to the cont[inuance] of this statt[ute] in the Bill of Monopolies, soe we needed not to conferr.

MARSHALL. Ad idem, with ——

DANVERS. And allso that we rely uppon the K[ing]'s promisse, and we need not bynde him to it by a lawe.

PRESIDENT. When a Bill is retourned to the Commons with amendements. Q. Whether yt may be re-amended, or noe?

Resolved Anno 39 Eliz. not to be. Vide in other former parlements, and 4to Jacobi. Their Lordships went to the Conference resolved to insiste uppon theis reasons with as much sweetenes as may be.

PRESIDENT to inferr and reporte.

    *   *   *   *   *

---

24 MAII, 1624.

[L. J. iii. 403.]

HAUGHTON. Touching the peticions of Sir Thos. Mounson, Sir Thos. Dallison, Officers of the Ordinance and Sir Ph. Cary; the E[arl] of Midd[lesex] his landes to be lyable.

Nowe other peticions. 1. L. Wylloughby. 2. Horseman. 3. Thelwell.

STEWART. That Wylloughby his peticion may be accepted, for debte uppon land. The other two come to late.

L. KEEPER. Yf the Bill passe yt wyll relieve them all. yf yee proceede to examine them, wyttnesses must be examined and much tyme spent, more then nowe can be spared. And the E[arl] of Midd[lesex] must have tyme to aunswere & examine, &c.

Agreed.   L. Wylloughbyes peticion to be sente to the E[arl] of Midd[lesex] to aunswere.

Message from the Commons by Sir Thos. Edmondes and others. The bill of Subsidye.

Adj. to 7 to-morrowe.

Die Martis, 25 Maii, 1624.

[L. J. iii. 404.]

Prayers.

Hodie 1ª *vice lecta est Billa Subsidii Temporalium.*

Pr[ince], a protestacion to be entred touchinge the judicature which the Commons reteyne by this acte.

Pr[ivy] Seale. The Judges to consider of a protestacion.

Reporte.   South[amp]ton reported the Bill for Reliefe of Creditors against such as dye in execucion as fytt to passe with a proviso, reade 1ª et 2ᵈᵃ *vice.* To be engrossed.

Reporte.   President reported the Bill for the County Palatine of Durham, without amendements, and the byll for levying of fynes in other mens names with one proviso. reade 1ª et 2ᵈᵃ *vice,* to be engrossed.

L. Keeper. To consider of the judicature reserved, &c.

Sheffield, and of the power gyven us by this Acte which *tacite* ymplyes, we olls have noe power of judicature.

*   *   *   *   *

Die Martis, 25 Maii, 1624, post m[eridiem].

[L. J. iii. 405.]

Hodie 2ᵈᵃ *vice lecta est Billa subsidii* for the temporal.

L. Keeper. The Judges first to consider of the 4 poyntes materyally to be considered in this bill.

1. Judicature to themselves.
2. Judicature seemed to be granted to this house.
3. Power of judicature over the Assistantes of this House.
4. Power to committ to the Tower, untill they be d[elivere]d by the Commons.

PRESIDENT. 5, that all proceedinges shalbe determined by them. The Judges to consider of this a[r]g[umen]t tomorrowe mourn-ynge.

*   *   *   *   *

MERCURI, 26 MAII, 1624.

[Report that the Judges' opinion is that the House is not prejudiced by the Bill of Subsidies. L. J. iii. 408.]

*   *   *   *   *

DIE JOVIS, 27 MAII, 1624.
[L. J. iii. 410.]

*   *   *   *   *

DIE [VENERIS,]ᵃ 28 MAII, 1624.

*   *   *   *   *

[Order to the Earl of Middlesex to pay 2000ˡⁱ to Sir Thos. Monson. L. J. iii. 418.]

DIE SABATHI, 29 MAII, 1624.

*   *   *   *   *

PR[INCE]. That the order made yesterday *post meridiem* against E[arl] of Midd[lesex] to pay £2,000 to Sir Thos. Mounson for the 6 Baronetts to be reversed and altered for that   viz.ᵗ To be referred to the King or the L. Keeper.

[Order accordingly. L. J. iii. 421.]

*   *   *   *   *

ᵃ Sabathi MS.

DIE SABATHI, 29 MAII, 1624.

[Address to the King by the Speaker of the House of Commons King's Speech in
reply. Lord Keeper's Speech. L. J. iii. 423.]

D[omin]us C[ustos] M[agni] S[igilli] ex jussu D[o]m[ini] R[egi]s prorogavit p[ræse]ns Parliamentum usque in diem Martis secundum diem Norembr[is] proximum futurum.

LORDS' DEBATES IN 1626.

[L. J. iii. 492.]

Le Roi.

The LL. and Judges stood untill the K. bad them set downe, but none were covered.

Kent with the capp.

Pembroc, Chambleyn, with the staffe on the left hande.

Ruttlande, with the sword on the right hande.

My LL.

Noe long speeche. The olde custome, by the Keeper at large.

L. Keeper, first on his knees with the King.

My LL. and the ——

You are here assembled by ——

To holde a Parlement, the generall ancient and powerfull councell, whereof yf we consider aright of the distance between a Monarche and subjects—conceave comforte in the constitucion, not only the Prelatts, Nobles and Grandes, but allso the Comons of eache degree to consulte of the great and weighty affaires of the K. and kingdom.

A greate—— Not to be thankfull to enjoy yt. All good hartes—— It behoves us all with united heartes to fixe our thoughts of counsell worthy of such an assembly.

Yt behoveth too to praise and blesse God that hathe putt the power of assembling Parlements in him whose vertue —— with his lineall discent ——

Stryve whether a —— Truly understand the trewe use of parle-ments. Wyttnesse his dayly accesse therto before his accesse to the Crowne, his frequent accesse to his never dying father.

When the Royal diadem discended ; first consultacion to meete his people in parlement.

To treate and consult with uniforme assent and affeccons of those things.

Nowe being thus assembled ; as his love and affeccon to call, soe the danger of the late mortallity, and the multitude of his occasions forbydds to prolong the sytting ; confynes the meetinge to a short tyme, me to a short —— as agreeable to the examples of best tymes.

To consult of provident and good lawes, the surest pyllars and buttresses of a kingdome.

The royall throne the fountayne of justice.

Good lawes the streames to despence the same to his people.

Study that this fountayne is not dry. They to receave such comfort as in the tymes of his best progenitors, wherin as most sensible of the publique ; so injury to this assembly, yf but doubted that they wyll not add any thing to.

Good lawes. This his Ma^ty hathe cause to desyre at this tyme more then any other.

His solemnity —— Oathe to ——

Noe tyme soe fytt to advyse and conferr of lawes with his people as at this tyme, his Ma^ty having ——

This is the summe of that I have to say touching the publique, as you may ——

The Commons to choose their speaker, and to present him on Wenesday next.

D^s Rex ad[jornavit] usque Wensday at 1 post Meridiem.

MERCURII, 8vo DIE FEBRUARII A° 1° RRs CAROLI.
[L. J. iii. 494.]

Dominus Rex.

[Approbation of the Speaker of the House of Commons, Sir Heneage Finch.]

JOVIS, 9 FEBR. 1625.

[L. J. iii. 495.]

Prayers.

Ep^{us} Carlile: Mulgrave excused.

ARUNDELL. That the order is to reade the order of the House before any Bill be reade.

Orders of the House reade.

1^a vice lectio of billa, for the meintenaunce of his Ma^{ts} revenewes.

PRESIDENT.

We^a exhibited to his Matie the peticion touching Religion begann by the Comons.

We joyned. Yesterday relacion.

Moved to sende a message to the Comons, that both they and we may by the mouth of the L. Keeper present our joynt and humble thanks to his Matie for his gracious answere, &^{c}.

CHAMB[ER]LEYN. To deferr yt till the Commons house be called.

SPENCER. The oathe of Allegeaunce to be gyven to all the LL. of the House ; especially nowe the King having bene so lately crowned.

Stet.

Stet.

Agreed.
Stet.

KEEPER. Comaundement yesterday from the Court of Starr-chamber. They being tender to touch uppon the priviledges of your LLp^s : vid. Informacion there by Mr Attorney against the L. Vaux and his brother, Mr. Wylliam Vaux: repeated the effecte of the Byll and what is there alleged against them ; which his L^p recyted out of a paper, firste econcerninge M^r W^m. Vaux, and then concerning the L. Vaux.

Complaint made to the Councell, his Matie was present, & gave order for the proceedinge in the Starrchamber.

Began at Reading. Purposed to be herde before the Parlement. All ready nowe. To be herde tomorrowe.

Not to be entred.

^{a} The portions in the brackets are crossed out with the pen.

Moved. They tender. Keeper comaunded to relate yt to the LL. for your direccion therein. 2 Judges appoynted to take the examinacion, & publicacion to be the first daye of the terme.

The L. Vaux preferred a peticion for staye. The L. Keeper referred yt to Mr. Attourney. He content, soe noe use be made of yt for delayes.

The L. Vaux his wordes under the peticion reade. The mocion made accordingly, the first daye of the terme, & by votes, publicacion not thought fytt to be stayed.

KEEPER moved for the LL. direccion herin.

WESTMORELAND. The Comittees for priviledges to be appointed, & they to heare this afternoone what the L. Vaux can say.

CHAMB[ER]LEYNE. The daye is tomorrowe [er]go.

RUSSELL. To speake your pleysure herin, whether president allready, or one to be nowe made?

DORSETT. The L. Vaux as a member of this House to be looked on and respected. To avoyde a president herafter against the LL. priviledges, but to proceede against his brother.

MARSHALL. Resolved by Mr. Attourney that this cause can take noe hurt by delay. To leave yt to the L. Keeper to graunt the L. Vaux his privilege, yf he demaunds yt, & not otherwise.

SAYE. Our priviledges are that we be free to attend the service of this House. He that makes himselfe uncapable therof not capable of the priviledges. The L. Vaux never sate here synce the order made to take the oathe of allegeaunce. Noe priviledge to be allowed him untill he take that oathe.

Question. Such of the LL. as thynke fytt that the priviledge of this House shalbe allowed unto the L. Vaux in this case, yf he demaunds yt.

SAY. The question, whether the L. Vaux, yf he take the oathe, shall be allowed the priviledges.

MARSHALL. To understande whether he hathe taken the oathe or not.

SAY. The Lord Vaux to be sent for &c.

The order 22 Junii 1625 reade touching the oathe of allegeaunce.   Feb. 9.
KEEPER. Moved to putt 2 questions.
   1. Whether the L. Vaux shalbe allowed his privilege, yf he
take the oathe of allegeance ?
                                                                   Not to be
   2. Whether he shalbe allowed his priviledge yf he take not   entred.
that oathe ?
The L. Vaux to be sent for.   Agreed.

*   *   *   *   *

The L. Vaux came whilest the last Bill was readinge.
The bill being reade and reported, the L. Vaux of his owne
accorde went forthe.
DORSETT & MONTGOMERY sent to him by the House to demaunde
of the L. Vaux whether he wyll take the oathe of allegeaunce or   Not to be
                                                                     entred.
noe.
Reported that his Lp. wyll very wyllingly take that oathe.
Noe question to be made of yt, but to allowe him his privi-
ledge &c.
The L. Vaux came in ; took his place.

Adj. to 9 on Satterday next.

Mervyne L. Audeley, Edwarde L. Vaux, dyd take the oathe of To be entred.
allegeaunce presentlye after the Courte was adjourned.

———————

SABATHI, 11ᵐᵒ FEBRUARII, 1625.   Feb. 11.
[L. J. iii. 497.]
   *   *   *   *   *

WESTMORELAND.   A Bill touching the encrease of offices and   Agreed.
fees, especially of lawyers fees, and the bill exhibited in parlement
to this purpose aⁿ 25 Eliz. to be sought out.
   *   *   *   *   *

Feb. 13.

LUNÆ, 13 FEBR., 1625.

[L. J. iii. 498.]

*   *   *   *   *

Feb. 15.

MERCURII, 15ᵗᵒ DIE FEBR., 1625.

[L. J. iii. 499.]

*   *   *   *   *

Feb. 16.

JOVIS, 16 FEBR.

L. J. iii. 501.]

*   *   *   *   *

Feb. 18.

SABATHI, 18 FEBR., 1625.

[L. J. iii. 502.]

*   *   *   *   *

Feb. 20.

LUNÆ, 20 FEBR., 1625.

[L. J. iii. 503.]

*   *   *   *   *

Reported an order for absence without proxies, &c.

MARSHALL. The same comittee to meet and consider of a newe order.

MONTAGU, e contra.

MULGRAVE. A respect to be had to the House, and to sende an excuse.

*   *   *   *   *

SAY agayne. 2 respects. 1. Those that come not at all. 2. Those that are in towne, and neither come nor send excuse.

Question. Whether yt shalbe recomitted or noe? Agreed *per* Agreed.
pluries.

The LL. subcommittees to consider of this order agayne.

Adj. to Thursday at 9.

JOVIS, 23 FEBR., 1625. Feb. 23.

[L. J. iii. 505.]

*   *   *   *   *

PRESIDENT. To dispatche Lowes bill this morninge.

MULGRAVE. The grande comittees for priviledges to meete.

NORTHE. Moved for direccons to receave those peticions only whoe cannot be relieved in other Courtes.

DENNY. *Ad idem.*

MARSHALL. That yt be left to discrecion.

*   *   *   *   *

BRIDGEWATER. Some of the Judges to assist the committee for peticions.

SAY. The comittee for peticions to offer to the consideracion of Ordered. the house what peticions they thynke fytt, and their reason for the same, and the House to direct them.

*   *   *   *   *

SABATHI, 25 FEBR., 1625. Feb. 25.

[L. J. iii. 506.]

*   *   *   *   *

The grande comittees for priviledges retourned.

PRESIDENT reported 4 orders thought fytt to offer.

1. An order that all LL. may knowe the danger for not coming to parlement at the firste.

2. For absenting from prayers to paye 8*s.* for every day. Noo excuse.

CAMD. SOC. Q

    3. After this session noc L. to be capable to receive above 2 proxies.

4. All proxies from a sp[irit]uall L. to be made to a sp[iritual] L., and from a t[emporal] L. to a t[emporal].

The sayd 4 proposicions were reade.

At the DUKE'S motion, the House is adjourned *ad libitum*.

1. The first read.

Leave out—uppon lawfull cause alledged.   .

DURESME. Except to the worde lawfull, to have yt (leave) only.

2. The second read.

3. The thirde reade. Noe L. to be capable of above 2 proxies.

DORSET, *e contra*, to be as aunciently.

SAY. Though *novum*, yett not evill. Newe orders made contynually. Noe restreint to priviledges. For none but hathe many in whom he may repose trust. *E contra*, the wholl House may be enclosed in 2 or 3, and their voices, with certein peeces of parchment.

BRIDGEWATER. That yt is against priviledges. Hitherto all hathe ben well, &c. Why not (?) so haste (?) That yt myght contynewe as yt hathe done, unlesse, &c.

MULGRAVE. *Ad idem* with Saye.

MENEVEN[SIS]. The Comittees for priviledges is to see the aunciente priviledges performed. This to be a probacioner.

BUCK[INGHAM]. *Ad idem* with Dorsett; and, as many worthy, soe none unworthy. This a restreynt to every particuler member, and sends him a begging to have his proxie accepted, &c. Not to [be] altered without the K[ing]s leave.

CLARE, *e contra*.

MARSHALL. Yt wyll preserve, &c. *Quære*, yf yt be a novelty.

PRESIDENT. Trust in proxies, [er]go, to be free. On the other syde, I never herde of any yll by yt, that one shoulde have many proxies. The Records to be serched, &c.

SAY. Why to looke for precedents to regulate our owne House by order. Greatest wisedome to prevent an inconvenience, before we feele the smarte of yt.

DORSETT. A noveltye, and a poincte of conscience, for the truste, &c. The precedents to be produced before the voate.

DURESM. A restreynt of your power.

STEWARDE. Precedents to be produced. I have known the trust soe precisely gyven in this House, that a L. hathe gyven his owne voate one way, and the proxie voate another waye.

RUSSELL. Noe precedents, but to prevent an inconvenience.

AWDLEY. The olde order to stand.

MARSHALL. Precedents: whether any new orders have been made or noe without viewe of precedent?

CLARE. Ad idem.

PRESIDENT. That precedents be firste viewed.

NORWICH. A noveltie to looke into precedents for making an order.

GREY OF W[ERKE]. To prevent an inconvenience, though noe precedent.

The House resumed.

3. BUCK[INGHAM]. Whether voated for a further tyme, or presently to be voated?

BRIDGWATER. Ad idem. To be respited.

To be voated in order.

1. The first putt to question.

Past generally, *nemine dissentiente.*

2. The seconde putt to the question, and agreed *per pluries.*

3. The thirde putt to the question.

They which wyll have this 3 order to be voated nowe presently, saye, content. They that woulde have yt deferred to another tyme, say, not content.

Agreed *per pluries* to be putt to the question presently.

3. Putt to the question.

Agreed unto *per pluries.*

4. Putt to the question.

Agreed unto.

* * * * *

Feb. 27.   LUNÆ, 27 FEBR., 1625.

[L. J. iii. 507.]

*   *   *   *   *

Feb. 28.   MARTIS, 28 FEBR., 1625.

[L. J. iii. 508.]

*   *   *   *   *

Amendments on the Bill of Armes reade 2da vice.

DURESME. Wardes or dyvisions to be added where hundreds, rapes, or wapentakes are in the bill.

WALLINGFORD. That the bastarde muskett be not omytted, but contynewed: and a penaltie against such as borrowe horses to shewe at the musters.

CLARE. The lyke penaltie for borrowing of armes allso.

*   *   *   *   *

March 1.   MERCURII, 1° MARCH, 1625.

[L. J. iii. 509.]

*   *   *   *   *

March 2.   DIE JOVIS, 2do MARCH, 1625.

[L. J. iii. 512.]

*   *   *   *   *

BUCK[INGHAM]. A message this morning from the Lower House in wrighting. Looking into his owne accions, the greatest happines that coulde happen; doubted whether he might answere yt there or noe. Requyred their LL^{ps} advyse.

The message reade, dated 1° *Marcii, a° 1° Caroli Regis, p* m.
BUCK[INGHAM]. The messenger that brought this stayes without for an aunswere, which he desyred to knowe of the LL.

Dyvers mocions whether to aunswere uppon an order from the Comons. That they sende hither to have leave from this House, or compleyne. Precedents recited that in the case of Mompesson, St. Alban, and Middlesex, when the LL. had but occasion to examine a member of the House of Comons, theyr LL^ps have firste sent to the Commons and demaunded their leave.

As touching the aunswere, Buckingham to doe yt as of himselfe, vizt.—

Noo aunswere from this House untill they shall firste addresse themselves hether.

I have acquaynted the LL. with the message *the Commons*^a ^{Altered by the} sent me, and when I have their LL^ps aunswere they shall have ^{Duke himselfe.} myne.

BUCK[INGHAM] reade his aunswere out of a paper.

I dyd accordinge to my duty.

KEEPER. Dyvers members of the House as are of the Councell of warre have received a warrant from the Speaker to appeare before them accordinge to the Acte of Subsidye, &c. Yett they in their duity acquainted the House with yt.

The acte of subsidy touching that parte reade.

They have leave according to the statute.

*   *   *   *   *

KEEPER. Whether your LL^ps wyll proceede nowe in this buissines of Buck[ingham]?

BUCK[INGHAM]. Desyred haste herin.

The Comittee of priviledges to consider of precedents, and then to debate yt tomorrow.

*   *   *   *   *

^a The words in italics were substituted for " they."

VENERIS, 3 MARCII, 1625.

[L. J. iii. 513.]

* * * * *

Buck[INGHAM]. As obedience to this House, soe he all respects to the Lower House.

To be resolved for his aunswere to satisfye them.

Whether he may aunswere with leave?

Whether, after resolucion; yf the Comons shall demaunde leave for the Duke to aunswere, that this may be allso resolved on, whether yt shalbe graunted or noe?

Moved. To take noe noatice what the Commons doe in their House. But to leave the Duke his owne will, which course the Comons take in lyke cases.

Moved. Reporte to be made of the precedents viewed yesterday by the Comittee of priviledges.

The L. PRESIDENT reported theis precedents, viz., aᵒ 25 H. 8, Phillips; aᵒ 18 Jacobi, Mompesson's, &c.; aᵒ 21 Ja: Middlesex.

Adj. ad libitum.

BUCKINGHAM desyred to have leave to aunswere the Commons by Councell.

Diversly debated.

Noe notice to be taken of the order made by the Commons
Moved. House.

Noe direccion to be gyven the Duke for his aunswer.

Duke to state the buissines. 1. Reade the orders. 2. Compare the precedents. 3. An order to prevent any inconvenience herafter. None to aunswere in the Commons House, unlesse he first aske leave here.

2 Questions. Priviledge of the House. Conveniency for the Duke.
Moved. 1. To enter a protestacion here to preserve their priviledges.
2. To leave the Duke to his owne mynde and desyre

Resumed.

Moved: Whether a conference to demaunded with the Commons,
&c., or a protestacion?
Question: Whether a conference is fytt to be demaunded with
the House of Commons touchinge the buissiness nowe in question
or noe.
Agreed, to demaunde a conference accordingly, of the priviledges
of this House.
CHAMBERLAIN. To be desyred at the Commons to knowe
whether

    *   *   *   *   *

DIE SABATHI, 4 MARCH, 1625.

[L. J. iii. 514.]

    *   *   *   *   *

Message to the Commons for a conference with them touchinge Buckingham.
the message which they sent to the Duke of Buckingham. Have
appointed a Comittee of 32. In the painted chamber.
Answered, they will meete presently.

    *   *   *   *   *

CANT[ERBURY], reported the conference.   Buckingham.
What they represented to the Commons. The answere was, they
are very gladd that the good correspondency which was, &c. A
larger comission then heretofore usuall, not only to here but to
aunswer. They fynding the course of their House that all things
sett downe ruffly in their clerks booke shoulde be viewed every
Satterday morning, amended their order. Read.
Desyred contynuance, & ——
This paper to be redelyvered.
CANT[ERBURY] remembred the 2 parte of the conference agreed
on yesterday.

Desyred to knowe whether that proposicion to be made to the Comons, or noe?

Agreed to be omytted.

MARSHALL. To retourne that the House is well satisfyed.

The Commons have certifyed the clerkes booke already according to this.

The Comons' order read this morninge to be entred.

The Comittees retourned to the Comons with this, that their order delivered this morning hath ben reade, and, yf that and noe other be entred in their journall booke, their LL^{ps} are satisfyed.

CANTERBURY returned and reported that the Commons made answere that nothing should herafter appear in their booke, but only this order nowe sente.

DUKE. To have leave to aunswere the Comons.

SOME. For leave.

OTHERS. Noe leave, till the Commons demaunde leave.

OTHERS. To be lefte to the Duke.

Propounded, that the Duke appoynte some members of the House of Commons, to saye what he woulde saye himselfe, yf he were presente; for that the first order is quashed, and by this order, noe noatice therof is as yet gyven the Duke. [Er]go, to sleepe.

This buissines to rest, untill some newe intimacion be made therof to the House.

The buissines touchinge the 2 peticions for the Erledom of Oxford deferred till Monday morninge.

Buckingham's buissines moved agayne.

BUCKINGHAM. Moved to have leave to sende unto the Comons, &c.

To be lefte to himselfe to doe what his Grace shall thynke good to gyve the Comons satisfaccion.

Ad. to Monday 9.

LUNÆ, 6 MARCH, 1625.   March 6.

[L. J. iii. 516.]

*   *   *   *   *

KEEPER. Moved for Wylloughby.[a]

SPENCER. The reference is to heare and certerfye. The privi-ledge to determine not graunted.

CHAMBERLEYN *e contra.* The King may referr yt to the LL. in such sorte as he please.

' The peticion & answere reade.

CURIA [?]. When a peticion is directed to the LL., and when to the King alone; and when this House is once so possessed of any cause, & when not.

BUCKINGHAM. Begged leave to sende his answere to the Lower⎫
House by Mr. Attourney ; and that his preface to his answere may ⎬ Left to
be herde, or ells to have this opynion of him that he woulde not ⎭ himself.
wyllingly offende.

MONTAGU. Moved to consider of the fortes & other defence of the Realme, *prout* a° 21 *Ja.*

*   *   *   *   *

DIE MARTIS, 7 MARCH, 1625.   March 7

[L. J. iii. 518.]

*   *   *   *   *

CANT[ERBURY] reported the ——.

In what state we stande now for the safety of the King and King-dom. Tyme requyres haste.

Dyvers hedds. Reports of ——? parcells from tyme to tyme. Somwhat don this day. To be communicated to you, viz.—

[a] One of the claimants of the Earldom of Oxford.

With the reporte of the M^r of the Ordinance for the viewe there. Small:^a fitt to be supplied.

Powder, most necessary. The stoare very small nowe that was wont to be.

Putt in mynde allso

1. What states &c. are confederats with us. Theis to be helde up with money to contynewe the warr.

2. Holde yt resolved that the potent enemy Spain wyll doe all the harme she can doe to us or our confederats. To provyde for safetye.

3. The meanes, nowe this season to sett out a fleete. Strength at home, encouragement to our friends abroade.

CHAMB[ER]LEYN. Mausfield his accion first resolved on by K. James to strengthen the Prynces of Germany. Misfortunes; yett the first countenance to bringe on Denmark, and putt lyfe to the Germans. Denmarke nowe in the field 50,000. Tylly by the nose. The Pr[inces] hartened.

States broaken by an army & faccion. The backe a dore stopped against by Denmarke.

Their league, and contribucion to the charge, 4 partes. The States to have of the goods, our King the land recovered. Buckingham sent to Holland. Denmarke ready to breake & treate for want of money. Buckingham caryed over 60,000^{li} in money, & pawned jewells for 30,000^{li} now.

Soe encouraged. France promiseth, Bethelem Gabor joynes & Sweden. Our armys nowe on foote. To keepe the warres from our owne doares, soe daungerous. Sett out a fleete. Paynefull.

2 proposicions—The fleete :—Denmarkes armyes to be meynteyned.

The fleete : 40 shipps ready ; 20 more ; 20 from the States. Furnished with municion & men.

Victualls :—wantes :—to be provyded this monthe. Money to be provyded for.

^a Small arms.

BUCK[INGHAM]. *Ad idem.*

ESSEX. When the Englishe went to ayd the States, they were not able to goe into the fielde without them, by reason of Spinolas greate armyes betwixt Breda & Grave, & the stronge faccions of the Arminians. But when the Englishe arryved, the Pr[ince] of Orange went presently into the fielde.

CHAMB[ER]LEYN. 3. by the Comittees to be presently don. 1. The fleete to be sett out. 2 Denmarks Army. 3. Mansfield meinteyned.

SAYE moved that before any conclusion yt may be propounded to the Commons allso.

BUCK[INGHAM]. To conclude only what to propounde to the Commons.

PRESIDENT. A conference when theis things are prepared firste.

CANT[ERBURY]. A preamble at the conference touching the dangers.

Message to the Commons by L. Ch. Justice, Mr. J. Yelverton.

The LL. demaunde a meetinge with the Commons this morninge in the painted chamber, about matters of greate importance, the LL. Comittees 40 : they a proporcionable number, to be presently in the painted chamber.

Annswerd. They have taken yt to their consideracion. & wyll retourne annswere by messengers of their owne.

CANT[ERBURY]. Whoe shall speake to the Lower House?

Canterbury
Chamberleyne } appointed
Buckingham
Carlyle added

The same relacion made, viz. the state of Christendom at the breacke of the treatyes & nowe.

WALLINGFORD. To lett the Comons[a] daungers and remedy, viz[t]. 1. Fleet. 2. Denmarke and Mansfield.

Necessary, but to make yt plausible to the Comons, add Ireland, & Dunkerke as the merchants may be guarded at home as well as an invasive, &c.

A fleete to offende Spayne. A lyke fleete on the narrowe Seas allso to defende the merchants.

[a] "know the"

WARWICKE. *Ad idem.*

DUKE. *Ad idem,* otherwise Dunkerk may putt over an army hither, during the invasion.

Agreed the Conferens to be for

1 { The fleete to goe to Spayne, & a fleete to guarde the seas.

2 { The Armyes of Denmarke and Mansfield to be meinteyned.

* * * * *

[Conference to be at 3 p. m.]

DIE MARTIS, 7 MARCH, P.M.

L. J. iii. 520.]

* * * *

The LL. returned from the conference.

CANT[ERBURY] reported that they delyvered unto them, 1, the inducement of the meeting uppon speeche that we sate 1 month & not provyded for our safety, & yett exasperated an enemy.

Left to their consideracion, &c.

They signifyed that they came to heare only, &c. Reports to theis House, & answer.

Ad. tomorrowe at 8.

MERCURII, 8 MARCII, 1625.

[L. J. iii. 521.]

* * * * *

JOVIS, 9 MARCII, 1625.

[L. J. iii. 522.]

* * * * *

SABATHI, 11 MARCH, 1625.   March 11.

[L. J. iii. 523.]

*   *   *   *   *

LUNÆ, 13 MARCH, 1625.   March 13.

L. J. iii. 524.]

*   *   *   *   *

DIE MARTIS, 14 MARCH, 1625.   March 14.

[L. J. iii. 525.]

*   *   *   *   *

PRESIDENT moved to proceed in the Comittee for municions,   Agreed.
&c., the Comittees to meate tomorrowe mourninge.

CLARE. That an order was made touchinge the reporte for   Mounson.
Mounson, aᵒ 21 Ja. Rs. the daye after, &c.

DORSETT. To refer yt to the L. Keeper now agayne.

CLARE. Mounson to peticion the King, yf he please, or exhibitt   Ordered.
his bill in the Chancery, as he wyll.

TREASURER. Mounson hath peticioned to the King, referred to   Mounson.
him, but his Lᴾ thought yt not for the King to recompence him for
a promise made by his officer, the Treasurer, uppon a bargayn.

Mounson to peticion the King (yf he please) against Middlesex,   Ordered.
but not for any recompense from the King.

CLARE shewed the povertie of Westm[inster], that the church-   Westminster
wardens, &c., dyd what they woulde for their reliefe of themselves,
and engaged themselves for their maintenance. London hathe had
much contribucion out of the collections.

Moved for some proporcion for Westminster, out of the remaynes
in the Bᴾ of London's hands.

Their peticion reade.

*   *   *   *   *

LINCOLN. That one of the members of the House is comitted. Moved we to proceede, as noe offence to the King, nor breache of the LL. priviledges.

KEEPER. A comandement from the King. Is comitted for a personall misdemeanour to himselfe, which is best known to himselfe, and which hathe noe relacion to the Parlement.

CLARE. That the House made [?] be putt into Comittee.

BRIDGEWATER. The Act not beinge in this House, and personall to the K[ing], knowen to him (in secreate) noe breache of priviledge. The coreccion [?] to be left to the King.

SAY. This may be extended further herafter against the priviledges, &c.

A Comittee in all duitye to attend the King, &c.

CARLILE. As lawful for the King to comitt him, as yt was for this House heretofore, &c.

Moved for an
entry to be
made of the
mocion of the
House for
safing of the
Priviledges.
PRESIDENT. A satisfaccion gyven before hand by the Keeper, as touchinge the justice of the House. The B^p of Winchester was tryed *tempore E.* 3 in the King's Benche, yt beinge the King's wyll to make his eleccion, notwithstanding the claim of the Parlement.

The House adj. *ad libitum*.

A mocion for a Comittee to serch precedent.

Resumed. Comittee named.

The subcomittees for priviledges read; appoynted to searche viewe and consider of the precedents, and to relate them to the House, and the L. Ch. J.; J. Doddridge, J. Y[elverton] to attend the LL.

To meet when they please, &c.

To reporte what they thynke fytt to the consideracion of the House.

To reporte when they are ready for yt.

Adj. to 9 to-morrowe.

MERCURII, 15 MARCII, 1626.

[L. J. iii. 527.]

*   *   *   *   *

TR[EASUR]ER. Uppon a mocion made yesterday, the L. Keeper delivered a message from His Matie that the L. Marshall was comitted for a misdemeanor to His Matie, &c.

His Matie dothe nowe avowe the former message, and that he hathe therin done justly and hathe not diminished the priviledges of this House.

Bycause the L. Treasurer spake lowe, yt was moved that the L. Keeper should reporte what his L^p sayd.

KEEPER. This: that whereas uppon a mocion made by himself— That the L. Marshall was restreyned, &c.

Avowed yt.

And that he knowes that he hathe therin done justly, and not diminished the priviledges of this House.

SAYE. Noe question, whether justly, &c. The future only, &c. Mediacion, yf the offence wyll beare yt, that he may sytt here during the Parlement, &c. A comittee to his Matie, &c.

BUCK[INGHAM]. Not here present yesterday, but herde that yf the King had been present himselfe, his Matie coulde not have been displeased with that which passed here.

Not to putt yt out of the course begun by the King, &c.

Q. Whether his Matie may in tyme of Parlement comitt a member of this House for causes knowne to himselfe, during the Parlement?

LINCOLN. The precedents to be shewen for yt.

CLARE. Wyll clere the precedent of Wickham. B^p of Wynchester, alledged the precedent out of a ligier booke of Westminster, 5° E. 3.

To proceede as was moved and agreed yesterday by the subcomittee, &c.

NORWICH. To avoyd the rocks that may breed distastes, &c., to his Matie.

Mocion to attend his Matie and humbly entreate his Matie to receave from the House the reason of their tendernesse of their privileges, &c., by our peticion, &c.

Co[VENTRY] AND L[ICHFIELD]. *Ad idem*, and to proceed in the inquisicion for precedents.

NORWICH. Noe proceeding till his Matie be attended.

Co[VENTRY] AND L[ICHFIELD]. *Ad idem*.

SAY. To proceed according to the order, or to reverse the order.

PRESIDENT. John B^p of Wynchester, 3 E. 3, for an offence to the Parlement House, and yett punnished by the King, vizt., endicted at the Kings bench, tryed there, and fyned. Priviledge claymed: denyed.

5 H. 4. Northumberland rayssed forces, &c.; came to Parlement, tendred his bill, &c. The King tooke his byll, and gave yt to the Judges. The LL. (to preserve their right) moved the King, and the reason is, for that the statut of 25 E. 3 reserved yt to the LL.

28 H. 6. De la Poole accused. Comitted. Declyned his peeres. Submitted to the King, whoe banished him. Beumond compl[ainan]t, and made protestacion to preserve the right of Peerage.

Moved for a protestacion for the Peerage, as he moved yesterday, and a Comittee to consider of the protestacion, but to staye the other.

Question. Whether the House shalbe putt into a Comittee or noe? Agreed, not to putt into a comittee.

DENNY. A peticion to the King, and goe on with the order.

STEWARDE. A protestacion only for the future.

ALII. Pro & con.

ST. D[AVIDS] MENEVENSIS. Cyted precedents *tempore Eliz.* Wentworth of the House of Commons, a mocion made there by him. The Q[ueen] displeased; she comitted him to the Tower, where he laye long, and no clayme made for him. For treason, felony, and breache of the peace, the King's prerogative lyes.

The King's Message.   Not to trouble the King after a double
message.   *Verba brigosa*, breache of the peace.
SAYE.   To proceed with the Comittee.
BUCK[INGHAM].   The question to be stated and kept.   The
protestacion only.
DORSETT.   To suspende the decision of yt as nowe.[a]
      Adj. tomorrowe at 9.

DIE JOVIS, 16 MARCII, 1625
      [L. J. iii. 528.]
*   *   *   *   *

VENERIS, 17 MARCII, 1625.
      [L. J. iii. 531.]
*   *   *   *   *

BUCK[INGHAM].   This daye the Comittee for municions to
attende this morning, and many Parlement men commissioners for
the navy to attend.
Moved to resolve on the thinges fytt, and then on the meanes.
This House hathe mett with the Commons heretofore.   Noe
answere.
A conference to consider of the redresse.
TOTTNES.   The Comittees first to meete in the painted chamber.
BUCK[INGHAM].   Noe exam[inacion] can be without the officers,
whoe are of the Lower House.   To sende for them, and a con-
ference at once.
MULGRAVE.   To sende for them first.
      Adj. *ad libitum*.

* This is followed by "The order made yesterday for a return of precedents suspended, but noe order to."
CAMD. SOC.   S

Resumed.

[Message asking the Commons to answer the propositions of the Lords.]

* * * * *

[Message from the Commons, "that they wylbe ever carefull of the safety of the Realme, mainteyning their owne priviledges."]

BUCK[INGHAM]. The Commissioners attende the Comittees for defence, &c. To consider whether to proceede, the Commons unwylling to confer.

PRESIDENT. To proceede.

DORSETT. To debate the particulers, and then to offer to them. To remember our owne priviledges; we to be as carefull of the comon welthe as they.

CARLILE. To putt in acte some what to shewe our zeale.

We to offer to gyve as much as ever any Peres did gyve: *prout* the Commons have offred for them selves.

BUCKINGHAM. The Comittee for priviledges to peruse precedents what hathe ben formerly done in matters of this nature. Howe we have proceeded anciently.[a]

Adj. *ad libitum.*

Resumed.

Agreed the Comittees to meete and proceede: soe they dyd.

* * * * *

- - -

18 MARCH, 1625.

[L. J. iii. 533.]

* * * * *

- - -

[a] In the MS. penstrokes have been drawn through this and Carlisle's speech, and " The Comittee to proceed " is written after Carlisle's speech.

*   *   *   *   *

MERCURII, 22 MARCH, 1625. March 22.
[L. J. iii. 536.]

*   *   *   *   *

BRIDGEWATER reported the peticion of the captives at Sally. The reference to the Masters of Trinity House. The relation of Cogin and prisoners that come from thence.

DORSETT. To be considered of by the Comittees for the safetye of the Kingedome, &c. He thought fytt that they shoulde be redeemed out of the common purse.

BUCK[INGHAM]. The King entended, when the next fleet shall goe out, to sende for theis prisoners, and to sende firste one (Fraunces Vernon) to deale for their redempcions.

BUCK[INGHAM] cleered himselfe touching his care of the seas synce he was L. Admirall, by shewing howe weake the Navy was when he came to be Admirall: howe a comission was granted: of the care of these to buylde newe shipps: of the lesseninge the charge, and yett the fleete encreased, from 50,000 per annum to 22,000.

That he hathe ever had 4 shipps to defend the coastes. He heares they have ben negligent. Of late since theis warres there have ben many shippes, sometymes 30, 20, 14. We have not lost the seas, we never fought battle. We never sawe enemy but we chaced them. They are to swyfte for our shippes to followe. Had not a storme happened, we had not had such losses by the Dunkirkers. But we have taken more of their shippes then they have of us.

SPENCER. Yt was enformed us at the comittee that 140 sayle are taken, most of them uppon our owne coastes, within this 2 yeares, and the faulte must be in some body. Whether in the execucion of them whoe are appoynted capteynes.

NORWICH. To speed the redempcion by a generall colleccion.

BUCK[INGHAM]. Wylling to satisfye such doubtes shalbe made in perticulers. Where the fault lyes. Compare tymes. The cause that stirres theis Turkishe pyrats. The journey to Algiers to extirpate them dyd incense them to come hether. But consider whether the pyrats were as stronge as nowe. The Spaniard or Dunkerke [n]ever soe stronge as nowe. But 22,000 per annum appoynted to defray the charge herof, which small summe is ympossible to defende the coastes from theis Turkes, from the Spaniards, and Dunkerks.

DORSETT. To redeme theis marriners out of the common purse.

SAY. An accompt for the moneyes collected for Algiers. Happely parte wyll remayne therof; the rest may be supplyed. That comittee to goe to the Lord of Canterbury, for that his Grace canott come abroade.

BRIDGEWATER shewed the greate ransomes demanded. A messenger to be sent from the King to deale for their easyer ransoms.

BUCK[INGHAM]. To sende a messenger presently—in the meane tyme

Comitted to the Comittees for priviledges, &c., who are appoynted to take the accompt of the colleccion for the captives at Algiers, &c.

L. Admyrall ⎫
Dorsett   ⎬ Added.
Episcopus Exon ⎭

EXON. A mariner ransomed there by a merchant of London for 12^{li}, for which he must pay the merchant 50^{li}. The meanest man's ransome is 10^{li}; others at 300^{li} or 500^{li}. Whether to redeme by money? 1. The sum soe greate. 2. That the Turkes tooke

lately 48 marriners out of one porte; and the Turkes bragge, synce
they are soe freely redeemed, they wyll take enough; [er]go,
some other course allso to be considered of besydes redempcion for
money.

DORSETT.   The merchant to be sent for whoe tooke 50ˡⁱ for
10ˡⁱ.

EXON.   Most of theis captives were taken as they came from
Newfoundeland, some within the Sleeve.ª

BUCK[INGHAM].   A man sente before hande to mediat their
ransom.   An embassador came from Algiers hether.   Had the
Turkes deteyned here delivered.   They promised the lyke of the
Englishe, and to joyne with us against Spayne.   This messenger
to deale for performance herof allso.   Yf they denyed, then
to ——

[Names of the Committee.]

Peticion of the Erle of Bristol reade.

KEEPER.   The King comanded him not to sende the writt.

BUCK[INGHAM].   He hathe ben offred to come to his tryall
(uppon his peticion to come to the Coronacion), uppon condicion.

The King sent him a letter, &c.   Requyred his answere, whether,
yf he were called to aunswere, he woulde make use of the pardon
in Parlement aᵒ 21 *Jacob. Regis,* unto which the E. of Bristol hathe
not as yett aunswered.

SAY.   To be referred to the Comittee for priviledges.   Agreed.

The Comittees for defence, &c., to meete this afternoone.

Adj. to 9 tomorrow.

———————

JOVIS, 23 MARCH, 1625.   March 23.

[L. J. iii. 537.]

*   *   *   *   *

ª *La Manche,* the Channel.

March 24.   VENERIS, 24 MARCII, 1625.

[L. J. iii. 539.]

*   *   *   *   *

March 28.   MARTIS, 28 MARCII, 1626.

[L. J. iii. 541.]

KEEPER. Message from the King that your LL^ps attende his Matie to morrowe at 9 in the hall at Whitehall.

*   *   *   *   *

BUCK[INGHAM]. A somons from the Lower House heretofor. Then wylling, hoaping to satisfye : —— Then leave: —— Had yt. I have the same occasion nowe. A message from the Commons of their voates against me. Deferred to proceed untill, &c.

I moved to have leave at first, in hoape to satisfye them. But setho they have proceeded to voate me, unherde, I respecte many persons in that House; but where they thynk to putt me downe by clamor, &c. : —— Not answere them.

2. And wheras, the other day; his Grace, &c. touchinge the defectes before his tyme ; he intended noe aspersion on his predecessor.

3. Whether he shall answere or noe to the Commons ?

Agreed, Noe Lord shall answere there.

To be perused [?] by the Subcomittee for privileges.   The Duke of Buckingham acquainting the House with a message from the Comons to his Grace, yt is ordered that he shall not answere them.

*   *   *   *   *

DIE JOVIS, 30 MARCII, 1626.

[L. J. iii. 543.]

Prayers.

BUCK[INGHAM]. His Matie comanded him to make some explanacion of what was sayd yesterday to bothe houses, touching his
Ma^ts demaundes of a large guifte; leaste his Matie may be thought to
have a desyre to breake up the Parlement, which he dothe not.

A meetinge with the Commons presently.

[Message for a conference.]

*   *   *   *   *

HERTEFORD reported the peticion of the E. of Bristol. Referred to the LL. comittees for privileges.

Their opynion that this House be suitors unto his Matie that this
peticioner may have his writt, & allso all others except whoe are
not to sytt, &c.

BUCK[INGHAM]. His Matie commaunded me to signifye unto
your LL^ps that he dothe not withholde this writt from Bristol for
any matter done in Parlement, nor dothe he intende to prejudice
your LL^ps priviledge herein. His Matie wyll sende him his writt,
but an intimacion to staye where he is, for that his Matie shall have
occasion to come hither in person, &c.

Copy of a letter dated 20 Januarii, 1625, written to Bristoll from
the King, wherin that he persuaded the King beinge in Spayne to
turn a Roman Catholique, &c.

SAY. To be entred in the Journall booke that, at the Erles peticion, his Matie hathe sent him his writt, & noe more.

Agreed.

MULGRAVE. Touching Herteford's reporte for the other LL.,
as they may have their writtes allso.

CLARE ad idem, and moved that Proxies of the absent LL. may
be lefte freely in the disposicion of him that gyves yt.

Aunswere of the message.

The Commons wyll as a Committee of their wholl House meet presently.

BUCKINGHAM. That such as he shall desyre may assiste him at this meetinge.

Adj. *ad libitum.*

The House went to meete with the Commons. Beinge retourned, the House was resumed.

*   *   *   *   *

DIE VENERIS, 31 MARCII, 1626.

[L. J. iii. 544.]

*   *   *   *   *

SABATHI, 1° APR. 1626.

[L. J. iii. 546.]

*   *   *   *   *

PRESIDENT. That the Comittees for defence dyd yesterday meet and call before them the Armorers, &c. before them, & understande by them what stoare of all maner of weapons they provyde monethly, & have appoynted a Subcomittee to sett the pryces.

And considering of the stoare of powder, they founde that salte-peeter, &c. cannot be made for want of sea coales.

Propounded, a fleete to goe to sea, & secure the Collyers from Newcastle.

The Subcomittee.

*   *   *   *

NORWICH renewed the mocion for a convoye to sea, to secure the coastes against Dunkerk, &c.

DURESM. Uppon noatice gyven of want of coales, he enformed that coales were plenty at Newcastle, yf they might be brought safe. 500 sale depende uppon this trade ; yf the trade loste, the shipping allso.

The place soe weake, that the enemy may enter (notwithstanding the castle), sack the towne and fyer the shippes. Some workes there begun by H. 8 may be fortefyed at small charges to defende the towne.

Yf the coale workes cease but a moneth, they wylbe all utterly loste, never to be recovered. Money must doe this, which is to be begun by the Commons House.

BUCK[INGHAM]. He hathe but 22,000 per annum allowed him for the narrowe seas, which will meinteyne but 4 shippes, yett he hathe 12 shippes victualled all for 2 moneths, some for 3, all save bere. He hathe complayned of theis daungers. The redresse must be here. Some have thought of an ymposicion on coales ; they dyd anciently belonge to the Admiralty, nowe the L. Maior hathe yt. Yf he may have yt, he wyll allowe yt all to secure the coastes.

CHAMB[ER]LEYN. An enginier sent downe to buylde a block-house ; fell sicke and dyed : yett soe viewed that a plott is taken and for 1200^{li} may be perfourmed, when the money is ready.

DURESM. Theis flankers which I spake of may be done for 300^{li}, and some supply of ordinaunce, which may be had from Berwicke, and another place.

PRESIDENT. A comittee for this, &c.

SAY. Some of theis 12 shipps to be sent to secure the collyers' passage, and to carry the ordinaunce which they of Newcastle have bought.

NORTHE, *Ad idem*, and the west coastes to be secured allso.

CONWAYE. Those 12 shippes are all ready ordered to be ymployed for the coastes of Kent and Essex and the trade into the countreyes. A comittee for money, for tonage, and pondage disposed of.

A comittee to provyde a convoye for every perticuler trade, or to

April 1.   barre up Dunkerk haven with a fleete, to pursue them yf they doe but styrre out.

BUCK[INGHAM]. Having but 12 shippes ready, he cannot disposse of them otherwyse then for our defense. Daunger for them to lye at anchor before Dunkerk. Our shippes not soe good for swiftnes as theirs, ours being stronge (but heavy) theirs light and swyfte. He hathe taken some of theirs and fytted them, and buylte others after their forme.

A Comittee for money.

SAY. He thought there had ben 30 other shippes ready. Renewed his mocion that the ordinaunce provyded by them of Newcastle to be conveyed to them.

A Comittee:—Whether any of the shippes may be dispossed of that way?

Adj. ad libitum.

Resumed.

L. KEEPER. Whether proceede touchinge Newcastle shipps?

Agreed.   The Comittee for defence, &c. are on Monday next to consider howe the Newcastle shipps may be secured.

*   *   *   *   *

April 1.

DIE SABATHI, 1° APRILIS, 1626, P.M.

[L. J. iii. 548.]

*   •   •   •   *

April 3.

DIE LUNÆ, 3 APR. 1626.

[L. J. iii. 549.]

*   *   *   *   *

April 4.

DIE MARTIS, 4to APRILIS, 1626.

[L. J. iii. 550.]

*   *   *   *   *

[L. J. iii. 551.]

*   *   *   *   *

CLARE. That dyvers Lords are absent, and yett sent noe proxies, which the LL. Comittees for priviledges have thought good to re-commende to the House.

HERTEFORDE. Proxies to such as sytt not in the House are of noe force; soe that 5 proxies graunted to the E. of Arundell; all their voates lost.

Then that viewing the presidents they fynde none that a Peere of this House can be comitted in Parlement tyme without judge-ment of his peeres, and the president alledged for yt out of a booke case aᵒ 3 E. 3 dothe not prove yt.

SAY. A comittee to attende his Maᵗᶦᵉ and to be humble suitors unto his Maᵗᶦᵉ for their priviledges, especially in respecte of the future tymes, which may otherwise be warranted by this precedent for the comittment of a Peere during the Parlement, farre otherwise then his Maᵗʳ nowe intends yt. The comittee to doe yt verbally to the King and receave his Maᵗˢ owne aunswere to yt.

MOUNTAGUE. Whether the order 15 Marcii dyd not suspende the serche for priviledges, &c. and the report to be made.

DURESM. That yt dyd.

CHAMB[ER]LEYN. Whether being suspended for a tyme, yt may be renewed without further mocion to the House firste made.   *The order reade.*

MONTGOMERY. *Ad idem.*

LICHFIELD. *Ad idem,* but pregnant proofes for the priviledges.

BUCK[INGHAM]. Question — whether the order were to sus-pende yt for that daye only or noe? Then, whether yt can be re-vyved by a pryvate committee?

PRESIDENT. *Ad idem :* and a further tyme to be taken for pre-sidents, &c.

BUCK[INGHAM]. He hathe herde the King's councell saye that

April 5.   they can schewe precedents that LL. of parlement have been taken and committed in parlement tyme, and that the precedents alledged are against the priviledge of the LL.

NORTH. Noe suspencion at all agreed on. Noe order at all made for yt: for he himselfe cryed, noe suspension.[a]

DORSETT. The question whether the former order was suspended or noe?[b]

31 for a Committee.   Question, whether the House to be putt into a Comittee or noe?

34 e contra.   ESSEX. That the former order was not suspended, or ells the

The Committee cleared.   comittee hathe comitted a faulte.

WESTMORLANDE. The Kings councell to shewe what precedents cann be produced that a Peere may be committed during the Parlement.

DEVON[SHIRE]. The committee made noe faulte. For their reporte not forbydden by order.

Question.[c]

This was putt.   Such of your LL[ps] as are of opynion that this cause *super tota materia* shoulde not proceede without a new mocion in the House say content: others saye not content.

37 contents.   Agreed yt coulde not be proceeded in, &c.

29 not contents.

*   *   *   *   *

CLARE. The King's councell to shewe the precedents which they have that a L. of Parlement may be committed duringe the Parlement.

The subcommittee to report to the House at the nexte accesse at their owne tyme.

Devon &			Dorsett
Clare	}	added	Duke
North			Holland
Wallingforde			President
Mansfield			Treasurer

---

[a] The words which follow, "and soe dyd others," are deleted in the MS

[b] See p. 129, note[a].

[c] Three forms of the question are here inserted, but are scratched out with the pen.

They or any 5 to meete on Thursdaye in Easter, and when they please.

April 5.
The King's councell to attende the LL. on that day in the painted chamber at 2 of the clock *post meridiem*.

*   *   *   *   *

Ad. to Thursday next weeke at 9.

_____

DIE JOVIS, 13 APRILIS, 1626.

April 13.

[L. J. iii. 554.]

*   *   *   *   *

___ _____

SABATHI, 15 APRILIS, 1626.

April 15.

[L. J. iii. 555.]

*   *   *   *   *

Hodie 3ª *vice lecta est billa pro Apparell.*

DORSETT. Against the bill, in respecte of the Apparell and Coaches, &c. allready made and provyded. But more especially for that the making of laces meintenyes at leaste 20,000 folkes, and yf we ennacte anythinge here whereby the ymportacion of forreyn commodities may be stayed, yt is to be doubted that other countreyes wyll doe the lyke with us.

Apparell.

ALII, *e contra,* noe ymportacion denyed: trade encreased, from laces to clothinge.   .

Billa prædicta pro apparatum putt to the question.

Agreed *nemine dissentiente.*

*   *   *   *   *

Hodie 2ᵈᵃ *vice lecta est billa* against scandalous ministers.

DURESM. That the last clause may be omytted, and thynkes yt straunge that the ecclesiasticall lawes are not sufficient to reforme the ministers without ayde of the seculars. Yt wylbe scandalous to them,

SAYE. Yt can be no scandal to the state to refourme abuses, &c.

April 15.   LANDAFF.   Rather to passe a lawe to ennable the BB. to con-
vent and punishe disordered ministers, according to the Bill, and
to barre all appeales from them,

ROCHESTER.   Dyverse very severely punished for theis offences
in the highe comission.

DORSETT.   With Landaff.

Billa prædicta against scandalous ministers committed.

*   *   *   *   *

April 17.   LUNÆ, 17 APRILIS, 1626.

[L. J. iii. 556.]

*   *   *   *   *

ESSEX.   The peticion of the Earl of Bristoll to be reade.

L. KEEPER.   He receaved a letter last nyght from the Earl of
Bristol requesting him to acquaint the King with the contents
therof.   And nowe he had received a peticion from the Earl of
Bristoll, with a copy of that letter annexed, which he redelyvered
to the Erles sollicitor, for that he had not as yett acquainted the
King with the said letter.

Ordered.   To be exhibited first to the Committee for peticions, and they are
to meete tomorrowe at 2 in the painted chamber, and to be proceeded on there according to the ordinary course.

*   *   *   *   *

April 18.   MARTIS, 18 APRILIS, 1626.

[L. J. iii. 557.]

*   *   *   *   *

PRESIDENT made reporte touching the proceedings of the subcomittee for priviledges uppon the comittment of the E. of Arundell.
The King's councell serched, and acquainted them with all that

chronicles or records can afforde, which the LL. have answered, and
declared their owne ——?

Firste was reade the precedents collected by the Comittee unto
eache of them in order.

CLARE. The proofe of the priviledge, &c., and the objeccions;
and answeres being herde, &c., to putt yt to the question touchinge
the priviledge, &c.

DURESME. To reade them agayne.

Reade accordingly.

SAYE. We were to prove our right of Parlement: not to be
arrested nor deteyned from hence during Parlement unlesse for
treason, felony, or breache of the peace. Remembred the judges'
opynion a° 31 H. 6, howe delyvered by them, and the L. Vaux his
case, for stayc of the suit in the Star-chamber (during the Parlement) against him.

Precedents offred to be produced, and when they founde noe
records they resorted to chronicles, all which you have herde.
Moved for the question to be putt accordingly.

Question: Such of your LL.ᵖˢ as are of opynion that the priviledge of this House is that noe L. of Parlement, sitting the Parlement, or within the usuall tyme of priviledge of parlement, is to be
(without sentence or order of this House) ymprisoned or restreyned,
unlesse yt be for treason or felony or for refusinge to gyve suertie
for the peace,ᵃ say Content.

They which are of a contrary opynion saye Not content.

Agreed *nemine dissentiente*.

DEVON[SHIRE]. That all reade this day may be entred in the
clerk's booke, and that some course may be thought uppon for a
remonstrance to be presented to the King.

[Committee appointed to consider of a remonstrance and petition.]

ᵃ The question is much altered by interlineations and corrections from its original
form, but the only change of importance is the substitution of the last words for "or
breache of the peace."

MERCURII, 19 APRILIS, 1626.

[L. J. iii. 562.]

Prayers.

PRESIDENT reported the peticion delivered by the Earl of Bristol to be presented to the House.

The peticion, the L. Keeper's letter, and the Erle's aunswere were reade.

The peticion reade 2da *vice*.

PRESIDENT reported the remonstrance to the Kinge of auncient right of Peeres, &c., and the peticion, &c.

Reade 1^a et 2da *vice*.

Approved of generally.

Moved that comittees for priviledges may attende the King with yt.

Others that the whole House myght goe with yt.

Agreed that the whole House shall presente this to the Kinge; and the L. President, the L. Stewarde, the E. of Cambridge, and the L. Greate Chamberleyn, to goe presently to the King to understande his pleasure at what tyme.

Defense of the Kingdome.   TREASURER. The Comittees for defense of the realme, &c. Paynes taken, &c. The merchants undertaking to provyde powder allowed of by your LL^p[s]. The merchants afterwards receded from their offer. I am to move the provision. Wante of money hinders yt, which in discharge of my duitye I thought good to imparte unto you, and that the comittee myght meete to consider what is to be done further for the provision of powder.

They went presently to [the?] ——

PRESIDENT. Wayted on the King. This day betwene 2 and 3 appointed in the presence chamber at Whitehall for the wholl House to attende the King with the peticion, &c.

The L. Keeper to present the peticion to the Kinge and to reade yt unto him.

PRESIDENT. Sally. Force to fetche them of. Treaty to redeme
them, or money to ransom them. Peticion to the King that a messenger may be sent to the King of Morocco to redeem them by
waye of treaty, and the Kinge to be moved in this by the L. President at his owne best conveniency.

*   *   *   *   *

DIE JOVIS, 20 APRILIS, 1626.

[L. J. iii. 565.]

*   *   *   *   *

KEEPER. The remonstrance delivered. Aunswere. He dyd
perceave that your LL^{ps} had taken a greate deale of care and paynes
in this buissines, and that yt was of greate weight, and therefor his
Matie would take time to consider theruppon, and gyve a full
answere in convenyent tyme.

*   *   *   *   *

VENERIS, 21 APRILIS, 1626.

[L. J. iii. 566.]

*   *   *   *   *

KEEPER. A message from his Matie. A peticion from the E. of
Bristoll soe full,&c. Cause to punishe him. Herde allso of your
LL^{ps} respecte in respect of his Matie, &c. Resolved to putt this
cause uppon the honor and justice of your LL^{ps}. That the E. of
Bristoll be sent for as a delinquent to aunswere the offences done by
him before his Matie went into Spain; after his Matie came into
Spayne; synce Bristoll retourned; and by this peticion, which
reflecteth ymediately uppon Buckingham, but obliquely uppon his
Matie. All which his Matie wyll charge him with, to be determined
by your LL^{ps}.

SAYE. The L. Keeper, with some others to be appoynted, to
render thanks to his Matie and assurance of the Peeres, &c., to
respecte his Ma^{ts} honour, &c.

CAMD. SOC.   U

April 21.   [Committee appointed "to attende his Matie with a message of thanks."]

CHAMB[ER]LEYNE. The comittees for priviledges to meete presently to consider on what manner Bristoll shalbe sente for.

*   *   *   *   *

Reporte of the Comittee concerninge the sendinge for the E. Bristoll.

TREASURER. They fynde him charged in the House by a letter reade in this House, and by a message delivered by the L. Keeper from the Kinge: thynke fytt that he be sent for by the usher of this House.

Ordered: The Clerke to make an order to brynge the sayd E. of Bristol hether by the gentleman usher.

Ordered
Read.   That the gentleman usher bryng the Erle of Bristol hether assooue as he maye.

PRESIDENT. The usher to be charged with him: tell him to come hether.

Ordered.   The House is to be called on Monday next.

*   *   *   *   *

April 22.   SABATHI, 22 APRILIS, 1626.

[L. J. iii. 568.]

Prayers.

L. KEEPER. Thankes represented to the King of your thanks touching the message he sent concerning the E. of Bristol. We brynge noe answere. Wee may perceive by his countenance that his Matie did receave it with all grace and good acceptance.

*   *   *   *   *

LUNÆ, 24 APRILIS, 1626.

L. J. iii. 570.]

Prayers.

BUCK[INGHAM]. The Lower House hathe sente me another message, that about 10 of the clock they wyll voate certeyne matters against me, and gave the messenger leave to take a noate of them, and that I myght take a copy of them at large, and expecte my answere before 10 this daye. I desyre to knowe whether I may answere them or noe.

Agreed, not to aunswer, uppon the respects of their former order 28 Marcii.[a]

DUKE. Sithe I shall not answere to the charge, yett to sende them an answere to the message.

Graunted.   Ordered.

The LL. doe not holde yt convenyent nowe to permitt the Duke to answere them.

The LL. doe not thynke yt fytt that the Duke shall answere in   Priviledges.
the House of Commons any charge there.

    *   *   *   *   *

LO[RD] KEEPER signified his Ma[ts] pleasure to this House, that for the peticion that was preferred to his Ma[tie] concerning the L. Arundell, that his Ma[tie] was takinge the same into his consideracion, and will returne an answere thereunto as soone as he can.

The House called.

Moved. The Erle of Somersett's name to be putt into the   Agreed.
Kallender, for that he hathe his writte.

WESTMORLAND. The Committees for priviledges to consider of those whoe have not sente their proxies.

DEVON[SHIRE]. All of the grande Committee to meete this   Agreed.
afternoone at 2.

LORD KEEPER. The Judges are comanded[b] to attende ellswhere, and to be spared. L. Tr[easur]er, President, Pryvy Seale, and Conway are to be ymployed by the King, and to be spared allso.

April 24.   L. KEEPER signifyed that the Archb. of Canterbury cannot
come unlesse he be caryed: wyll come yf he may be carryed, and
sett whilest he speaks, for he canott stande.
Approved, &c.
Adj. to 9 tomorrowe.

April 25.   DIE MARTIS, 25 APRILIS, 1626.
                              [L. J. iii. 571.]
        *   *   *   *   *

PRESIDENT reported the buissines done yesterday.   Began with
a comendacion of the LL. care to preserve rights and justice, &c.
4 things.

Ordered.   1. Proxies }
             2. Lycence } Determyned.   To be approved by the LL.

Ordered.   3. Touchinge fees of the officers.
             4. In contemplation only.   For serch to be made by the sub-
comittee, howe a Peere sent for shalbe demeaned.

Ordered.   To reporte imediately to the House.

MONTAGUE reported the accompt touching the colleccions for
London and Westminster, and what remayned in the hands of the
L. Maior of London: vid.—
The remayne in the B^p of London's hands.
And that the B^p laid out 19^{li} more then he received at Oxford,
and gave 40^{li} out of his owne purse.
There remaynes in debt [?]
And 11 dioces have brought in nothing.
The sum remayning of the said collection comes to ——
The remayne of this colleccion, parte to be distributed among the
parishes by the Comittee; parte to the redempcion of the captives
at Sally.
The Comittees to consider howe much of this remayn shalbe dis-
tributed[a] amongest the parishes, &c.; and yf the[y] fynde any sur-

[a] "this amongest." MS., the first word being left unerased by mistake.

plusage therof, then that and the remaynder of the other 11 dioces,
and the remaynder in the Archb[p] of Canterbury's hands, to be converted towards the captyves of Sally.

The order at Oxford confirmed for the absence from the fast, and   V[e] ordered
hee[a] that dyd not then paye to paye nowe double for bothe tymes.   at Oxford
                                                                      10 Aug. 1625.
And the Clerke of the Crown to receive yt and to be converted for
Sally allso.

The summe demaunded for caryage of the briefes not to be
allowed, but to be considered of how farre to be abated.

The peticion of the Countes of Bristol reade and ordered.

Mocion to what tyme the House shalbe adjourned, whether to
Satterday or noe?

BRIDGEWATER.   Whether the Comittees to meete, &c.?   Yea.

*   *   *   *   *

SABATHI, 29 APRILIS, 1626.

[L. J. iii. 573.]

*   *   *   *   *

CLARE.   Reporte of the subcomittee for priviledges.

1. By a message delivered by the L. Keeper from his Ma[tie] of 4
generalls concerninge the Earle of Bristoll, wherof the laste is a perticuler, takinge noatice of his peticion to the LL. scandalizing the
Duke of Buckingham and by refleccion his Ma[tie], and therefore, &c.,
prout in the m[essage].

Your LL[ps] thot good that the Comittee for priviledges shoulde
consider, &c.   They reported that the E. of Bristoll stood charged
by a letter and the message, and to be therefore sente for [by] the
gentleman usher.

The order theruppon.

A consideracion arose, howe a L. sente for shal be demeaned.

We called the Clerke, and demaunded the letter, which he had
not.

---

[a] MS. "hee," &c., the "hee" being inserted above the line in the wrong place.

April 29.   We considered the message. 1. Wherefore we forbare to meddle with the E[arl's] peticion, vizt, for that we conceaved him to be restreyned for matter of State, but we dyd yt for that other matters were fitt to be first proceeded in.

The peticion of the Countesse of Bristoll, and the order we have allso considered.

For the seconde, we serched for precedents of the lyke, &c.

A° 50 E. 3. W. L[ord] Latymer, J. L[ord] Nevill, and some other auncyent [?] which for brevity I omytt.

We had precedents allso of latter tymes.

Ep^{us} Wigorne, *tempore Jacoby Rs.*, Ep^{us} Norwicen: Ep^{us} Landaven: Nowe thus yt standes. The E. of Bristol is brought up, and in the custody of the gentleman usher: the consideracion we leave to your LL^{ps}, what shalbe further done with him.

The message 21 Aprilis, and the order reade: the peticion of the Lady Bristol, 25 Aprilis, and the order theron reade.

DORSETT. The former precedents to be rules to guyde ourselves by. He is only accused, not charged, [er]go, to come and sytt in his place as others have done.

PRESIDENT. Of the same opynion, yf the cause stood alyke; but the order is to come before the House, not into the House.

DURESM, *ad idem*. Tender, where the King is soe farr engaged. The presidents alleadged touching the BB^s are of complaints fynding them in the House, wheras Bristoll is not here, but sente for to be brought hither.

NORWICH. He was charged parlamentarily and with particulers, which were read, and I demaunde[d] to knowe whether I shoulde aunswere in my place, or at the barre, and directed to aunswere in my place. The charg against Bristol is not soe. A letter reade, not by way of a charge. The message sayes that the King wyll charge him; —— ? by a judiciall charge. In the meane tyme I conceave he ought to come to his place.

SAYE. *D[istan]cia* inter charge and accusacion. Instaunced in the case of the Erle of Middlesex, who aunswered his accusacion in

his place, his charge at the barre.   Other precedents proove this to
be the course.   He is not sent for as a delinquent, for he is not
examined, &c.   He sytts here, for his proxie is here: [er]go, he is
to be in his place.

BRIDGEWATER.   Our order, and the message to be considered of.
I was at the drawing of the order, and some desyred yt to be
expressed in the order to be sent for as a delinquent.   Some LL.
resolved yt to be all one.   He cannot be sent for but as a delinquent.   He cannot come to sytt here, but by an order.

DEVON[SHIRE].   Yt is agreed on all sydes that a L accused and
charged, &c.

Touching the order, yf made sodainely, and uppon noe grounde,
we may alter yt uppon grounde.

MONMOUTH.   Bristoll is prisoner to.the gentleman usher.

DORSETT.   The subcomittee appoynted to serche for precedents,
which was to some end, &c.   Yf noe charge appears against him,
to sende an officer for him, and then he may come and take his
place.

SAY.   To answere in the House, is to aunswere before the
House.

The Erle remaynes nowe in the custody of an officer for that the
House happened to be then adjourned for certeyne dayes.

CLARE.   To resolve howe to proceed.

DYVERS.   To sende for him.

TREASURER.   He is ordered to be brought hither.   He is in
custody.   Q[uery] whether to aunswere to his charge or delivered
out of custody.   The charge is by the King himselfe.   Yf you discharge him out of custodye, you dissavowe your owne order.

ESSEX.   Orders heretofore not soe constantly observed, but
altered uppon reason.

CHAMBERLEYN.   The order of the House must be firste reversed
ere he can be sett free.

WESTMORLANDE.   This order may be considered howe farr yt
bynds us.   The Subcomittee hathe not yett allowed yt, but stopte

at yt on Satterday laste, which was the last tyme they viewed the booke.

NORTHE. To sende for him to be brought to the barre, and then comaunded to come to his place.

CONWAYE. Yf the orders made to be broake, yt is as great breache of the priviledges as any thinge can be. Remembred the message, and the order. Understood as delinquent; for he was then the King's prisoner by restreynt.

CLARE propounded, the Earl of Bristol is sent for, but the usher hathe not retourned him brought. There is but an accusacion yett against him, and noe charge. He is here by proxie. Q[uery] whether you wyll withdrawe the officer, and leave him at his house untill the charge be brought.

BUCK[INGHAM]. Yt may be my owne case, and, yf yt be, I shall not be ashamed yf there be a barre betweene me and your LL^{ps}. This bussines was in agitacion many parlements since, and then in your opynions he stood not a condemned man. He was not a prisoner *ab origine* by this King, but by the deceased. The King that nowe is offred to lett him remayne in that tranquillity which a man in his state coulde have wished, soe he woulde acknowledge his errours. He desyred to come to his justificacion. His Matie offred yt, soe he woulde make no use of the pardons of K. J[ames] nor his. Nowe the K. reposseth trust in your LL^{ps}. Yt wylbe a shewe of favour to discharge him before he be herde.

The message from the King and the order to be sente for; and under custody in his owne house. Agree with a delinquent. Yf you wyll alter yt, to debate it firste.

CO[VENTRY] and L[ICHFIELD]. Uppon the orders.

MOUNTAGU. I was earnest that he shoulde be sent for as a delinquent : we were satisfyed that to be brought before us dyd tantamount. To take the same course which was taken against Middlesex, he sate in his place till he herde the charge, &c.

MONTGOMERY. He was a prisoner before the parlement began.

WARWICK.   His writt of somons released that restreynt, *prout*   April 29.
in the Earl of Northumberlands case a° 18 Ja. Rs.

DORSETT.   To be resolved whether a writt sent with a letter :
and whether the Earl is here as a prisouner.

SAY.

PRESIDENT.   A writt enlargeth a restreynt.   But this case
differres—

1. The letter is not here which doth charge him.

2. The House is not possessed that the Earl is come.

That the Grande Comittee may take this into their consideracion.

NORTHE.   Maxwell sent his man yesterday to the Comittee to
signifye that the Earl was come, &c.

DORSETT.   Yf the writt of somons dothe discharge his restreynt,
then he comes as a Peere, but whether a writt sente with a restreynte
dothe discharge him or noe ?

The Comittee of priviledges to consider of yt, and whether he
brought as a delinquent or noe?

TREASURER.   That the gentleman usher on Monday may make
his retourne, and the Grande Comittee to consider in the meane tyme
what shalbe then done.

On Monday mournynge next the gentleman usher to retourne to
the House what he hathe done uppon the order hee receaved from
the House for brynging the E[arl] of B[ristol] before their LL.ps,
and then the House to be putt into a Comittee.

Adj. to Monday at 9.

LUNÆ, PRIMO DIE MAII, 1626.   May 1.

[L. J. iii. 574.]

*   *   *   *   *

MAXWELL.   That, according to the Order, he hath brought up   Agreed.
the Erle of Bristol, and is ready to doe further as they[r] LLps shall
appoynte.

To brynge him before theyre LL^{ps} presently.

L. KEEPER. A message from his Matie. To receave from Mr. Attourney what the offences are against the Erle of Bristoll.

Mr. ATTOURNEY came to the Clerks table to charge him.

MULLGRAVE. To consider whether Bristoll shalbe present at the charge or noe.

PRESIDENT. He must then come to the barre.

Ordered : to be brought to the barre presentlye.

* * * * *

MAXWELL. To knowe in what fashion he shall bring Bristoll to the barr.

Agreed : To keeele at his firste coming, being for an accusacion of high treason ; and the L. Keeper to wyll him to stande up, and to tell him that Mr. Attourney is to charge hygh treason, and other missdemeanors.

Bristoll brought to the barr; kneeled.

KEEPER. To stande up.

Sente for to heare your charge of high treason, &c.

BRISTOLL. That he exhibited his peticion, he beinge a Peere . of the realme is charged theruppon with Treason, and desyred this to be taken into consideracion, that he had informed the late Kinge of the unfaithful [?] service of Buckingham. He vouched the Lord Chambleyn, and he laboured he myght be clapt up in the Tower presently at his cominge up, and since he laboured to keepe him from this King's presence, and nowe he is charged for treason.

He hathe ben often Embassadour, came home never taynted. Laboured to be herde by K. James. He promised yt. I pray God yt dyd him noe hurte. For the promisse he vouched Pembrock.

Desyred to consider that this House is possessed of his accusacion by his peticion.

Requyred that his charg[e] may be rec[eived] ag[ains]t Buck-[ingham] and Conway first, and then to proceed against him, and not to invalid his testimonye ag[ains]t the Duke and him by the K[ing]'s charge.

He speakes for the K[ing].   He is free, and desyred not to be
impeached till his charge of soe highe a nature be first herd.

He d[elivere]d in his 2 charges in writinge w[hi]ch the LL.
commaunded the Clerke to receave, and soe he dyed.

Withdrawen.

BUCKINGHAM.   Loathe to interrupt Bristol when he was speaking. He hathe ben his friend. Went with that intencion into
Spayne, and gave him assurance therof before the King. Some
mistaking ; whether when the Kinge of Sp[ain] being sensible of
the honor the Prince had done him in cominge thether, &c. Bristol,
he knewe the state of Sp[ain] soe well that the Prynce myght well
reposse his buissines on him. Yett I advised that Cottington myght
be addressed allso to Olivares, &c.

This he tooke to be a crosse to him personally, and we grewe to
some heate there. Yett reconcyled, and caryed himselfe with all
respecte to him afterwards.

At his retourne, he reported nothing to the late Kinge, nor to
bothe Howses, but at the comaundement of this Kinge. And ever
desyred the Kinge to putt an ende of this buissines, and to question
him.

His Matie was loathe to sende his owne Minister.[a] But nowe,
he styrringe the matter ytselfe, the case is alltered ; yt is himselfe,
not the King, that brynges him hither.

CONWAY desired the charge against him to be herde presently.

Mr. ATTOURNEY. That he rec[eived] his Ma^{ts} comandment to   He had not
leave, and soe
proceeded not.
attende this day to gyve the E[arl] of Bristoll his charge. Moved:
Whether the E[arl] of Bristoll shalbe herde first or noe?

The peticion of the Erle of Bristol reade, which was exhibited
19 Apr.

PRESIDENT.   The question is not of his person as a Peere, but of
the reason. Yt stands not with honour nor justice to preferr him

---

[a] " to trial," or some such words, appear to be omitted.

May 1.   in his charge in priority before the K[ing]'s charge.   His to be
herde in his tyme.

NORWICH.   Whether this House is or may be dewly possessed of
Bristoll['s] accusacion?   Yf it be, then his had priority of tyme.   His
peticion an accusation.   When his Matie reposed the tryall in this
House, he allso referred yt to the orders of this House.

ESSEX.   Bothe the charges to be reade.

CARLILE.   The K[ing]'s letter reade here before the peticion,
and soe the K[ing] hathe priority of tyme.

DORSETT.   The Comittee reported him charged with that letter.

NORTHE.   The charge ag[ains]t Bristol and the charge ag[ains]t
Buck[ingham] to be both read.

The E[arl] is interested in them bothe.

Adj. ad libitum.

BUCK[INGHAM].   That Bristoll's accusacion ag[ains]t him may
be herde in such tyme as all what he can saye against me may be
of force, &c.

Clare.   *Ad idem.*

BUCK[INGHAM].   Bristol shewes his arte of delayes.   The K[ing]'s
accusacion ag[ains]t Bristol concernes not him, but the K[ing]
and Bristol only.

The accusacion of Bristol ag[ains]t him is of treason, &c., and a
touch uppon the late K[ing]'s deathe.   Prayed, yf he prove yt not,
then he may have *lex talionis.*

And after much debate,

BUCK[INGHAM] desyred that they myght be bothe reade.

Agreed.[a]

And the charge to be read against Bristol first, then his against
the Duke.

Resumed.

---

[a] " Resumed " is added here in the MS., but it should no doubt have been erased
when the word was entered lower down.

Agreed, bothe charges to be reade presently, in the Erle of Bristolls absence, by a generall acclamacion.

And yett, Dorsett speakinge agaynste yt, yt was putt to the
Question.

Such of your LL^ps as are of opynion that theis charges shalbe
reade presentlye, say content, and such as are of a contrary opynion
saye, not content.

Agreed per pluries.

Mr. Attourney begann with a preamble of the [Earls] peticion,
and the K[ing]'s message

The K[ing]'s charg[es] are for offences of high nature, from un-
feithfullnes to treachery.

The honor of the K[ing]'s father, his owne and the kingdom, and
safety and peace of Christendom.

4 parte[s]
prescrybed by
the K[ing]

1. Whylest in Sp[ain], before.
2. Whylest the Pr[ince] was there.
3. After his retourn.
4. Offence in the peticion.

He wyll begyn with the last:

1. The quallitye of his person.
2. Of his ymployment.
3. Of the persons whom he offended.
4. And the tyme.
1. A gentl[eman], &c. honoured with degrees.
2. An Embassador of highest quallitye. The Palat[inate] and
   maryage of the Pr[ince] and that the tymes of his negociacion most daungerous, when, yf opportunity omitted,
   the negociacion lost.
4. And the tyme of the peticion in parlement, to rayse dif-
   ferences betweene the Peeres and the Kinge.
3. The person. Disrespecte to his M[ajesty].

Peticion. Much unthankefullnes.

Thankes to the LL. for his somons, none to the Kinge; a greate disrespecte, and arg[u]ment of pryde with subtilty, he slyghted his Maᵗⁱᵉ; ever ready to obey, &c. and yett p[rese]ntly wayved his Maᵗˢ knowne direccion.

Against his owne knowledge, the K[ing]'s pleasure signifyed by some others, and the termes the letter of the K[ing]'s pleasure sent by the L. Keep[er], a missive letter.

Then taxeth the K[ing] and his father of open injustice. For 2 yeares past highly wronged, and not permitted to aunswere for himself. This is ag[ains]t his owne certeyn knowledge, for he receaved a charg in wrighting and retourned answer in wrighting.

Hereby he hathe offended the patience of the K[ing]; otherwyse he had not herde of his accusacion at all. This only, disrespecte and unthankefullnesse to his Maᵗⁱᵉ for a Peere of this realme openly to traduce.

2. Tymes. { Before the K[ing] went into Spayn.
{ Whylest the K[ing] was there.
{ After the K[ing] came home.

He dyd deale unfeithefully, treacherously, and traiterously.

1. Offended his M[aste]r whoe ymployed him.
2. His Maᵗˢ chilldren.
3. His countrey.
4. The peace of Xtendome, God, and religion.

1. Grossly neglected the duty of an Embassador, not feithefully advertising, ever reporting that certeinty in the K[ing] of Sp[ain] to be such that the last K[ing] was misled.

In not following precyse instruccions, as by his letters.

2. He missinformed touching the maryage and porcion, &c., and [protracted?] the tyme soe long, &c. By his false intelligence, the Pallatinat lost, &c.

3. As much as in him lyeth, he hath betrayed the wholl kingdom; being more a servant to the K[ing] of Sp[ain] then to the K[ing] of Englande, which shalbe proved by a testimony from Spayne of their liberall proffers to him.

4. Peace of Xtendom, the Palat[inate], Germany, Bohemia; all,

through his miscarriage in his embassage. Fallse to God and religion. By his letters often perswaded for a connivence, and toleracion of religion in England.

When the Prince was in Sp[ain] what was kindled before, there burst out, and was acted at full.

Obj[ection]. He reported but the protestacions of Sp[ain]; followed his instruccions. Be yt so; yett he is a foolishe Embassador that wilbe cosened with protestacions. Credulitye the greatest faulte that can be. He selldom sent any letter to England, but he expressed his greate opynion and affeccion of Sp[ain], that his Matie had not more feithefull counsellors iu England then in Spayne.

This not out of his want of knowledge or experience, for he woulde often boaste of his wytt, and that he had as lythe be reputed a knave as a foole.

The instruccions hathe ben ever to dispatche, and not to spyn out tyme. Taken noatice of yt, yett complyed with them:[a] take heed you putt them not out of their pace; but never wrote, take heed that you be not cosened by them.

The motives that drewe him to this were, 1, ambition, and 2, covetousenes.

1. Unwilling to comunicate: rather forbade others to intermedle in yt. Whensover the question came whoe were in the faulte, he was ever readyer to lay yt on Englande, and the ministers of his K[ing], then on Spayne and the ministers therof.

2. Covetousnes, his rewardes: his owne wordes, when questioned about the difficultyes or ympossibillityes of his embassage, he answered, I wyll looke to my instruccions, and make my fortunes out of them.

The Prynce his being in Spayne.

Bristoll much troubled at his coming, least his former jugglinges myght be discovered. The Pr[ince] adventured to discover the truthe. Greate honor. God drewe him of[f].

Bristoll's caryage. Religion. He had many tymes advysed a

[a] *i.e.*, with the Spaniards.

favourable hande to the Catholiques here. But Br[istol] first attempted the Pr[ince].

B[ristol]. Sir, why come you hither?

P[rince]. You knowe as well as I.

B[ristol.] Servants canot serve feithefully unlesse they knowe your mynde truly. Yt is here reported that you intende to change your religion.

Shortly after, B[ristol] meinteyned that the state of England never dyd anythinge of greate consequence but when they were under the Pope of Rome.

The tyme of this intimacion, when the Pr[ince's] affeccion to that lady was expressed.

Observe the stat[ute] of 27 Eliz. and 3 Jacobi.

The proffer of the matche of the K. of Boh[emia's] son with the Emperor's daughter, and he to be bredd up in the Emperor's corte. He perswaded yt, and replyed, without some such greate accion the peace of Xtendom coulde never be effected.

The articles.

The publique to be sworne unto.

The pryvatt to be signed only.

Yett intruded to the Pr[ince] as yf he were to be sworne unto bothe, and contested with the Pr[ince] about yt, and after confessed he was mistaken, and the pryvat articles were for religion.

Newe articles from Rome clogged. Pr[ince] woulde be gon: perswaded. But perceaving by the newe Junct of dyvynes that he must stay till the sprynge, he woulde [be] gone, &c.

Buck[ingham] feared delaye. Bristoll slyghted yt. The Pr[ince] promised to staye. The Junct of divines resolved that the Infanta coulde not goe till the sprynge. Then Bristoll, that the Pr[ince] was tyed to staye by his promisse, though before that yt shoulde be but a punctilio.

The Palat[inate] being urged to be restored, or ayde from the K[ing] to recover yt. Br[istol] aunswered they are not tyed to us in that.

Putt a lye uppon his owne M[aste]r by sayinge, &c.
Extoll the courte of Spayne. You must neither hunte nor
hawke, nor eate your meate with quyett, yf you have warres with
Spayne.

After the Pr[ince] was retourned out of Sp[ain], the Palatinat
beinge offred, &c., the Pr[ince] contented to signe articles for the
maryage firste, and after varyed from, Olivares saying that the
person of the Count Palatine was not intended. Bristol was
comanded to urge Olivares to this, and they justifyed that the
Palatine himselfe was never spoaken of, &c.

Pr[ince] seeing he was thus cosened, he resolved to retourne,
leaving the powers with Br[istol], but sent a letter of limitacion by
Clerke, &c., *prout* in the narracion by Buckingham.

Br[istol] promissed to obey theis restriccions punctually. Yett
he sette a short day for the weddinge, soe shorte, &c.

Concluded.

Rather then loose his owne childe, soe he calld yt, he would
rather hazard the losse of the Palat[inate], &c., then his owne ends,
&c. Howe yt hathe intangled the state, &c. Howe theis tende to
highe treason, leave to your judgement, and that you would direct
this into a legall waye.

The Erle of Bristoll's articles reade ag[ains]t Buck[ingham].

His articles against the L. Conway reade.

SPENCER. We expected greate matters, *montes parturire, et
nascitur ridiculus mus.*

DORSETT. To proceede ag[ains]t Bristol nowe, and afterwards
with his articles against the Duke.

ATTOURNEY. To sett this buissines into an order, what course
shalbe taken in the K[ing]'s cause.

DEVON[SHIRE]. Bristoll to be here to morrowe, and charged
by Mr. Attourney.

PRESIDENT. To be indicted, *prout* Berkley, aº 4 E. 3; 21 R. 2,
Arundell and Warwic; 28 H. 6. Suff[olk] and to be comitted.

May 1.   WESTMORLAND. The usher to carry him back, and bryng him hither agayn to morrowe.

DORSETT. The Judges to delyver what in other courts ought to be done.

MULGRAVE. The Judges to resolve us of the precedents.

L. KEEPER. Whether the clerke may gyve copyes, or noe?

Agreed.   Agreed, to gyve copyes of bothe, aswell of the articles against the Duke as of those against the L. Conwaye exhibited by the Erle of Bristoll. The Judges withdrawne to consider of the presidents.

Beinge retourned, The Judges declared,

1. What fourme we use in comitments in cases of treason, yf accusacion and good matter appe[ar] then we comitte him, yf he be within the stat[ute] of 25 E. 3, but yf yt be out of that statt[ute] the Parlement must declare whether yt be treason or noe.

2. 35 H. 8. Yf the treason be beyonde the seas, an endictement before comissioners, &c. or bill by way of Attaindre, w[hi]ch must passe bothe Howses.

And we comitt none, unlesse some witnesse be first examined. Lefte yt to the LL. in this case.

MULGRAVE. We desyred to knowe whether by the presidents avouched yt wyll appe[ar] that a Peere is to be comitted uppon a bare accusacion.

WESTMORLANDE. The precedents to be perused by the Comittee for priviledges, and Bristoll to be comitted to the gentleman usher in his owne house. Accesse of friends to be permitted him.

Agreed   NORTHE. The K[ing]s charge against the E[arl] of Bristol to be herde firste, and then the charge of the Erles against the Duke, but yett soe as the Erles testimonye against the Duke be not prevented, prejudiced, nor impeached.

Reade and ordered.

Bristol at the barre agayne; kneeled; stood up.

KEEPER. The LL. with a greate deale of honor and justice have taken into consideracion bothe the Articles, &c.

Resolved the K[ing]s charge to be first, yett soe as, &c. *ut supra.*
Prisoner, &c. accesse of friends, &c.

Bristol, he conceaved that his articles were treason, and therefore requyred that the Duke myght be indicted of treason by the Attourney generall.

Withdrawen.

Adj. to 9 to-morrowe.

DIE MARTIS, 2ᵈᵘ MAII, 1626.

[L. J. iii. 579.]

Prayers.

L. KEEPER. The last nygh[t] his Maᵗʳ, and comandement—message. Knowledge of the Articles per Bristol. Many of them such as his Maᵗⁱᵉ knowes more than any man of the Duke's sincere caryage. That touching the declaracion, he and you all knowe him to be interessed.

Bristol longe concealed. Thanks that you have gyven noe way to [t]he Erles mocion, to putt the Duke in some restreynt. Thereby you have eschewed ——

Confident that a difference betwen a delinquent app[ear]inge, and the recriminacion. *Non jure parium.*

CARLILE. Whether a Peere accusinge another here of high treason, and delyveringe his charge here, may at that same tyme delyver the same charge to the Commons?

DORSETT. This is recriminacion and calumniacion. We had some debate whether to be comunicated, and he hathe strowen papers of yt ellswhere.

To accuse the Duke here, the right way. To the Commons is to accuse as of not competent judges, &c., and sought to prejudge the cause, and a high cryme, and next to the cryme of treason the highest.

MULGRAVE. Howe can we take noatice what is done with the Commons? To proceede to th' other.

SPENCER. By common fame. To sende to them to knowe of yt.

CLARE. Remembred the accusacion of the Commons against Ep^us Lincolne: uppon fame. To proceede in the other.·

MENEVEN[SIS]. The Comons sent a message hither of an intendment of this House to move for money, &c., and after they desyred that they myght preserve their priviledges intirely. The LL. here to doe the lyke.

CLEVELAND. When Bristol comes to the barr, then to demaunde of him whether he hathe caused any such Articles to be d[elivere]d unto the Commons or noe, and soe to proceede as cause shall requyre.

DORSETT. He can produce authors, and wyll at your LL^ps comaunde.

LONDON. Yt is as yf Bristol had receaved gravamen here. And yt is in nature of a libell being exhibited there *coram non Judice*, to sende to the Commons. That they take noe noatice of it, for that this House is possessed herof.

NORWICH. We were tender to take any noatice of a message heretofore to the Duk[e] from the Commons. Yt comes not to us in a parlementary waye.

SAY. To consider whether they have intrenched uppon our priviledges or noe. To enquyre on common fame: not to judge uppon yt.

Moved to knowe first, whether a man maye not informe this House and that, of any offence at one tyme.

BRIDGEWATER. Yll to question the Commons. But yf we fynde any humors amongst our selves, they to be cured; and this is done by one of this House. The Commons have done us noe wronge. To proceede to the buissines of the daye.

PRESIDENT. Consider: 1. The facte; 2. the power of the

Comons ; 3. whether this and the Commons House may [occure?]ᵃ May 2.
in one and the same proceeding.

1. The facte is not pertinent to the Comons. An unworthy
thing, and to be damned, proceedinges uppon comon fame. The
injury ; the acte of the partie is to be questioned.

2. He exhibited his bill here in poynt of treason, and there allso.
Here yt is propper. There they have noe power to proceede.

3.

To tell him of yt roundly when he is at the barre, and after proceede to judgement.

ALII. Not to be charged with yt.

ESSEX. Not to be tollde of yt untill he hathe answered the
K[ing]'s charge first, least yt myght disturbe him, &c.

BUCK[INGHAM]. The question not to be asked him till he hathe
herde his charge and aunswered yt, leaste yt disturbe him in his
aunsweres.

SAYE. Not satisfyed whether our priviledges are intrenched on.
Being but by enquirye, the Erle not to be asked question nowe. Yf
you entende to punishe him, then not to drawe the grounde of his
punishment out of his owne mouthe.

DURESME. Yf the Erle hath subscrybed to the Articles
d[clivere]d to the Comons, then he hathe declyned the justice of
this House : and a calumnye.

MULGRAVE. To resolve firste whether yt be an offence to
presente to enquyrors, &c.

KEEPER. To knowe what course to take with Bristol. Mr.
Attourney firste to pen the charge, and then to delyver him the
hedds of the charge, and he to aunswere.

ALII. He to have tyme to aunswere.

TRE[ASURE]R. To be indicted first, before we examyne the
cause. Nowe the hedds of the cause to be redd unto him. Then
to consider howe to proceede. Whether to have him indicted first

---

May 2. in the K[ing]'s bench by direccion from thence, which beinge cer-
tefyed hither, your LL^{ps} then to proceed.

L. KEEPER. Noe hedes to be d[elivere]d him, yf he be to be
indicted. The Attourney to shewe howe to proced.

ATTOURNEY. 2 wayes. 1. By bill in Parlement. 2. By byll
of indictement, which yf founde then to be remitted hither, and the
LL. the Peeres to proccede theron.

PRESIDENT. This is the legall way: the Attorney generall to
exhibitt a bill of endictement for the K[ing] in the K[ing]s bench.

KEEPER. The Attourney to be directed.

ATT[ORNEY]. Parte of the cause is of crymes acted beyond the
seas; for them a comission is to be had according to the statt[ute].

Agreed. KEEPER moved that Mr. Attourney proceed and provyde an
indictement, to be retourned hither on Satterday next. Yf he
doubte of the fourme, to conferr with the Judges. And yf any
greater difficulty, soe that there shalbe cause to resorte to their LL.,
then their LL^{ps} to be acquainted with yt.

MULGRAVE commended to their consideracion, whether this
indictement wyll not prevent or prejudice the testimony of the Erle
of Bristol.

Agreed that, till he be convicted, his testymony remaynes good.

CLARE. Touching treasons beyond seas, there are precedents of
a complaint by the Commons of such, and procceded on in Parlement without any comission.

KEEPER. The comission is uppon a statute of 35 H. 8 for them
to take an indictment.

Ordered. ESSEX. Mr. Attourney to proceede with preparacion, but the
House not to be concluded till their next meeting on Thurseday,
and the subco[m]ittee for priviledges to serch in the meanetyme.

Ordered. The L. Keeper to move his Matie for the House for a speedy and
gracious aunswere unto their peticion on the behalfe of the Erle of
Arundell.

Adj. to Thurseday at 9.

DIE JOVIS, 4to MAII, 1626.

[L. J. iii. 580.]

*   *   *   *   *

L KEEPER. Moved for the House. His Matie aunswered that yt is a cause that he hath a greate deale of care, and is wylling to gyve you satisfaccion, and hathe yt in his consideracion, but hathe ben interrupted with other beuissines, wherin Mr. Attourney hathe good occasion of much conference with him, as you are acquainted, and wyll with all as convenience gyve your LL^{ps} satisfaccion and retourne you an aunswere.

*   *   *   *   *

DEVON[SHIRE]. Reported the serche of precedents: founde one that gyves them satisfaccion in the case of the E[arl] of Northumberl[and] in 5° H. 4 Parl[iamen]t, and had caused the roll to be brought hither,

Which was reade.

L. KEEPER. Mr. Attourney to be sente for.

Mr. Attourney came.

KEEPER. Whether he shall propounde anything or noe?

CLARE. The Attourney to brynge in the hedds of his charge.

The order 2 Maii reade.

MULGRAVE. Not concluded or resolved on that an indictement shoulde be, but the hedds of the charge to be firste d[elivere]d by Mr. Attorney, and the House to consider of the offences.

Mr. Attourney to brynge in the hedds of the charge against the E[arl] of Bristoll on Satterdaye next. And then the House to consider of the further proceedinges.

SAY. Mr. Attourney to charge Bristol, and, his aunswere and proofes beinge herde, and considered of by the House, then to proceede as the cause shall requyre.

CANT[ERBURY]. Thankes that he hathe leave to speake syttinge. Commended the care of and wisedome of their LL^{ps} to

May 4. procecde with all warines and caution asswell for posteritye as the presentc.

His observacion of the K[ing]'s message, priority to the K[ing]'s charge. Approved. Bristoll's testymonye preserved. Hyghly praysed. To procecde as you have begunn. To weigh whether by indictement or noe. Much commended the other waye. The partie to be herde firste.

Bristoll the other daye in passion prayed a byll of indictement myght be putt in in the K[ing]'s bench against the other.

Moved. Mr. Attourney to gyve the charge, the partye to be herde, &c.

Mr. ATTOURNEY, with leave. He had lefte his papers at home. Whether he shoulde come with Articles, or be prepared to gyve his charge.

L. KEEPER. Whether he shall brynge proofes or noe?

Mr. ATTOURNEY. That he cannot make ready the proofes so soone. Moved that he myght gyve the charge, and the Erle aunswere, and uppon his aunswere the LL. to consider therof, and then to directe the proofes.

SAY.

PRESIDENT. The way propounded may be a greate prejudice to the cause.

Mr. Attourney to drawe up the hedds of the charge, and to open them, and cleere them to your LL.ps before the partie be called to his aunswere. Your LL.ps to judge uppon the heddes. They beinge determyned, then to call the Erle to his aunswere.

Explayned the president of the Erle of Northumberland's case, nº 5 II. 4, to be in respecte of the stattute, and briefly opened the articles against Bristoll. The hedds to be first herde, before Bristoll be called to his aunswere.

DEVON[SHIRE]. To knowe firste whether yt be treason or noe, before he be indicted.

The House adj. *ad libitum.*

TRE[SURE]R.   Yf the treason be within the compasse of the
statt[ute] of 25 E. 3, then the proceedings knowen by the usage.
Yf within the statt[ute] of 35 H. 8, then the forme is there sett
downe.

Touchinge the examinacion of the truthe of the case, you must
heare all the proofes and determyne the lawe before the tryall, which
is unfytt.   The heddes of the charg or the indictement rather to be
herde, and to determin whether yt be treason or noe.

Then to be indicted firste and afterwardes tryed and herde.

CLARE.   Not to make a faulte before we knowe yt to be a faulte.
Before the indictement, first the hedds of the cause to be herde and
the parties answere.

DEVON[SHIRE].   An order of Parlement 28 Maii, 1624, reade:
for the triall of Peeres, *pro consilio*, &c.

NORTHE.   The charge to be d[elivere]d to the House firste,
before he comes to the barre.

PRESIDENT.   The case of 3 R. 2 [Imperea's?] case.   An Embassador slayen in the streetes.   Proceeded on thus in parlement.   First
the lawe.   Declared to be treason.   Then the parties endicted.

TREA[SURE]R.   *Probabilis causa* sufficient for an indictement.   But
good proofes at the tryall.   The jury to fynde accordinge to the
evidences.

Precedents to be serched, whether any examinacions have been
taken formerly before an indictement.

The hedds of the charge to be herde firste.   Then to receave his
aunswere and tyme appointed to goe to tryall.

DEVON[SHIRE].   Whether a Peere may be allowed counsell and
wittnesses after his indictement, at his tryall; according as is ordered
to be allowed him by the order, 28 Maii, 1624.

DORSETT.   Doubtes of yt (for that yt is against the lawe)
whether he may be allowed counsell upon the order of this House.

ALII.   The order is for tryalls here.

SAY.   To consider of the cause well, before any L. be proceeded on judicially. For the indictement wyll leave a blemmish on a Peere, though he be cleered.

DORSETT. Bristoll to be herde before any other procceding.

MULGRAVE. To pursue the precedent of 5 H. 4.

BUCK[INGHAM]. Double interessed in this buissines, as a Peere; as accused.

1. To be resolved on firste, whether the proceeding ought to be here, or in the K[ing]'s bench. He here.[a]

2. The heddes to [be] considered of, and to conclude whether such an acte be treason or noe; not naminge the partie. Contented you doe soe with me, or howe you please. But you to proceed against Bristoll with all the caution that may be.

After the hedds considered of, then to proceed, either by de-lyverye of the charge at the barre, or sende yt him, and here his answere.

CLARE. The Parlement is not tyed to any forme. 4 E. 3, one forme, 5 H. 4, another. That of the Embassador, deathe a cleere facte, and soe the facte alone debated before the proceedinge.

PRESIDENT *prout antea.*

Et alii alias.

BUCK[INGHAM]. First heare the hedds, then declare whether the thing be treason or noe, not naminge the partie.

DEVON. To heare the proofe allso before yt be putt into an indictement, or any other coarse of proceedinge.

DORSETT *ad idem,* and to examine yt well first.

Et alii ad idem, but not to be out of this House.

TRE[ASURE]R. To have a taste of the evidence and proofes only.

PRESIDENT. 2 things granted.

1. Hedds to be d[elivere]d by Mr. Attourney.

2. They to be d[elivere]d him here or sent him.

The other 2 doubtefull.

BUCK[INGHAM] *prout antea.*

---

[a] *i.e.* He thinks it ought to be here.

NORWICH. The case to be stated generally. But the particulers
to be herde firste, &c. *prout* Buck[ingham].

COMPTON, SAY, et ALII. To resolve (before the House is resumed) of the question or conclusion of the debate at a Committee.

Resumed.

KEEPER. The questions—

1. Mr. Attourney to prepare the hedds of the charge against the
E[arl] of Bristol, and brynge them in on Satt[ur]day.

2. The Erle of B[ristol] to receave the charge at the barre then.
Mr. Attourney to brynge in the hedds of his charge on Satter
daye, and the Erle to be here then allso at the barre to heare yt.

Mr. Attourney is only to open the charge against him.

3. When the Erle hathe herde his charge, the LL. wyll determyne
whether he shall answere presently, or at what other tyme, according as occasion shalbe ministred from the Erle, or otherwise. But
the Erle is not to be inhibited, yf he wyll answere presentlye.

4. After the Erle hath answered the charge the LL. wyll then,
and not before, resolve into what way of procceding to putt this
cause.

5. This cause of the E[arl] of B[ristol] is to be reteyned wholly
in this House.

6. After the charge is brought in, and the Erles aunswere, their
LL.ps to procede to heare Mr. Attourneys proofes amongest them-
selves, and then to putt the cause into way of proccedinge in this
House.

Adj. to Satterday at 9.

---

*　　*　　*　　*　　*

L. KEEPER moved. Mr. Attourney desyres that in respecte you
have herde what the nature of the cryme is agaynst the Erle of

Bristol, that the Clerke of the Crowne in the K[ing]'s bench shall attende at the readinge of yt here, accordinge to a precedent of former tymes.

Denyed, in respecte of the order 4to Maii, that this cause shalbe kept within this House, and the Clerke of the Crowne of the K[ing]'s benche is noe minister of this Courte.

*   *   *   *   *

The Erle of Bristoll brought to the barre, kneeled, stood up. ·

[Charge against the Earl of Bristol, L. J. iii. 582.]

BRISTOL, for himselfe, craved pardon for earenest speeches the other day, and sayd yt was a faulte which herafter he would amend, confessing yt to be a passion which he was much subjecte unto : and thankes for this course of proceeding.

Desyred to knowe from Mr. Attourney whether this be his wholl charge or noe.

ATTOURNEY. He hathe comaundement to open noe more against. Peradvent[ure] uppon the opening some particulars may aryse which shalbe urged against you, but noe newe.

2. Desyred to knowe his relation, for he had the honor to sitt in the Starrchamber, where the order is to have a relator, and so desyred to knowe his accuser.

Mr. ATTOURNEY. The K[ing] himselfe with his owne mouth dyd dictate all his relacion against the Erle, and what was added, corrected many thinges.

BRISTOLL. He woulde not conteste with the K[ing]. But he hath posteritye. And therefore an humble suytor that his Matie woulde not take indignacion at his owne defense.

And as touching his offences to his Ma^{ty}, he wylbe ready to perfourme any submission to his Matie. Desyred that some meanes might be made that he might make yt personally to him.

That he woulde be pleased to sett himselfe here on his throne of justice, and declare that he leaves the L. Duke and him on equall termes, and that nether of their causes may be advanced before the other.

2 peticions.

1. For his personall submission to the K[ing].

2. For a declaracion for the equallity of his cause and Buck-[ingham].

To represent to his Matie that his accuser may not be his judge.

Yt wylbe a disservice to his Ma^ts service herafter.

To the charge ytselfe, he hath answered them once all over, and doubt not but to cleere himself therof before your LL^ps.

He expected a remonstraunce of some practisse with Spayne, as for rec[eipt] of 20,000^li for delyvery up of the townes, as Brill and Flushing: for delyvery of the K[ing]'s shipps to serve other nacions ag[ains]t our owne relligion; revealing of my M[aster]'s instruccons, which none above 2 dyd knowe of, for treating, &c.

Prayed to have his charge in wrighting, tyme to answere: counsell assigned him.

A greate difference betwene Buck[ingham] whoe is at large, and in the K[ing]'s favour, and him. Moved that—

As touchinge the L. Conway, a minister; that in my particuler he may not meddle, nor use the K[ing]'s name ex officio against him, he being Secretary.

For the particuler dispatches of his embassage may be brought into the House, and he have use of them; and the dispatches of Sr Walter Aston allso.

That his late Matie having in the presence of many LL. here present that I had neither comitted treason nor felony, and per-mitted dyvers to come to me.

That his Matie that nowe is hathe sayd he thought me an honest man, and that he thout my fautes* criminall, and hathe lately sayd soe, in the presence of some of the LL. and others, and an offer made me lately by the L. Conway, and a pardon, vizt, the corona-

---

* Apparently " not " is omitted here.

May 6.   cion pardon, then thought enough for me: nowe, all is made highe treason, contrary to his Ma^{ts} promisse, &c.

He coulde never gett redresse from his Matie by meanes of the Duke of Buck[ingham], wherefore he addressed his peticion, which touching Buck[ingham] the Duke's cunninge is to make the K[ing] a partie against me, and for accusinge him, I am made a highe traytour and the Duke a judge to voate against me.

Desyred the LL. to distinguishe of this.

He had ben to tedious, but desyred to have leave to present his case to him.

At the Prince his coming from Sp[ain], in favour with the K[ing]. At his retourne allso.

That in Sp[ain] he acquainted the Pr[ince] in Sp[ain] with the particulers which he was to wryte into England against Buck[ingham], and the Pr[ince] forbadd him not. I acquainted the K[ing] my master with yt, which the Duke of Buck[ingham] had sight of, *et hinc illae lacrimae.* He laboured Rich[mond] [a] and Cambridg [b] to deale with Pembrock that I myght be committed to the Tower, though but for a tyme, and desyrd Pembrock to speak his knowledg here.

Then in the Parlement House, he accuseth me of the Pr[ince] his going into Sp[ain], which he wyll prove was plotted by Buck[ingham] with the Spanishe Embassador, and many other contra-rieties in the Parlement House. Much daunger threatened. I offred to come presently: but answered that I myght staye and come at leysure.

Yett I came, and beinge at Callys I coulde gett noe shipp to wafte me over, least I should come before the Parlement ended.

At my cominge to lande, a single lettre was sent me from the L. Conway not to come to the Courte, but remayne in my owne house.

The K[ing] sente me worde that the Parlement was soe incensed ag[ains]t me, that yt was not safe to bryng me thither, as my

    [a] The Duke of Lennox.   [b] The Marquis of Hamilton.

desyre was, but within a fewe dayes I shoulde have an ende of my May 6. troubles.

Interrogatoryes were sent me, and I answered them.

The K[ing] sente me worde he woulde see me.

The K[ing] sett a day for those to be sent: much delayed: a lettre from Conwaye that they were ready, but he thought yt better to accomodate the matter.

A comission granted.

Their answere.

The K[ing] sente a messenger to me to wryte Buck[ingham] a fayre lettre, and all shoulde be well.

Then Mr. Clerke sente me from the Duke that all shoulde be well, soe I woulde retourne to the countrey and not come to the Courte, and he to disposse of the Vice Chambleyne's place.

I shewed Clerke some papers against the Duke. He requyred a retractacion. Denyed. All reconciliacion broaken of.

Then a proposicion that I shoulde satisfye the K[ing], the Pr[ince], and him.

I answered Buck[ingham].

I peticioned the K[ing]. The K[ing] sente me worde by Buck-[ingham] that I had satisfyed him, and therefore I had my free-dome.

Uppon this I came up, with an intent to come to my lodging at Whitehall.

Crossed by the Duke. The K[ing] sente me a message to make noe acknowledgement unlesse I woulde frely confesse my selfe faulty; and the Duke sent that message that I shoulde confesse my selfe guilty, and thus yt stood with me when the K[ing] sickened and dyed.

When this K[ing] came to the Crowne he gave me gracious speeches. The Duke wished me, &c. I desyred my writt of somons and had yt. Wrote worde that I desyred to knowe whether my coming myght be pleasing to the K[ing] or noe. The K[ing] ——

Quyett. Till when I desyred my wrytt. A lettre reade here,

May 6. wherewith I was charged, with an intent to fryght me, and copyes of this lettre divulged.

Then I peticioninge for my right, and ag[ains]t him, I am made a traytour.

Desyred to take into their cares his cause, whoe hathe putt himselfe wholly into your hands, &c.

                    Withdrawen.

ESSEX. The clerke to reade the noates which he hathe taken.

PRESIDENT. Bristol to pen the hedds of his owne desyres, as they may be trewly presented to the K[ing].

CHAMBLEYN. Bristoll to have tyme to doe this.

DEVON[SHIRE]. Chambleyn to delyver his knowledg of that for which Bristol vouched him.

CHAMBLEYN. Cambridge that in some discourse with Buck-[ingham], Buck[ingham] tollde him that through some nycenes in Richmond, him and me, he suffred in his cause, and moved him that Bristoll myght be comitted to the Tower.

KEEPER moved,

Agreed. Bristoll to putt in wrighting the shorte hedds of those peticions which he desyres this House to present to the Kinge on this behalfe.

To be allowed councell for his owne defense.

Tyme to answer.

Copy of his charge to be d[elivere]d him.

Bristoll at the barre agayne.

L. KEEPER. Tolde [him] he should have copy of his charge : he shoulde have counsell allowed to pleade for him, to name them here.

He named	Agreed.
Serjeant Henly	Tyme is graunted him to
Brampston	consider whom he wyll
Noy	have of his counsell.
Littleton	

L. KEEPER. Touchinge the tyme of his answere.

[BRISTOL.] Desyred tyme till this day sennight, by reason of some dispatches of his in the country

Mr. ATTOURNEY. That he had direccions to charge him with noe further dispatches then from 1621.

[BRISTOLL.] Then he requyred that on Monday next he myght signifye when he shalbe ready to answere.

L. KEEPER. For the hedds of his peticions which he desyred the House to present to the K[ing] and what ells he wyll desyre them to [be] mediators for him to the K[ing].

[BRISTOLL.] Promised to doe yt on Monday next, and retourned most humble thanks to their LL^{ps}.

Withdrawen.

Mr. ATTOURNEY, with leave, moved for direccions. When the Erle of Bristoll shall come back to make his defense? Howe he shall provyde himselfe for proofes, vid. some lettres and dispatches to be shewed and wytnesses to be produced?

CHAMBERLEYN. The Erles aunswere first to be herde.

The clerk to gyve copyes of this charge.

CHAMBERLEY[N],

SAY. The dispatches which shalbe urged against him to be brought hither, as the House and Bristoll may have use of them.

DORSETT. The K[ing] to be peticioned herin first by the House, and yt is one of Bristolls peticions.

Maxwell may leave Bristoll in his house, and not tyed to be continually with him.

*   *   *   *   *

DIE LUNÆ, 8 MAII, 1626.

[L. J. iii. 587.]

Prayers.

L. KEEPER. Comandement. Message.

May 8.   Bristol made request to have counsell. Understands the not using of counsell for a defendent in cases of treason and is an ancient fundamentall lawe of his kingdome. And therefore his Matie desyres that, forasmuch as he hathe comitted this cause to the honor and justice of this House, that your LL^ps woulde proceed with that caution that that ancient and fundamentall lawe may receave noe prejudice nor blemishe.

q. of the LL.   BUCK[INGHAM] desyred to knowe what the words spoken by Chambleyn.

CHAMBERLEYNE. Hamilton tollde him that Buck[ingham] feared that the Duke of R[ichmond's] nycenes and myne myght doe some hurte to the cause.

BUCK[INGHAM] explayned the maner of this. When he herde that Bristoll was cominge over.

I dyd feare that yf Br[istol] should but gett the care of my M[aste]r, he myght by some words he would use to him subverte all.

He ever desyred Br[istol] might come to his publique tryall here in this house; yett he ever sayd this, that yf the E[arl] of Br[istol] were his brother, he thoughte the fittest lodging for him was the Tower.

L. KEEPER repeated the message agayne.

MULGRAVE. First to see what Bristoll wyll peticion this daye, and then ——

CLARE. *Non est norum.* Dependes uppon an order made in this House in the Parlement a° 21 Jacobi, after the E[arl] of Midd[lesex] had rec[eived] his tryall. To consider whether that order shall stande or not.

CHAMBERLEYNE. Tyme is not yett, till yt be resolved yt be treason or noe wherewith Bristoll is charged, and then to consider what to doe uppon this message touchinge his counsell.

SAY *ad idem* and to be allowed couucell in the mean tyme.

Not settled.

The peticion of the Erle of Bristoll reade and exhibited this daye, touching his Ma^ts owne testimonye, and to move his Matie to

declyne his owne testimonye and his sorrowe for his Ma^ts dis- May 8.
pleasure, and prayethe that the persons of Buck[ingham] and his,
and their causes may remayne in equall termes.

To make his submission.

The dispatches of 1621. 22. and 23 to be brought.

That the L. Conwaye may not use his Ma^ts name *ex officio.*

The names of his Councell.

Tyme for 8 dayes respeat for answere.

An order that Mr. Maxwell may present such further peticions
as he shall have occasion herafter to present.

Reade agayne after the House was putt into a Comittee.

The peticion dyvided into parte[s]. 1. Touchinge his Ma^ts accusacion and testimonye.

NORWICH. The Judges to be consulted with, how farre in their   Agreed.
courtes, in cases of felony or treason, the K[ing]s testimony hathe
ben used.

DORSETT. Mr. Attourney to delyver whether the K[ing] wyll
use his owne testimony or noe.

ATT[ORNEY]. As farr as he hathe looked into t[h]e proofes,
there is very little or noe use of the K[ing]'s testimony for any
thinge which the K[ing] affirmes of his owne knowledge, but that
yt may be proved by one or 2 other proofes.

Besides the K. was then Prynce, and soe a subjecte.

The judges to be sente for to be here to morrowe morninge.

This particular to be shewen them, and the Judges to gyve their   Agreed.
opynion therof to morrowe morninge.

MR. ATTOURNEY. A worde mistaken in the Erles peticion,
vizt, that the King is a Relator, which is ——?; to be altered.

He to be admonished to alter that worde.   Agreed.

2. The seconde poynte touchinge equallitye betweene Buckingham and him.

BUCK[INGHAM]. In this particuler he wyll desyre noe other
Judges then their LL^ps.

May 8.   DORSETT. Some grounde for[a] his excepcion against the K[ing]. But none to take away Buck[ingham]'s testimonye allso.

And as unjust to except against him that shalbe his Judge, by accusinge him of the same offence.

The seconde poynte reade agayne.

CONWAYE. Uujust: he is a prisoner allready, hathe ben att the barre and accused of high treason.

PRESIDENT. Here is noe contestacion betwixt Peere and Peere, but betwene the K[ing] and him.

CHAMBLEYN. The E[arl] to peticion the K[ing] yf he please, and not the House; but when the House hathe herde the cause wherewith he ——

Then noe doubte but the House wyll deale nobly and justly.

CANT[ERBURY]. The House not to be mediators to the Kinge. After this cause comes into debate, &c.

3. Touchinge his personall submission to the K[ing].

DIVERSE. Unfytt till he be tryed and cleered, for the House to doe yt.

SAY.

4. For the dispatches to be brought hither for him to have use therof.

Mr. ATTORNEY. That what he shall offer against him, that to be comon.

Agreed.   CHAMBERLEYN. And those allso whom he shall requyre in particuler to be brought hither.

But noe copyes to [be] gyven out.

BUCK[INGHAM]. Nothing to be allowed but the originalls, and noe copyes.

5. Touchinge the L. Conwaye, not to use his Ma[ts] name *ex officio* as Secretarye.

DORSETT. To be restreyned unto his particuler onlye, and not to looke backwarde.

---

* In the MS. "touchinge" has been left unerased before "for" inserted above the line.

CONWAY spake in defense of his owne reputacion touching the articles exhibited by Bristoll. May 8.

Prayed to suspende their judgement till proofe.

Touching his particuler, he never yett wrote any lettre unto Br[istol] but upon the K[ing]'s owne direccion, and that Br[istol] knowes well; for he hathe enquyred after my lettres, and the King hathe ben moved in yt, and justifyed my lettres. He never dyd any thing *ex officio*.

CHAMBERLEYN. Yf Br[istol] hathe any desyre to peticion this, he may to the King ymediatly himselfe, yf he wyll.

TR[EASURE]R expl[ained] the meaninge *ex officio*.

PRESIDENT. The peticion is that he may not doe yt, nor that he hathe done yt: [*er*]*go*, needes not to be restreyned.

Reade agayne.

SAYE. Conceaves yt concernes not the future only, but his testimony allso for the tymes past.

MULGRAVE. This last poynte to be sent to the Erle, and he to explayne yt. Agreed.

1. The councell to be allowed him.

CANT[ERBURY]. To be deferred at this tyme.

ALII *e contra et varie.*

SAY. Yf this be not allowed, you receade from your order.

DORSETT.

The firste order, 28 Maii, 1624, reade.

The order allso, 6 Maii, 1626, reade.

BUCK[INGHAM]. To debate the justnes of the first order, whether yt be not against the fundamentall lawe of this lande.

TRE[ASURE]R. Conceaves the House intends to heare his aunswere, and have a taste of the proofes, and then to discusse whether yt be treason or noe.

In other courtes, councell is allowed at tryalls in poynte of lawe, but not further.

Propounded, to gyve a precedent that canot be excepted against, viz.

May 8.   You intende to examin wyttnesses yourselfes to satisfye you
whether yt be treason or noe, to this his councell canot be admitted.

DEVON[SHIRE]. To have councell in the meane tyme to advyse
with.

PRESIDENT. Not to pleade for him.

MULGRAVE. Ment by the order to have councell at all tymes.

RUSSELL. The reason of our order was for that at the comon
lawe the Judges are the parties councell, to directe the lawe; wheras
here they be not the Judges, but we, who have noe experience of
the lawe, and therefore we thought yt fytt to allowe councell in this
case.

DORSETT.   } Whether this order can be of force against
CHAMBERLEYN.   } a fundamentall lawe of the Kingdome.

CLEVELANDE. We may gyve a rule for tryalls here in this
House.

DEVON[SHIRE]. The last order is not against the fundamentall
lawe, for yt app[ear]es not yett whether he shalbe tryed for treason
as yett, or noe.

PRESIDENT. Yt is against the lawe for the partie accused at the
barr to have his councell.

An order *contra morem majorum*, and ag[ains]t *jus publicum*.

BRIDGEWATER. To advyse with his counsell, and they to speake
in poynte of lawe.

SAY. To allowe him councell to advyse withall, and yf any
thinge shall fall uppon the examinacion or his aunswere, then to
advyse with them allso.

Resumed.

Message from the Commons by Mr. Vicechamberleyn and many
others,

That the Comons desyre a conference betwcen a Comittee of both
Howses yf you soe please, at such tyme after this morninge when
you please.

BUCK[INGHAM]. Desyred expedicion.
The afternoone appoynted.

BUCK[INGHAM]. Gyves thanks for yt and desyred to have leave to be there, and occassion to speake in the generall.

PRESIDENT. They to explayne this. Yf we may not confer.

CHAMBERLEYN. Aunswere (as they doe us often) we wyll gyve them a meeting.

DORSETT. Reporters to be appoynted.

ESSEX. To be answered first.

Aunswered.

A committee of this wholl house wyll gyve meetinge[a] to a Committee of the wholl House of Commons at 2 this afternoone to receave what shalbe propounded to their LL^{ns}.

CLARE. The House to sytt this afternoone.

DORSETT. Reporters to be appoynted. They have appoynted 8. All to be reported.

To be as at Oxford, whe[re] Comons appoynted dyvers to take noates, and then 1. President. 2. Chamblcyn. 3. Devon. 4. Dorsett. 5. Say. 6. Bridg[water]. 7. Clare. 8. Norwich. Theis 8 to have convenient places, and to sytt firste.

SAYE. Touching Bristoll's peticion not to peticion to the K[ing] for him in some points; yett the things not to be rejected.

CHAMBLEYN. So settle this to morrowe morninge, and nothinge to be entred as yett, as concerninge the Erle of Bristoll's peticion.

Adj. to 7 tomorrowe .

MARTIS, 9 MAII, 1626.

[L. J. iii. 589.]

Prayers.

BUCK[INGHAM]. To gyve the Commons a speedy meetinge agayne this morninge about the buissines concer[n]ing them.

---

[a] These two words are erased by a pen-stroke, evidently by mistake.

May 9.   Message to the Commons.

That the LL. desyre that that meetinge which was begunn yesterdaye in the afternoone, and not then perfected, maye goe on presently this mornynge, yf yt may stande with their conveniencye.

*   *   *   *   *

Aunswere to the message.

They wyll sende answere by messengers of their owne.

Message from the Commons That the gentl[eman] whoe was ap-
poyted to proceede in the next parte of the charge is nowe visited
with sicknes, whereby the House is enforced to make use of one of
his assistants, and therfore desyre any other tyme to be appoynted
for this meetinge after this morninge.

Viz'., the pre-   BUCK[INGHAM].   That in respecte the Commons are to treate
amble of the   of some buissines concerninge the K[ing] this afternoone, and
subsidye.   therefore to move that this meetinge may not be till to morrowe
mourninge.

ALII *e contra* for this House hathe noe noatice what buissines is
there

Much debated.

Agreed to be to morrowe at 8.

Aunswered.

The LL. have appoynted to morrowe mourninge for this meetinge agayne, in respecte that the gentl[eman] originally appoynted
to delyver a parte of that charge may have his healthe against that
tyme, or his assistant the better provyded to perfourme the same.

L. KEEPER.   The auncyent orders of the House is not to speake
but once to one thing.   Requyred an interpretacion whether he
hathe spoaken once may, uppon newe reasons arysinge, speake
agayne or noe.

Resolved to the contrarye and none to speake twyce, unlesse he
be mistaken in his speeche, and hathe leave gyven him to explayne
himselfe.

DORSETT. ⎱   Whether he may speake agayne yf a new matter
SAYE.   ⎰   be moved.

Buck[ingham]. The L. Keeper to holde the speaker to the matter in question and not to goe from yt.

Tre[asure]r. None to speake twyce, though to explayne himselfe, till the L. Keeper hathe demaunded of the House (uppon his request) whether he shall have leave or noe.

The order reade.

None to speake twyce, nor noe newe matter, &c.

Confirmed.

And yf any L. stands up and desyres to speake agayne, or to explayne himselfe, the L. Keeper to demaunde of the House, firste, whether he shalbe admitted to speake or noe.

Say. Yf the cause requyre much debate, then the House to be putt into a Comittee.

Northie. The K[ing] to be moved to prevent the recourse of the citisens to the countrey fayres, for that they are nowe soe much visited.

Northie. There is a remayne of the generall accompt, &c. some small proporcion to be allowed for Westm[inster], &c. and the mayne of that remayne to be for Sally.[a]

L. Keeper remembred the buissines of the Erle of Bristoll's peticion appoynted for this daye.

The Judges sente for.

* * * * *

Ordered. Every L. to sytt duringe a committee, that the House be not disturbed.

The House was putt into a Committee.

Devon[shire]. The Judges to have a copye of the firste parte of the Erle's peticion.

The firste parte reade: touchinge the K[ing]'s accusacion and testimonye.

Essex. The Judges requyred to delyver their opynion. L. Ch[ief] J[ustice] desyres tyme to be appoynted for them to conferr thereof firste, and an order for yt.

[a] For redemption of prisoners from the Sallee rovers.

That parte of the peticion reade agayne.

The Judges to have a copye of soe much.

MOUNTAG[U]. To add that the K[ing] was then Prince, as Mr. Attourney desyred yesterdaye.

CANT[ERBURY]. Mr. Att[or]ney to be sente for firste.

DORSETT. Bristoll requyres that neether his Ma^ts accusacion nor testimony may be used.

MULGRAVE. Mr. Attourney, that he is Relator for the Kinge, &c.

CHAMBERLEYN.

LONDON. Br[istol] says he woulde not have the K[ing] to be a wyttnesse, for that yt is uppon a pryvat conference between his Matie and him. The civill lawe allowes yt. *Ubi judex non potest esse testis, hoc non tenet in summo Magistratu, quia non est judex proprie dictus, sed fons judicii;* and this case the K[ing] hathe referred to this House, soe that the House is Judge.

CLARE. We are all Englishemen, *et nolumus leges Angliæ mutare.* The Judges to resolve us howe farre the K[ing]'s testimony may be used.

PRESIDENT. The case to be agreed on, which is thus:—Wordes treasonable are spoaken to a Prynce. The Crowne discends uppon that Prynce. The question is, howe farr the testimony of the K[ing] for what was spoaken to him as Prynce may be used.

SAY. Not determyned whether treasonable or not.

CHAMBERLEYN. Leave out that word.

ESSEX. We to knowe the Judges' opynion of that only which Br[istoll] demands in his peticion.

MULGRAVE, *ad idem.*

DORSETT. And of that which Mr. Attorney demaunds allso.

TRE[SURE]R. The case to be sett downe as yt is in the K[ing]'s charge, and the Judges' opynion to be demaunded theron.

MA[STE]R ATTOURNEY. But lytle syngle testimony of the K[ing] to be offered. He wyll first open what he shall urge of the K[ing]'s testimony, and then the Judges opynion to be asked.

NORWICH. The question to the Judges to be first generall.

That beinge resolved of, then the particuler question to be putt to the Judges. May 9.

The Judges to resolve howe farre in cases of felony or treason, &c.

ESSEX. A comittee to drawe the question to be resolved on by the Judges.

*   *   *   *   *

The House resumed.

*   *   *   *   *

[Committee appointed " to sett downe the question.]

CHAMBERLEYN reported on this [manner?] in wrighting.

The questions to be proposed to the Judges which they are to take into consideracion and delyver their opynions to the LL.

1. Whether in case of treason or felony the K[ing]'s testimony is to be admitted or not?

2. Whether words spoaken to the Prynce, whoe after is Kinge, make any alteracion in the case?

DORSETT. For the tyme when the Judges are to delyver their opynion.

L. CH[IEF] J[USTICE] desyred Satterdaye next.

Agreed.

LINCOLN. The King to be moved touching the Erle of Arundell.

ESSEX. A comittee to be named to attend his Matie herin.

[Committee to attend the King.]

NORTHE. To agree on the words to present unto his Matie.

To desyre an answere, and, for that their LL^{ps} have longe expected yt, that his Matie woulde gyve a gracious answere.

[Petition for the King reported by the Committee].

*   *   *   *   *

DIE JOVIS, 11ᵐᵒ MAII, 1626.

Prayers.   [L. J. iii. 591.]

REX.

Tho K. Keeper and Tre[asure]r by the State.

REX. My LL. The cause of my coming to day is to expresse
the sense I have of all your Honors: for he that toucheth any [of]
you, toucheth me in a very greate measure. I have thought fytt
to take order for punishinge of some insolent speeches spoaken to
you by way of digression yesterday.

I have ben to remisse heretofore of speeches conceringe myselfe,
for that Buck[ingham] his ymportunity would not suffer me to
take noatice therof, least he might be thought to have sett me on.
And as he might come the sooner to his tryall. As touching the
accusacions ag[ains]t him, I can be a wyttnes to clere him in every
one. I speake not this to take any thing out of your hands, but to
shewe the reason why I have not heretofore punished insolent
speeches against myselfe. But nowe I hoape you wylbe as sensible
of myne honour, as I am of yours. I have noe more to saye unto
you at this tyme.

Et sic exiit Ds. Rex, and the L. Keeper attended his Maᵗⁱᵉ forthe
as he dyd at his cominge in. Being retorned, L. Keeper went to
his seate on the wooll sacke.

Jurati.

PRESIDENT reported the message to the K[ing] touching the
E[arl] of Arundell from the House 9 Maii, which was d[elivere]d
yesterday in the afternoone.

Reade the message *prout* 9ᵐᵒ Maii.

A gracious and present answere.

Aunswere reade, in wrighting allso.

My LL. I dyd lytle looke for such a message from the House.
I have ben of the House, and dyd never see such a message sent
from one House to another. When a message comes fytt[a]
your Sovereigne, I wyll gyve an aunswere.

[a] Left blank in MS.

The other LL. desyred me to knowe the exception. The K[ing] May 11.
sayd that his exception is to the peremptorines of the tyme for a V^e papirum.
presente answere, &c.

Message from the House of Commons, d[elivere]d by Sr The Duke of Bucking[ham] was p[re-s]cute.
Nathanaell Rich.

That the Knights, Citisens, and Burgesses of the House of
Commons, &c. V^e papyrum.

Aunswered.

The LL. have rec[eived] the message, and wyll in due tyme take
yt into their consideracion, and retourne an aunswere by messengers
of their owne.

BUCK[INGHAM]. Your LL^{ps} see what accusacions come against
me from the Commons. Howe I stood in their opynion heretofore,
you knowe. They have done me a favour to delyver me out of
their owne house to your LL^{ps}.

Whylest I defende my innocency, I wyll not mei[n]teyne that I
have not erred, an incident to emynent officers.

He reade yt out of a paper. q. Yf to be cutred.
V^e that, if his Grace wyll gyve yt.

Be sensible that he hathe longe suffred in his reputacion bothe at
home and abroad, and therefore desyred expedicion, but without
precipitacion. He dyd absent himselfe of purpose when Bristoll
was herde here, and soe woulde doe nowe.

But the Comons inviting your LL^{ps} to punishe me aforehand, I
wyll not gyve way to them, but referr myselfe to your LL^{ps} judgements, &c.

CLARE. A comittee of the wholl House was appointed, and 8
reporters. When that is reported, then to consider of an answere
to this message.

SAY. I suppose this buissines is settled, and therefore speake
touching that of the Erle of Arundell. The same Comittee to
attend ehis Matie this day to explayne the meaninge of the House
touchinge their desyre for a present aunswere, vizt, that they ment
only a speedy aunswere; and, considering what a precedent this

May 11.   may be to posterityc, that his Matie be pleased to gyve us leave to
peticion for his gracious aunswere.

DEVON[SHIRE] *ad idem*, and gave this reason, that uppon serch
of precedents Mr. Attorney sayd that there were some precedents
against the LL. priviledges herin; yett uppon viewe therof they
proved to be none. But this, yf not granted, wylbe a main precedent against us.

PRESIDENT. The word present to be made speedy.

BUCK[INGHAM]. Leave out speedy allso, and make yt only a
gracious aunswere.

The message reade without that worde "speedy" or "present."
Reade.

The first word "gracious" omitted, and made "your Ma^ts
aunswere."

PRESIDENT. That the 8 appoynted to reporte unto the House,
what was d[elivere]d at the Committee, that they have agreed to
compare their noates, and hoppe they shalbe ready for their reporte
on Satterday.

NORWICH. Yt being his tourne to reporte that which was
spoaken by the last man yesterday, at which the K[ing] tooke such
just excepcions this day, and therefore moved to be directed howe
farr he shall make reporte of that.

Agreed, that he is and ought to reporte all to the House, and
nothing spoaken or delyvered there is to be imputed to the
reporter.

And not to quallifye the same in any parte.

MULGRAVE. Bacon made his owne reporte very truly, though
he was accused of dyvers crymes by the Commons, for which he
was afterwards punished.

*   *   *   *   *

SAY.   { To reporte all that was d[elivere]d by the
BRIDGEWATER. { Commons touching Buck[ingham]; and to
make use of their papers; or rather, to reade the same out of their
papers.   Agreed.

L. CHAMBERLEYN. To move the K[ing] when the former   May 11.
Comittees shall attend with an explanacion of their former peticion.

CLARE. The Judges that are assistants to be at the Comittees
herafter.

DEVON[SHIRE]. The reporte is to be on Satterday, and the
Judges reporte then allso.

L. KEEPER. The Judges coulde not attende yesterday p[os]t
m[_]eridiem], being Wensday, for that they then meet together all
to consider of errours out of the K[ing]'s benche.

Adj. to Satt[u]rday at 8.

DIE SABATHI, 13 MAII, 1626.   May 13.

[L. J. iii. 593.]

Prayers.

ESSEX. The Judges to delyver their opynion touchinge the
K[ing]'s testimony in cases of treason or felony.

JUDGES. Wee purposed to have mett uppon those questions on
Thursdy laste in the afternone, Mr. Attourney desyrous to knowe
the tyme and to attende. In the interim Mr. Attourney brynges us
a message from his Ma[tie] and a [signifie?] of his. That his Ma[tie]
dothe conceave that this cause dothe concerne the right of his
Crowne. The questions beinge generall, and not knowing howe
dangerous yt may be to the future: [er]go, he thought yt not fytt
that we shoulde gyve any resolucions herin; yett contented we
shoulde, uppon mature deliberacion, delyver our opynions freely
and evenly uppon any particuler question that shall aryse concerninge the case of the E[arl] of Bristoll.

DEVON[SHIRE]. Whether to deferr this, or proceede to the
buissines of the daye.

The Judges have leave to retourne to their courts.

PRESIDENT reported the K[ing]'s answere to the peticion as yt
was penned.

The worde " presente" was not pleasinge unto him, by cause he never knewe yt used from one House unto another, but nowe ——

L. PRESIDENT reported that which was d[elivere]d at the Comittee of the wholl House of Commons 8 Maii.

[Report of the Charges against Buckingham, L. J. iii. 595.]

The House being moved to be adjorned to the afternoone,

THE DUKE. That yt myght be adjourned till Mondy.

For answere : many thinges reported otherwyse then there spoaken. Somcthing shorte; somwhat more. Shorte to be amended. But what is more, yf they have assisted any synce by addicion, he is gladd and wyll answere fully to all.

Nowe generally. For his owne abillityes or defectes, he wyll leave to examinacion. For gettinge of the places, &c., he dyd nothing but by the K[ing]'s commands, as he wyll prove. For Rocchell, the K[ing] is master of warr and peace, and to gyve noe accompt. Denyed the words " Judge by the event." Yt was an engagement of the late K[ing] his owne against Soubyse unreasonable rebellion, as he can prove yt, and wyll make app[ear]e. He gott him free of a farr larger promise, and, had the Prynce of Orange lyved, he had soe wrought with him that the Dutche shipps had not gone thither, and they wrought all the mischeife; for ours laye at anchor and dyd nothing. All delayes used by him, till the K[ing] expressly wrote. He hyndred their buying of 20th shippes more, all which he wyll make app[ear]e fully and cleerly.

Touchinge the brybes from the East Indian shippes, he wyll make yt app[ear]e that they gave him the first noatice what they ought him, &c.

Wyll prove he never treated with any man for offices, and that which was gyven was ymployed to the K[ing]'s use, &c.

Adj. to Monday, 9.

15 MAII, 1626.   May 15.

[L. J. iii. 609.]

*   *   *   *   *

[Report of the remainder of the Charges against Buckingham. L. J. iii. 610.]

DORSETT. We have had noates, &c.; but he that spake last omytted somwhat, which he desyred myght be added. 1. The comparison of the greate sums. 2. Comparison, not forgetting the veneryes and venefices of Sejanus.

BUCK[INGHAM]. Touchinge the deathe of the late Kinge, soe   q. si; et
good to me, that I never herde him spoaken of, thoughe in the   quatenus.
beste times, but yt brynges affliccion to [me?] : nowe, spoaken of in
this maner, much distempers me, and adds the more affliccions,
being condempned by that House allready, which heretofore had
commended me.

The late K[ing] comanded me to sende for that phissique, which
I had used in my sicknes, and sent one himselfe. I besought that
tryall myght be made therof, and yt was uppon Mr. Palmer, and
that encouraged the K[ing] to take yt, and 2 chilldren, and 1 man
of myne own.

In my absence he took yt himselfe before I came. I questioninge
one of the bedchamber for suspectinge me, his [Majesty] sayd that
none but devills would speake of any such thinge.

Touchinge his kyndred advaunced, I wyll not in this call my
accusers my enemyes, for, yf they were, they woulde fall uppon
worse then this, yf they had any thinge.

Compelling the L. Robartes to buy honour. The receyit of soe
much. Many thinges reported more then commanded, wyll answere
in wrighting, but this nowe, that the money went in my name, but
ymployed wholly to the K[ing's] use, and much more of myne
owne allso.

This, he had noe charge to accusse me of from the Commons,
viz', to accusse me of a patron of Heresye, the Pelagian Heresye,

which opynion I never herde of before. I was never fedd with any other mylke then of the Church of England, &c.; and I hoape never to lyve to have any other opynion of the Church of England, then to lyve and dye in yt, &c.

" That man," whereby he hath condempned me before he herde me. I wyll shewe that generall councells have erred, and I hoape that this allso.

Somewhat added, somewhat omytted.

SAY. That Buck[ingham] may shewe where any thinge hathe ben omytted, or added, that yt may be rectifiyed.

BUCK[INGHAM]. I spake yt not to taxe any of your Ld^{ps}, for I admyre that you have done soe well. I wyll shewe what was omytted, &c., yf ymposed on me. What was added, I am [contented?] to answere. But mean not this of your LL. I cleere you all.

PRESIDENT. What I reported was from the parties owne mouthe after he came from the conference. The partie then mollifyinge yt.

Reade yt agayne, and sayde that theis words were d[clivere]d unto him by the partie himselfe.

BRIDGEWATER. Some aspersion on me, touching the restreint of the gentl[eman] that made the prologue. Desyred the tyme of the restreint, and his noates myght be conferred, and the noates allso of all the rest of the LL. whoe tooke noates.[a]

The peticion of the Erle of Bristoll reade, for councell to be assigned him, and Mr. Maxwell to delyver his peticions herafter.

BUCK[INGHAM]. That the noates taken may be compared.

SAY. To knowe uppon what grounde.

BUCK[INGHAM]. I thought you had ymposed uppon me to shewe what was omytted, &c., and that is the grounde.

[a] Here follows, carefully erased with a thick penstroke:—
"DORSETT. The Prologue. Spea[ker], having spoken of the deathe of the late Kinge, added: " I am commanded by the House of Comons to take care that nothinge myght reflecte uppon the honour of the deceased K[ing], nor the K[ing] nowe lyving."
In the margin is: " The E[arl] of Dorsett says he wyll sett this downe himselfe."

SAY. With leave graunted. Your L^p hathe allready specifyed   May 15.
that.

Adj. *ad libitum.*

Agreed, to be shewen for any particuler, but not in generall.

BUCK[INGHAM]. I have yt taken in characters.

The reportes to be brought in first.   Agreed.

Then the noates yf occasion requyres of any particuler.

Resumed.

SAY. To reade his noates himselfe, as he hathe taken them. And reade them, &c.

DORSETT. Whether there be any precedent to have theis reportes entred?

Precedents were cyted: vizt, of the E[arl] of Midd[lesex].

BUCK[INGHAM]. I wyll not declyne yt.

BRIDGEWATER. This hathe not been long used. The precedents to be perused.

BUCK[INGHAM]. To bringe in their noates.

MULGRAVE. Never agreed to be [don?]

BUCK[INGHAM]. Moved to have the noates of those that are here.

DENNY, CLARE, &c. Noates shorte taken, not to be entred· nor used. A worde here, and another there. May conduce to memory, but incerteyne, and may conduce to your owne prejudice.

BUCK[INGHAM]. Yt is the fashion of this House to make reportes out of their memory, or noates, and rectificacion by noates and memoryes.

DEVON. My noates are so shorte that you can make noe judgement out of them.

Adj. *ad libitum* agayne.

PRESIDENT produced his noates and reade them.

" I am comanded by the Comons," and vowed that theis were his noates; but what he reported he had out of his owne mouth.

BR[IDGEWATER] read his noates. " Phissiq[ue]," &c.

May 15.   Tender in examinacion; not to reflecte uppon the person either of the deade or present K[ing].

DORSETT.   My noates are the lyk.

SAYE.   " Enumeracion of the particuler charges.   Administring of phissique to the deade kinge without advyse of Councell. Wherin, &c."

Resumed.

Quere howe
farre I shall
enter thes pro-
testacions, and
the occasion
therof.

BUCK[INGHAM].   Not to reflecte uppon the dead nor lyving Kinge, viz'., on the deade K[ing] touchinge poynts of Goverment, uppon this K[ing] touchinge the phissique.

DEVON[SHIRE].   Not mente soe.

NORTH.   Not mente soe, and every man to delyver his sense.

BUCK[INGHAM].   He soe conceaved yt then, &c.

SAY.   This may trenche uppon all our loyalties.

DORSETT.   Buck[ingham] to explayne himselfe.

BUCK[INGHAM].   Explayned himselfe that by the orders of the House you can not speake of yt ther.

Adj. *ad libitum* agayne.

Resumed agayne.

Every man[a] to make his protestacion whether he herde Sir Dudley Digges speake any thinge that might be interpreted treason, &c.

GREY OF WARKE.   Protested he herde him not speake yt, nor any thing that myght [be] thought treason.

DENNY *ad idem*.

DORSETT.   Not to speake of Digges his meaninge, but his wordes.

BUCK[INGHAM] *ad idem*.

DEVON.   Yt concernes us to tell our opynions of the sense of words allso, what he intended thereby.

NORWICH.   To sett downe the words and what our conceiptes were.

<hr>

^ " mant" in MS.

NOWELL.   I understood noe yll meaninge, nor any thing spoake that might be soe conceaved.

BRIDGEWATER.   I desyre not to be taught what to saye, but to knowe unto what to speake.   The words to be first agreed on.

DORSETT.   Not to cleere the partie prisoner without leave first from the Kinge.

SAY.   To cleere our selves

TRE[ASURE]R.   The words to be sett downe and agreed on.   To be expounded, when the partie is called in question.   We are not taxed.   Neede not cleere our selfes.   Not taxed by the K[ing].

BUCK[INGHAM].   I desyred only the words.   We to proceed noe farther least we distate his Matie.

SAY.   The LL. words that spake last are, that the words were such, that so touched ――

Protested on his honor that he conceaved not that Diggs had any such intencion, neether were his words soe: neether dyd he conceave them such.   Yf he had, he woulde have presently reprehended him.

MOUNTAGUE.   Protested as much.

GREY OF WARKE, *ad idem.*

NOELL, *ad idem.*

RUSSELL, *ad idem.*

NORTHE, *ad idem..*

CROMWELL.   Uppon his honor and salvacion, *ad idem.*

VAUX, *ad idem,* and he herde noe such thing.

DUDLEY, *ad idem.*

SCROOP.   He is not tyed to make any protestacion.

MORLEY, }
PERCY,   } *ad idem.*

Ep[iscop]i:

ST. DAVID.   Not speake without comandment.

SARUM.   He herde nothinge that myght touch the [King]'s honor.

LANDAFF. The words which he spake are such as the [Earl?] [a] spake, but canot conceave his meaninge.

CHESTER herde nothinge that he could conceave dyd touch the K[ing]'s honor.

Co[VENTRY]and L[ICHFIELD]. Uppon his faithe herde nothinge, neither can conceave anything that myght, &c.

ROCHESTER herde the words; hoaped he had noe yll meaninge, for he prayed for the K[ing].

NORWICH. No rationall construccion can be made of any thing that can touche the K[ing's] honor.

DURESME. Desyres to be sylent, for that the words are not stated. The gentl[eman] had noe wyll to reflecte any thing on his Ma[tie], but the words being spoaken must be taken as they are. They may be yll taken, yett he prayed for the K[ing], and I think in his harte he ment well, &c.

LONDON. Conceaves not what the words were, nor any question putt for this. He herde them not when they were spoaken.

WYMBLEDON was not present.

SAY. Uppon his honor and before God, I dyd not apprehende that the gentl[eman] dyd speake or intended to speake anything that myght reflecte.

ROCHEFORD. Ad idem, to his understanding.

MULGRAVE. According to his former protestacion.

CLEVELAND ad idem.

BERKS[HIRE] ad idem, at large.

WESTMORLAND. Not charge his memory further then his noates ; after all the charges, &c. Recyted the words. Protested, he thought he had noe yll intent.

BOLLINGBROKE. Protested that nothing which was spoaken by Diggs coulde reflecte on the K[ing].

CLARE. Protested that his noates are that the conclusion of

---

* I think the letter is an " E," but I am not certain. If so, it means, I suppose, the reporter, the Earl of ——.

Digges was uppon all the charges, and not uppon this, protested *ut*
alii.

HOLLAND. He ought to be expl[ained] and questioned,

DENBIGH. Protested he herde nothing that ——.

CARLILE. Not to speake till comaunded.

CAMBRIDGE. He herde lytle, but nothinge that can touch the
K[ing]'s honor.

DEVON[SHIRE]. Tooke noates, nothing that can touch the
K[ing]'s honor.

WARRWICK *ad idem.*

NORTH[AMP]TON. He herde not the directe words, but he
herde nothinge that myght touche the honor of the Kinge.

BRIDGEWATER. I doe confesse I thynk this protestacion is
somewhat to soone. I wyll not trust my memory, nor penn soe
much as to determine the words, much lesse wyll I enter into the
thoughts of him that spake them. But touching my owne, &c. at
that tyme, &c., *prout alii.*

MOUNTGOMERY. I herde nothing come from him that coulde
reflecte on the K[ing]'s honor.

EXCETER. Was not present.

DORSETT. I have d[elivere]d the words; lett him be the inter-
preter himselfe. But I conceaved them not to be treason. Yett I
then thought them soe ambiguous, that he woulde be troubled for
them, and cyted Salisbury for them.

NOTTINGHAM. He herde his words. But coulde not make
any construccion that any way myght tende to the K[ing]'s dis-
honour.

LINCOLN, *ad idem.*

ESSEX, *ad idem.*

HARTEFORD, *ad idem.*

OXON, *ad idem.*

KENT, *ad idem.*

BUCK[INGHAM]. Noe question is stated. He spake the words,
as is confeste by many. (He sayd, he woulde quytt the K[ing]'s

service, soe he myght have freedome of speeche, &c.) Yf you wyll not speak of wordes by cause your noates are not here, howe can you speake of the generall?

Leave the interpretacion of the words to ——.

PRESIDENT. I thynk certeinly that he meant a savinge of all what he had sayd, for the K[ing]'s honour.

But here is a dislocacion of the words, and soe they des[e]rve and requyre an explan[ation] from the partie.

The gentl[eman] himselfe, when he gave me the words, protested he had not thought nor intencion to reflecte anything on the K[ing]'s honor, and so.

TRE[ASURE]R. Not present.

CANT[ERBURY]. Not present, but bounde to speake of the pious and duitifull respecte of the K[ing to his father.

DEVON[SHIRE].

The peticion of Bristoll for Councell to be assigned him.

Adj. agayne *ad libitum.*

The president of 5 H. 4 reade.

Much debated whether to be allowed councell or noe.

Resumed.

CARLYLE. | The order 28 Maii 1624 to be shewen the
DEVON[SHIRE]. |

K[ing], and that yt was made when he, as Prynce, was presente.

KEEPER. To peruse the book whether the Pr[ince] was p[rese]nte or noe.

WESTMORLANDE. A committee to sett downe the message to the Kinge.

The order 28 Maii 1624 reade.

The order 6 Maii 1626 read.

A precedent aᵒ 6 R. 2, where councell is denyed to Sᴿ ——

q. This of the L. Keeper. L. KEEPER. To delyver a message, vizᵗ.: A serious debate of this matter, fynde an order 28 Maii, 1624, the Prynce himselfe

p[rese]nte.   An order 6 Maii, which dothe not touch the fundamentall lawe.

Question.   Whether a message shalbe sent this nyght to the
K[ing] or noe?

Agreed *per pluries.*

KEEPER.   To agree on the message.
Recyted the same as before.

The message 8 Maii.

The order 28 Maii.

The order 6 Maii.

Question.   Whether that message shalbe delyvered to the K[ing]
this nyght or not, by the L. Keeper?

Agreed *per pluries.*

Adj. to morrowe at 9.

DIE MARTIS, 16 MAII, 1626.

[L. J. iii. 627.]

*   *   *   *   *

L. KEEPER.   I dyd yesterday delyver that message which you
requyred late: for the p[rese]nte he coulde not make an answere.
I to wryte agayn this alternoone, and to signifye unto you that he
wyll retourne you an answere with all the sp[ee]d he cann.

*   *   *   *   *

LINCOLN.   Answer to be retourned to the comons message.
Buck[ingham] whom yt concernes to withdrawe himselfe in the
meane tyme.

CONWAYE, *e contra, quia* the K[ing] sayes he can cleere him of
all that is complayned of by the Comons, and as touching that
before us, they not to be judges, and we spurres, &c.

After much debate the Duke offred of himselfe to goe out.

PRESIDENT.   The question is, first, whether we shall thynke of
makinge an aunswere to the Commons.   Here is an accusacion of

May 16.   the Commons, but noe profe nor answer, and till the aunswere, we cannot judge, and, though the Duke desyres·to goe out, yett yt wylbe against our priviledges; for from E. 3 to the E[arl] of Mid-d[lesex] his case, noe L[ord] accused here went out until his aunswere.

Adj. ad libitum.

Debated firste, what shoulde be in question. Whether the peticion of Bristoll, or the declaracion of the Comons, or the message, &c.

But not stood uppon.

Then whether the Duke shall withdrawe himselfe, or not, duringe the debate?

Much and longe debate. The Duke to have noe voate.

Resumed.

TRE[ASURE]R. The Duke's presence wylbe necessary to be p[rese]nte, &c.

NORTHE. Agreed, none to sett here whylest his owne matter is in debate, &c.

CLARE. Whether to retourne an aunswere to the Comons peticion or noe. Yf yea, then to sende aunswere to this effecte, vizt., that the order is not to sequester any member of this House untill he hathe aunswered his accusacion, and to signifye to them the tyme is gyven him for his aunswer, &c.

ALII <i>e contra</i>.

Debated, whether the message from the Commons 11mo Maii hathe trenched on the LL. priviledges or noe. And what answer is to be sent to the Commons.

MENEVEN[SIS]. The priviledges of this House are trenched uppon by the Commons by their message 11mo Maii.

Adj. ad libitum agayne.

Debated, whether that message dothe trenche on the LL. priviledges or noe.

That was declyned.

The message to be agreed on.

Resumed.

DORSETT.   ⎱   To sett downe the answer to be sente the Com-
SAY.   ⎰   mons.

*   *   *   *   *

BUCK[INGHAM]. Desyred tyme to advyse what councell to have, and when to make his aunswere, which he woulde very shortly resolve[a] on.

DORSETT reported the aunswere conceaved by himselfe, and reade yt.

SAY reade his draught of that aunswere.

ESSEX. To reade noe aunswere at all untill the Commons have sente agayne.

Question. Such of your LL.ps as are of opynion that the message to the House of Comons shoulde be forborne till further consideracion, say content; others, not content.

Voated.

Counted *per* Essex *et* Carlile.

The proxies called for, not reade.[b]

Adj. to 9 to morrowe.

DIE MERCURII, 17mo MAII, 1626.

[L. J. iii. 629.]

*   *   *   *   *

L. KEEPER delyvered a message from his Ma[tie] in answere of that to him concerning Bristoll. Advised therof:—Referred to your LL:—Fundamentall lawes not:—Pleased to discend:—As app[ear]e to:—Content and gyves full licence in this particuler, that the Erle

----

[a] " Resolved," MS.

[b] Here follow these words erased : "SAY. Yt was agreed, noe L. to sytt here duringe the tyme his owne buissiness is in debate. Moved. the Duke to putt in his."

may have councell to advyse and pleade for him. As touchinge the order of 28 Maii, 1624, not satisffyed with that generall order.

Ordered, Mr. Serjant Hedley, Mr. Ser[j]eaunt Bramston, Mr. Serg[ean]t Crawley, and Mr. Anthony Lowe to be of Councell with the Erle of Bristoll to advyse with him in his cause and allso to pleade his cause for him.

Signed by the Clerke and sent to the Erle, and the Erle is to sende worde when he wyll sende his aunswere.

BUCK[INGHAM]. Whether he shall aunswere the wholl charge or such parte therof as you shall appoynte, or the aggravacions allso.

All the charge, and the charge only, but not the aggravacions.

A question was moved whether the reportes of the aggravacions shalbe d[elivere]d to the Clerke or noe to be entred.

BUCK[INGHAM]. Desyrous to aunswere the aggravacions, that he myght clere the matters therin, and to noe other purpose.

MULLGRAVE. That they may be brought in, and entred, beinge reported (as the manner is), and when the Duke is cleered (as he doubted not) then they may be taken out of the booke agayne.

SAY. The clerke is bounde to enter the reporte by virtue of his oathe. Yett yf the D[uke] be cleered (as he doubtes not) then to be taken awaye, and the roll allso.

DORSETT. Hereafter noe aggravacions to be brought in together with the articles. This to be prevented by some order.

BRIDGEWATER. Noe copyes of the aggravacions to be d[elivere]d unto any.

MULGRAVE. Except to ourselfes.

TRE[ASURE]R explayned what aggravacions are, viz[t], noe parte of the charge, but only a recytall of the particulers of the charge and inferences, used at the examinacion or tryall of the cause. At the tryall heretofore, the K[ing]'s councell was not permitted in this House to use any. The partie is not to aunswere. Keepe them forthe, till you have cause to make use of them, either at the examinacion or tryall.

WALLINGFORDE.   Such aggravacions as concerne the facte to
be here, &c.

SHEFFIELD.   A comittee to take out those scandalous partes as
are not pertinent, and the rest to be entred.

NORTHE.   To be d[clivere]d to the Clerke only, and not
recorded, and then the House, and the Duke allso, to have resorte
to them, but not to be brought in as records, nor noe copyes to be
gyven.

DURESM.   To resolve what charge you wyll imposse on the
Duke, and the Duke to have lib[er]tie to aunswere any parte of the
aggravacion, yf he please.

CHAMB[ER]LEYNE.   The charge.   The L. D[uke] to rec[ieve].
The reportes to the Clerke, and he to keepe them secrete.   The
Duke only to have resorte unto them, or any of the House.

Theis aggravacions to be delyvered unto the Clerke to be kepte   Ordered.
by him closse from all save from the members of this House, and noe
copyes to be d[clivere]d unto any save unto the members of this
House.

The L. Duke to aunswere to the engrossed charge sent up by   Ordered.
the Commons, but not to the aggravacions, unlesse upon perusall
theroff he shall fynde any thinge fytt to be answered.   And yf the
House fynde fytt that the Duke shall answere any parte of the sayd
aggravacion, then he is to answere them allso.

The L. Duke to have use of the Originall aggravacions for   Ordered.
expedicion.

The conclusion of the Commons' declaracion reade, wherin they
requyre a savinge of replicacion unto them.

Mr. MAXWELL.   The Erle of Bristoll desyres to be herde this
afternoone.

Ordered:—The Erle of Bristoll to make his aunswere on
Frydaye next, yf he be able, and Mr. Attourney to be here
then.

The Erle of B[ristol] is to chooce whether he wyll aunswere
either in the morninge or afternoone.

May 17.   And Mr. Maxwell is to warne the K[ing]'s councell to attende accordingly,

LINCOLN. To renewe our humble peticion to the K[ing] by the wholl House on behallfe of the Erle of Arundell.

The L. Chamberleyne to knowe when the House shall attende his Matie.

ESSEX. A comittee to drawe up the peticion.

*   *   *   *   *

PRESIDENT reported the peticion from the House unto the K[ing] touching the Erle of Arundell. He reade yt.

1.

2. Approved of.

NORTHE. The L. Chambleyn to ——

Adj. to Fryday, 9.

May 19.   DIE VENERIS, 19mo DIE MAII, 1626.

[L. J. iii. 631.]

*   *   *   *   *

CHAMBERLEYNE. The K[ing] is pleased that the House attende him this afternoone at 2, at Whitehall.

*   *   *   *   *

Bristoll called for to the barre.

BUCK[INGHAM]. That he myght retyre, least he shoulde gyve some distaste to the Erle of Bristoll.

Graunted, and so he dyd retyre.

Bristoll at the barre. Kneeled. Wylled to stande up.

KEEPER. You have rec[eive]d Mr. Atto[rney's] charge. The LL. expecte your answere.

[Answer of the Earl of Bristoll. L. J. iii. 632.]

L. KEEPER. Yf you have any thinge ells to saye.

BR[ISTOL]. Yf Mr. Att[orney] wyll saye anythinge to me, &c. To proceed.

B<small>R</small>[ISTOL]. Unequallity, being under restreynt, to followe any May 19. thing against Buck[ingham]. Urged their LL^{ps} promisse of an equallitye.

His councell enfourmes him that there is noe treason ag[ains]t him in the charge, save one that comes nere a statt[ute] touching relligion. To take such course by resolucion with the Judges, or otherwyse as you please, that yt may be declared whether his case be treason, before he be further proceeded in. That he may have libertye to examine wyttnesses.

A paper lefte with the Prynce.

Protested against the, &c.

Cleered the Duke of Buck[ingham] of any intencion of yll in his acte to the late K[ing]. Indiscrecion.

M<small>R.</small> A<small>TTOURNEY</small>. Br[istol], that noe matter of forme or legallity shalbe taken holde of to his prejudice; promissed to take holde of the matter only, not of the forme. Desyred allso that, as Bristoll dothe, the House may directe the course howe the wittnesses may be examined, and howe proceeded further.

Br[istol] withdrawen.

A<small>TT</small>[ORNEY]. To have a copy of this answer.

Granted.

Then when he hathe perused the answere, he wyll move the LL. further; but, in the meane tyme, the House to take some course for exam[ination] of wyttnesses.

L. K<small>EEPER</small>. Mr. Attourney to advyse with the K[ing]'s councell.

First^a before he was brought, his councell to be encouraged.

The Erle to have leave in the company of Mr. Maxwell, the Read and Usher, to goe abroade and take the ayre for his helthe's sake; ordered. granted at the Erle's humble request.

Ordered.

C<small>ONWAY</small>. Bristoll hathe touched upon me in some poyntes.

^a This word is preceded by "Bristoll called to the barre agayne, but." Erased, without anything else being substituted.

May 19.   Suspende your opynions of me untill that comes to be spoaken of, and his answere herde.

Bristoll at the Barre agayn.

KEEPER. Your peticions at this tyme the LL. canot settle; but wyll in due tyme. For your helthe, to goe abroad. That the LL. have assigned you councell, and the K[ing] wylling to yt. Yt is neither the K[ing]'s meaninge nor the LL., but that they should freely councell you without any doubte at all, or any discouragement.

BRISTOL desyred his humble thanks to be retourned to his Matie and their LL^ps.

*   *   *   *   *

_____

May 20.   20 MAII.

[L. J. iii. 645.]

*   *   *   *   *

L. KEEPER. His Ma^ts aunswere reade.

*   *   *   *   *

The K[ing]'s aunswere reade agayne.

A mocion to referre this to the Comittee for priviledges.

Ordered.   Referred to the Comittee for priviledges, to meet on Mondaye next p'.m. to consider whether the priviledges of the House ar preserved, and how to proceede to preserve the same, and they to reporte to the House.

*   *   *   *   *

BUCK[INGHAM]. 8 shippes and pynaces thought fytt to serve the shippes to Newcastle, which wyll amount to 17,000^li per an[num], which may be meinteyned by the measurage of coales in London, which anciently belonged to the Admiralty. Desyred that yt may be converted to that purpose. The Citty hathe offered, &c.

Moved the Cittye to be called hether, and to consider of their
right to this measurage of coales, and of the contribucion to meinteyne Dungen-nesse.

And 5*s.* on the tun allowed to by the K[ing] for buildinge of
shippes above soe many tonns. To consider of this, and howe to
settle yt agayne, and the disposinge therof, and of what moldes to
buylde those shippes. For nowe greate, for lastinge. The enemy,
nymble shippes, which wyll not laste longe; the shipprights to be
called for and to consider, &c.

Referred to the comittees for municions.

Devon[shire], Conway, Wimbledon added.

To meete on Wensdaye next.

*   *   *   *   *

LUNÆ, 22 MAII, 1626.

[L. J. iii. 647.]

*   *   *   *   *

DEVON[SHIRE]. To sende for Mr. Att[orney] to knowe when
he wylbe ready to make his proofes ag[ains]t the Erle of Bristoll.

Sente for.

Mr. Attourney came.

L. KEEPER. Whether you have considered of the answer?

Mr. Att[orney] reade yt, and taken noates.

Moved to name a comittee to take exam[ination] on bothe sydes.

[Committee named, L. J. iii. 648.]

BUCK[INGHAM]. That yf he shalbe ready to aunswere the com-   Granted.
pl[ain]t of the Commons, before Mr. Attourney shalbe ready to
proceede in the charge ag[ains]t Bristoll; that he may not staye,
but proceede to his answere.

And that he may have councell allowed him.   Graunted.

May 22.   And that, yf the K[ing] wyll gyve him leave, then to have some
Referred. of the K[ing]'s councell that attende here.

Referred to the Comittee for priviledges.

The Committees to examyne wytnesses touchinge the K[ing]'s charge against the E[arl] of Bristoll, and the Erles defense.

To meete on Thurseday next in the afternoone, to have power to subdyvyde themselves yf they please.

Ordered.   Mr. Attourney to begyn on Thurseday to produce his proofes and wyttnesses, yf he be ready.

And yf the E[arl] of Bristoll wyll produce his proofes and wyttnesses, then he maye, or when he please.

The wyttnesses to be sworne in open House.

Denyed To be considred of in due tyme.   BUCK[INGHAM]. His charge consistinge of many hedds, that he may be judged for eache as he shalbe ready to make his answere after exam[ination].

R[esponsi]o.   To be considered of in due tyme, and then to be soe disposed of as he may not be confounded with the multiplicitye of charges at one tyme.

Adj. to Wensday at 9.

May 24.   DIE MERCURII, 24to MAII, 1626.

[L. J. iii. 649.]

*   *   *   *   *

BUCK[INGHAM] desyred a tyme to be appoynted for ——

Ordered.   Ordered. The Duke of Buck[ingham] may putt in his aunswere to the charge of the Comons the firste sitting daye after Whytsundtyd.

Reporte.   PRESIDENT. Reported the peticion agreed on by the Committee of priviledges touching the E[arl] of A[rundel], and their priviledges.

Reade the same.

Ordered to be presented to the K[ing] by the wholl House.

The L. Carlyle and L. Carleton to goe p[rese]ntly and knowe the
K[ing]'s pleasure when they shall attend.

Reported all-o touchinge three of the K[ing]'s Sergeants to be of
the Duke's councell, vizt.,

Serg[ean]t Richardson, Crew, Damporte; allowed by the Comittee
yf the K[ing] shall allowe them.

DEVON[SHIRE].   To be resolved whether this House may call
any others to assiste, when theis 3 of the K[ing]'s councell are
allowed to the Duke.

DUKE.   Contented to be allowed but any one of them, or 2, or
none. Desyred to have one of them.

S[E]RG[EAN]T DAMPORTE with leave.

That the K[ing]'s Serjeaunts are tyed by their oathe not to be
of councell against the Kinge. Soe that his conscience woulde not
permitt him. Otherwyse he was very readye.

MENEVEN[SIS].   Some othes are of that nature that a condi-
cionall is naturally to be understood, though not expressed, which
may be dispensed with. He moved allso to knowe whether his oathe
may not by the fundamentall lawes of the land be dispensed with.

SARUM EP[ISCOP]US.   An oathe promissary may be dispensed
with by the partie unto whom yt was mad.

Adj. *ad libitum.*

Resumed agayne.

The Serg[ean]t's oathe to be brought hither to morrowe morninge,
and the Judges to be here then.

*   *   *   *   *

DIE VENERIS, 26 MAII, 1626.

[L. J. iii. 651.]

Prayers.

L. KEEPER.   My LL. His Matie hathe wylled me to signifye to
your LL^ps that he dothe mervaylle that his meaninge in his last

answere shoulde be mistaken. And for the better cleeringe of his yntencion, hathe comanded me to delyver unto your LL^{ps} his further answere, which is that your LL^{ps} last peticion was soe acceptable to his Matie that his intent was then, and he is still resolved to satisfye your LL^{ps} fully in what you then desyred.

All buissinesses to be adjourned till Frydaye nexte.

Adj. to Fryday next at 9.

DIE VENERIS, 2do JUNII, 1626.

[L. J. iii. 652.]

* * * * *

L. KEEPER. A message from the K[ing] touchinge the E[arl] of Arundell.

He reade yt.

The Clerke reade yt allso.

That his Matie hathe thought of that buissines, and hathe advysed of his greate and pressinge affayres, which are such as makes him unwyllinge to enter into disspute of things doubtefull. And therefore, to gyve you cleere satisfaccion touchinge that cause, whereby you may proceede more cheerfully in the buissines of the House, he hathe endeavoured, ass much as may be, to rypen yt, but cannot yett effecte yt, yett is resolved that by Wensdaye sennight at furthest he wyll either declare the cause or admitt him to the House. And addeth further uppon the worde of a Kinge, that yf yt shalbe sooner rype, which he hathe good cause to expecte, he wyll declare yt with the soonest. And further, that yf the occassion doe enforce to staye to the tyme prefixed, yett he dothe not purpose to sett such a shorte ende to the Parlement, but that there shalbe an ample and good space betwene that and the ende of the session to disspatche affayres.

Dyvers moved to adjourne the House.

Dyvers e contra.

Adj. ad libitum.

Dyvcrs to adjournc, &c. For that the reassurringe of buissi-   Jnue 2.
nesses wyll queytt their claymc of priviledgc, and soe this delaye
wylbe a president of the breache of their priviledges, &c.

Alii to proccedc in respectc of the weight of buissinesses nowe in
hande.

Alii in respectc of the K[ing]'s promisse, he havinge not prefixed a daye, and that that is a waye of gayne to the priviledges;
and allso in respect of Arundell himselfe, that he may come hither
with the K[ing]'s favour, &c.

Others that the priviledges are allready broaken, and cannot be
healed but by the Erle of Arundell's cominge and syttinge in the
House.

Some ——

        Resumed.

All other buissinesses to be adjourned but this of the E[arl] of
Arundells concerninge the priviledges of the House, and the House
to meet thereon to morrowe mourninge, and to be putt into a
Comittee to consider therof.

    Adj. to 9 to morrowe.[a]

DIE SABATHI, 3 JUNII, 1626.

[L. J. iii. 658.]

   June 3.

  *   *   *   *   *

L. KEEPER. A message; that his Ma[tie] hathe ben very desyrous
to avoyde as much as in [him] lyeth all d——   and
and desyrous to thynk of any expedient that may stande
with the buissines, and yett gyve your LL[ps] all sattisfaccion.

—— [b] Your LL[ps] adjourne the House till Thurseday next.

Agreed to gyve his Ma[tie] thanks.

    Adj. to Thursdye next at 9, and all buissines.

---

[a] Repeated twice in MS.   [b] Word obliterated by a blot.

DIE JOVIS, 8 DIE JUNII, 1626.

[L. J. iii. 654.]

*   *   *   *   *

L. KEEPER. A message from the Kinge, That on Satterday last he sente you worde that on this day he woulde this day.

To take away all restreynt.

Arundell came to the House.

ARUNDELL. Rendred to the K[ing] all possibble thankes for taking of his restreynt from him, and to your LL^ps. To have a good opynion of him. Protested his feithe and allegeance to the Kinge.

CHAMBLEYNE. That the Duke of Buck[ingham] his answere be nowe reccaved.

NORTHE. That thanks, &c., to his Matie, and that some entraunce be made that this restreynt of a Peere without cause shewen be not drawen into a consequence herafter.

CANT[ERBURY] *ad idem.*

Referred to the Committees for priviledges, &c.

Peticion of the Erle of Bristoll reade. To be sente for presentlye.

BUCK[INGHAM]. Touching the charge of the Comons, and their aggravacions. Yf his answere to the charge gyve their LL. satisfaccion, he hoapes the aggravacions wyll fall of themselves.

He reade much out of a paper.

He wonders not at the charge; but had they knowen the perticulers, or gyven him any invitacion to have opened the perticulers unto them, he doubtes not but their LL^ps had not ben troubled with them.

Much in cleeringe the House of Commons, and that himselfe shalbe cleered allso by them.

Concluded with an humble supplicacion that he may delyver in his answere in writinge:—

Which his Grace delyvered to the L. Keeper, from whom the Clerke receaved yt, and the Duke's councell reade yt at the barre, the Duke standinge in his place.

After the reading of the answere, the Duke made a shorte speeche and desyred expedicion for the examinacion of his cause, and soe withdrewe himselfe.

CONWAY. That he myght putt in an answere to the charges ag[ainst] him by Bristoll, and to have cou[n]cell allowed him, and tyme appointed.

Bristoll brought uppon his peticion.

L. KEEPER. What he woulde propounde.

BR[ISTOL]. Ready nowe, in the afternone or to morrowe.

Withdrawen.

Agreed to be at 2 p^t m.

Called agayne, and soe signifyed to him; for that the LL. purposse to gyve him an honorable hearing.

Adj. to 2 p^t m.

DIE JOVIS, 8vo DIE JUNII, 1626.

Post meridiem..

[L. J. iii. 668.]

Prayers.

BRISTOLL at the Barr uppon his peticion.

Sorry the occasion of your troubles, &c.

Move ——? 2.

1. Charge against him treason.

2. The articles exhibited by him as an Embassador concerning Buck[ingham's] unfeithfull[ness].

For the 1.

Howe he comes to stande here arrayned here of treason.

Lynked with priviledges.

3 yeares.

When the Pr[ince] came out of Sp[ain], kyssed his hand, &c.

But synce this Parlem[en]t, his wrytt stayed, though formerly he had yt. Added nothing to his former offences. Buck[ingham] [beyond?] helde on. Soe his crymes encrease.

Noe mediacion could gett his writt, brought to the lowest estate before. First, all his estate seised: his places taken away, and to pull up his honor from rootes, his writt stayed. Mediated by his lettres to the L. Keeper: had his writt with a lettre of restreynt.

That you may see my restreynt is not auncyent, I wyll produce 2 lettres of Mr. Sec[retary] Conwaye offred me soe as I woulde keepe my selfe as I was, &c., I myght lyve secure.

Not permitted to defende my innocency, for that wyll laye dishonor on the Kinge.

Thus we must all be involved in this, not to defende our selves, &c.

Sente for as a traytor, contrary to all other proceedinges I ever observed in other causes.

The order of this House, noe Peere to be restreyned without yt be for Treason, &c. Pray God yt tourne not to our prejudice: all charges to be for treason herafter against [a] man restreyned.

His snyte touchinge the poynt of treason. A man to be accused of treason, a hundred to one yf he escapes. I have had an honourable favour of the Parle[men]t, but that ended, none wyll advyse me; therefore, for all your Honors I beseech your LL^ps that I may be tryed here, &c.

For his particuler: that Mr. Att[orney] wyll make yt knowen whether he wyll proceede in the charge of treason or noe. Yf he wyll, then to assigne some inference, and that yt may be tryed and determined.

Not to lyve longe under the name of traytor without proceeding.

For the further proceeding: that the dispatches of Mr. Walter and himselfe may be brought in by inventorye, he to have the one parte; and when Mr. Att[orney] moves for the K[inge], that I may attende allso. Thus much for his own perticuler.

I have ben many yeares ymployed as Embassador. Yf Mr.

Attourney shall not reply, then to take noatice that I shall [lose][a] the . The most materiall poynt of my defense. Not open the misteries without leave of the K[ing].

Having served the K[ing] thus many yeares. The D[uke] of B[uckingham's] power is such that I cannot gett leave for any message to be d[elivere]d to the K[ing]. I sent my son. Conway sente worde that what I had to say I shoulde speake in the Parlement House.

Loathe to doe yt, unlesse for his owne defense. Yett when Mr. Att[orney] hathe replyed, that he myght shewe somwhat to 2 or 3 of your LL[ps] rather then openly.

Touching Buck[ingham].

That his accusacion of Buck[ingham] is noe recriminacion, but originally intended by him theis 2 or 3 yeares against the Duke. Besydes, the Duke hathe noe charge against me.

Buck[ingham] charged me for the Pr[ince] going into Sp[ain]. I, that the Duke plotted yt 6 moneths before. Buck[ingham], that I sought the conversion of the Prince. Protested the contrary. I, that B[uckingham] dyd carry him thether of purposse that he myght be converted to Popery, and brought him cunningly to a conference for that purposse.

I am charged with the losse of the Palatinat. But I wyll prove there is more fault in Buck[ingham] for this then in all the men of Englande.

I am charged with breache of the peace. Buck[ingham] moved yt. Olivares answered, yt wyll not prosper, being gyded by such an hand as his. Yett he sware yt.

I acquaynted the Pr[ince] with my lettres against Buck[ingham]. The Pr[ince] unwylling at the first I shoulde sende them; that yt were fytter some other shoulde wryte of them. Yett I answered. The Pr[ince] withstood yt not. Soe I sent those lettres, soe that nowe theis cannot be sayd to be recriminacion. When I sawe the K[ing] last, he sayd I had never offended him. Tollde my wyfe soe.

[a] There is a blank in the MS.

June 8.   I wrote some 16 lettres since: yf any unduitefullness found in them, contented to be judged a traytor; soe, I may be firste herde.

I here as a traytor.

Contrarywise Buck[ingham] being accused by me (a publique minister of the State) goeing abroade.

1. An equallity betweene him and B[uckingham].

2. The Att[orney] to proceed ag[ains]t him.

And yf he doe not make yt appe[ar] that the Duke of B[uckingham] hathe served the late K[ing unfeithefully:—this K[ing]—: the narracion in the other Parlement very false:—then, &c.

The K[ing] to leave them both on equall termes.

The hedds he hathe gyven in are only hedds.

The LL. to putt yt into a legall course, and the proofes shall not be wanting.

Prayed an equallitye.

Concl[usion], that he may wayte on in the outer roome, whilest any thing is moved against him, aad that the hedds of his requeste may be redd.

Which he d[elivere]d, and they were reade.

Bristoll withdrawen.

Adj. *ad libitum.*

CARLILE. This but a foundation of a digression. Moved the accusacions and all myght be herde together.

DEVON[SHIRE]. The perticuler requests only to be nowe considered of.

Much debated.

1. The firste parte of the peticion reade.

Whether the charge be treason or noe?

Mr. Attourney was comanded to shewe whether he wyll proceede, &c.

Mr. ATT[ORNEY]. That he rec[eived] the charge from his Ma[tie], and is ready to produce his proofes.

For the case, Mr. Attourney says yt is layd downe in the charge June 8.
allready.

His interr[ogatories] are ready, and some wytnesses.

SAY.   That the Comittee maye meete to morrowe.

ATT[ORNEY].   The House wyll not sytt then for the wytnesses
to be sworne.

NORTHE.   The L. Keeper to be here and the House to sytt to
morrowe at 8, and then the wyttnesses may be sworne on bothe
sydes, and noe other buissiness done for that tyme but this by the
House.   Then the Comittee to proceed to the examinacion, and
then the House to determyne whether yt be treason or noe.

2. That his owne and Sʳ Walter Aston's dispatches may be
brought in, &c.

ATT[ORNEY].   He hathe copyes of his owne, any dispatches
that he shall demande, to be ——

Any dispatches that the Erle shall demand to be brought in, and
he have the use of them, and of any others that shalbe produced
against him.

3. That his Maᵗⁱᵉ ——

To be considered of as occasion shalbe offred.

4. That he come to the House with Maxewell, &c.

Granted.

The firste reade agayne.

1. The House to sytt to morrowe at 8, and such wytnesses to be   Ordered.
sworne as Mr. Attourney or the E[arl] of Bristoll shall produce.
And then the Comittee to proceede to take the examinacions; and
the answeres to the rest of this parte of the peticion to be deferred
to further consideracion after full examinacion taken by the Committees and reported to the House.

2. All such dispatches as Mr. Attourney shall make use of   Ordered.
against the Erle, to rest here to be used by the Erle for his defense.
And the House to be suytors to the K[ing] for any other dispatches
to be brought hither for the Erle's defence, as the Erle shall per-
ticulerly name.

June 8.
Ordered.

3. When any such occasion shalbe offered, the House wyll then consider what course shalbe taken herin.

Ordered.

4. This to be graunted.

SAY. A reason to be gyven the Erle why the wholl parte of the first parte of his peticion is not graunted.

1. To his favour.

2. Yf declared within the compasse of treason, then —— (v[id]e papyrum).

The Erle at the barre agayne.

The L. Keeper tolde him what ——

CARLILE. Expressed his joy of all impediments removed. Moved the Comittee for defense and safety of the Kingedome (consideringe of the daungers nowe threatened and prepared against us from all places) to meete uppon the firste opportunitye.

Adj. to 8 to morrow.

<hr>

June 9.

VENERIS, 9 JUNII, 1626.

[L. J. iii. 669.]

*   *   *   *

L. KEEPER. A message from the Kinge. Observed with what duitye you had proceeded towards him all this parlement, and of your care to provyde for the safety of the Realme, and that he doubted not but you had seen the fruicts of your labours had money ben supplyed, &c.

Had written a lettre to the Speaker about yt, a copy wherof he had sente unto their LL^ps.

Enter the lettre.

Which was reade.

Message from the Commons by Sr Humphrey May and others.

That they have herd that the Duke of Buck[ingham] hathe putt in his answere to their charge ag[ains]t the Duke, and therefore requyre a copye of that aunswere, as they may reply thereunto, yf June 9. need be, and sende up their proofes.

Aunswered.

The LL. doe resolve to take their message into consideracion, and to send aunswere by messengers of their owne, with all convenyent sp[ee]d.

This is referred to the LL. Comittees for priviledges, and they to Ordered. meete theron this afternone at 2 in the p[ainted] ch[amber].

Bristoll at the barre.

Moved that his Secretary beinge sicke in the countrey, that he may be examined by commission.

Mr. ATTOURNEY. That the interrogatories may be firste viewed.

BR[ISTOL]. That his charge ag[ains]t Buck[ingham] may be putt into a legall forme by the K[ing's councel, and prossequuted.

Jurati pro Comite Bristol, to make trewe answeres to such questions as shalbe demaunded of them by the LL. Comittees, vizt.

The peticion of the Erle of Bristoll read, that the K[ing]'s councell may charge the Duke of Buck[ingham].

The K[ing]'s councell to take consideracion of the hedds d[eli- Ordered. vere]d in by the Erle of Bristol ag[ains]t the Duke of Buck[ingham] and of such other informacions as the E[arl] shall gyve them, and putt them into the forme of a charge ag[ains]t the sayd Duke, and to present the same to the House on Tuesday next.

Jurati ex parte D[omi]ni R[eg]is v[e]r[su]s Comitem Bristol.

Sr Dudley Digges.

Endymion Porter.

ESSEX. Carlile added to the Comittee for priviledges.

Adj. to 9 to morrowe.

SABATHI, 10 JUNII, 1626.

[L. J. iii. 671.]

*   *   *   *   *

BUCK[INGHAM].   The Commons have requested copyes of my
aunswere.   Desyre that when yt is sent downe you wyll recom-
mende yt unto them with haste.

One thinge he had reserved in his answere, desyringe some
assistance for leave from his Matie to open some secreats touchinge
the buissines of Rochel, which otherwyse he durste not doe, but
nowe His Matie had gyven him leave to doe yt.

Desyred that his further aunswere to that of Rocchell may be
added herafter.

That a member of this House hathe taken lib[er]tye to speake
ag[ains]t me agayn.   Unworthy of any aunswere; but sythe he
had alledged this ag[ains]t him, he woulde forbeare to sytt here
untill his cause be herde, which his Grace desyred their LL^{ps} to
expedyte.

And soe he departed.

Reporte.

THE L. TRE[ASURE]R reported that the Comittee for priviledges mett; and, seekinge for precedents, they fynde yt ordinary
for the Commons to replye unto their accusacion, and that they
ought to have a copye of the Duke's answere, and that they may
sende up their proofes and wyttnesses to be examined here.

Agreed, the copye to be sent them.

Agreed, that a supplye of the Duke's aunswere touching Rochell
be added, and viewed fyrst by a Comittee.

SAY.   That the LL. Councell doe consider of yt, and sett yt
downe themselves, either in a schedule or otherwyse, as they shall
thynke good.

His councell were sent for.

CONWAY. To renewe the mocion begunn by Carleton; viz', that the comittee for defense of the Kingedome may meet, &c. For many matters moved by the councell of warre are stopped for wante of money.

But he moved in respecte of many matters that canott be deferred, the daungers are soe greate, as apperes by many advertisements, especially by the Pr[ince] of Orange; of a liste of an army preparing there at the leaste of 40,000 men, with the names of the commaunders. They gyve yt out for Irelande, but intended for England, and 1º Julii *novo stylo* appoynted for the day. This apperes allso by many other advertisements and lettres intercepted, and the pylotts sente, &c.

[*Er*]*go:* hygh tyme for counsell; and though there be noe money, yett the realme must be mainteyned, and this House fyttest for that councell. To make some lawes fytting for the fyndinge of forces to defende the same.

DEVON[SHIRE] *ad idem*, and the sooner the better.

Agreed. This Committee to meete on Monday next in the mourninge.

All the LL. Lieutennants are added to the Comittee for defense of the Realme.

Bristoll's peticion reade for wyttnesses: reade and granted.

Ordered. The Erle of Bristoll, with Mr. Maxwell, to have leave Reade and ordered. to goe to the King's councell at such fyttinge place as they shall agree on, to informe them touching the charge to be drawen by them against the Duke of Buck[ingham]. And yf the Erle be sicke, then one or more of the K[ing]'s councell to resorte to him, and to receave his informacions, and to acquaint the rest herewith. And the K[ing]'s councell are requyred to appoynte an indifferent place for their sayd meetinge, and gyve the sayd Erle noatice therof.

*　　　*　　　*　　　*　　　*

The Duke's answere amended by an addicion to the 7th Article in margent.

June 10.

Message to the Commons.

That the LL. have sent a copy of the Duke's answer. Yt is the Duke's humble desyre to their LL^{ps}, and their LL^{ps} recommend the same to them that their reply may come up with the soonest.

The subcomittees and Comittees for priviledges, &c., to observe their former dayes.

Carleton, Grandison, and all the LL. of the Councell of warr added to the Comittee for defense.

*   *   *   *   *

June 12.

DIE LUNÆ, 12 JUNII, 1626.

[L. J. iii. 673.]

*   *   *   *   *

Bristol at the barr.

His peticion was reade to that purposse.

Humble suytor for expedicion of his cause, in respecte of the charge, and his sicknes.

That Mr. Attourney may hasten his wyttnesses, and some day this weeke appoynted for publicacion. And that 2 lettres which he lately receaved from Mr. Secretary Conway may be reade.

Reade. { The one dated 25 Febr., 1625.
{ The other 24 March, 1625.

And one other wrytten from Sr Kenelm Digby, dated 27 May, 1625.

The peticion of the Erle of Bristoll reade, that his charge be hastened.

R[esponsi]o. Mr. Attourney to be sente unto to be here in the afternoone.

Adj. to 3 p^t m.

LUNÆ, 12 JUNII, 1626 Pᵗ M.

[L. J. iii. 674.]

Reporte of the Comittee for the defense of the Realme, per Cant-
[erbury].

Many proposicions which tended to goode effecte, yett nothing
soe concluded as needes any reporte.

An accident fytt to be reported, of some sharpenes of speech
betweno twoe LL. there: that an order myght be settled to proceede at their meetings without any asperitye herafter.

ESSEX.   Thatᵃ the words myght be sett downe, &c., by a com-   Denyed.
mittee.

CLARE.   An order to avoyde the lyke herafter.

MULGRAVE.   A Comittee to sett downe an order.

Referred to the subcomittee for priviledges to sett downe an order
to prevent the lyke ynconvenience herafter.

To meete this afternoone, at the rysinge of the House.

The subcomittee reade.

Mr. Attourney, being demaunded what daye may be assigned for   Bristoll.
publicacion of wittnesses, aunswered, he hoaped some daye this
weeke, for that Sʳ Walter Ashton is nowe come to towne, but coulde
not appoynte a daye.

But wyll examin such as sworne by Bristoll p[rese]ntly, &c.

Wᵐ Bosswell, Batchelour of Divinity, sworne, ex parte comitis
Bristoll.

MR. ATTOURNEY.   That he and Mr. Sarg[ean]t Crewe have ben
with the E[arl] of Bristoll, and agreed that his owne councell shall
drawe up the charge ag[ains]t the Duke of Buck[ingham], and the
K[ing]'s councell wyll advyse on yt and present yt to the House so   Approved.
soone as may be.

*   *   *   *   *

ᵃ A penstroke is drawn through the words "Essex. That," probably by mistake.
The idea meeting with no favour, Elsing may have intended to obliterate the speech,
but on second thoughts inserted the marginal note instead.

DIE MARTIS, 13 JUNII, 1626.

[L. J. iii. 675.]

* * * * *

MR. ATTOURNEY moved:

Desyred to rec[eive] direccions from the LL. in the buissines nowe dependes.

Dyvers wyttnesses' names gyven in by the Erle. Yf he wyll examin this afternoone, he wyll attende to examyn them allso, and to examin others to morrowe.

And whether he may produce any to be examined for the K[ing] of him selfe?

Named Sr Wm Curteyn, Ph. Burlemacchi, Ph. Jacobson, [   ] Rollstrolph, S^r Ro: Pye.

The Clerke is to make a warrant for their apperance to be examined here.

Mr. Attorney. Touching the charge ag[ains]t Buck[ingham].

Br[istol] had an order.

S[er]g[ean]t Crewe and I wayted on Br[istol]. After some discourse of yt, we thought yt fytt that his owne councell shoulde drawe yt up, and shewe yt unto us, which is not yett brought unto us.

Mr. Att[orney] to produce his wyttnesses to morrowe at 8, to be sworne then, and examined afterwards.

Report per CANT[ERBURY]. The Comittee examined one wyttnes.

Br[istol] thought yt to his prejudice, for what Mr. Att[orney] examines ag[ains]t him is not published, but what is taken in exam[ination] for Br[istol], being taken by the K[ing]'s councell, they knowe yt presently. He moved therefore that an indifferent course may be taken. Either some other then the K[ing]'s councell to take the exam[inations], or the partie examined to sett downe his owne exami[n]acions, and they to be kept closse till publicacion granted.

A mocion that some of the M[aste]rs of the Cha[ncery] might   June 13.
attende to take the examinacions, and to be sworne to keepe them
privatt.

Sʳ Robert Rich, Sʳ Edward Salter, Sʳ Peter Mutton appoynted.

Whoe were presently sworne to keepe closse and secrete all such
examinacions as they shoulde take, untill publicacion.

Reporte *per dominum* PRESIDENT for a rule that all asperity of
speech be prevented betweene the LL. either in the House or at
Committees.

He reade the order.

CLARE. That the Comittee myght receave satisfaccion allso in
the House. To be added.

To be entred in the Roll of Orders.   Ordered.

WARWICK. The subcomittees thynke fytt the clerke drawe up
a roll of the judgements in a° 18 Ja.

Ordered, and the Subcomittee to viewe yt firste, and then to be   Ordered.
retourned by the clerke into the Chauncery.

CONWAY remembred the articles ag[ains]t him by Bristoll 1°
Maii. A suitor that he may putt in his aunswere to them.

Ordered.

He delyvered his aunswere presently, which was reade.

For which the L. Conway gave their LLᵖˢ thankes.

A mocion, that Bristoll may replye unto this aunswere, yf he   Ordered.
please.

*   *   *   *   *

MERCURII, 14 JUNII, 1626.   June 14.

[L. J. iii. 678.]

*   *   *   *   *

Jurati ex parte Domini Regis: George Gage, George Digby,
Tho. Wake, Phillip Jacobson, Phillip Burlemacchi, Sʳ Wyll. Cur-
teen, Sʳ Roberte Pye.

*   *   *   *   *

DIE MERCURII, 14 JUNII, 1626, 1ᵗ M.

[L. J. iii. 679.]

*   *   *   *   *

Juratus in causa Domini Regis versus Comitem Bristoll; Sʳ
Walter Aston, Kᵗ.

*   *   *   *   *

BRISTOLL at the barre.

Mr. Att[orney] hathe called dyvers to be examined whoe are
straungers to him.

Mr. Att[orney] refuseth to reply.

1.   Moved that Mr. Attorney may shewe to what poynt he wyll
examin them, or ells that he may not be concluded by them, but
may examyne them allso, &c.

2.   And that he may have the dispatches, &c.

3.   And yf the deposicions of these straungers prove not any parte
of the charge, that they maye be burnte.

4.   That he may produce a lettre which he receaved from the K[ing],
which he hathe kept secreate.   Yett yt is published, and a copy
therof reade here, produced by Buck[ingham].

Desyre the copy may be brought forthe and examined by the
originall, and that then he may be herde to speake to that lettre,
which he supposeth to be surreptitiously gotten.

Ilis peticion to that purposse reade.

Withdrawen.

CONWAY denyed that that lettre was surruptitiously gotten, and
avowed the same to be dictated by the Kinge himselfe, and desyred
their LLᵖˢ to consider of Bristoll's taxinge his honour on this manner; and avowed the copye, and protested his feithefull service to
the Kinge, &c.

The Erle of Bristoll's peticion exhibited this day was reade in 4
partes.

The firste parte reade: That he be not concluded, &c. June 14.

MR. ATTOURNEY. That the E[arl] of Br[istol] may not be
permitted to reade those lettres which he produceth to prove, as he
is informed he dyd.

All denyed he reade any at the Committee.

He may produce his lettres to be proved, but not to publishe them
till tryall.

To the firste parte this answer was gyven, viz.

Such lettres wherein *arcana imperii* are conteyned, as he affirmes, Ordered.
he may produce them to be proved, and yett to keepe them secreate
till he hathe cause to use them for his defense, and then, though
publicacion be graunted, he is not to be concluded from them.

That for as much as Mr. Att[orney] hathe not replyed, &c., to To the 2. 3.
sett downe to what points of his charge or the Erles answere he in-
tendeth to exam[ine] them.

Mr. Att[orney] is to examine none, but to meinteyn the poynts of Ordered. To the 2 and 3.
the charge, or to contradict the Erles answer.

Aunswered in the 2. 3.

That the lettre reade here (v^e 30 Marcii) by the Duke of Buck- 4. Not answered nowe.
[ingham] may be brought into the House, &c.

Mr. Attourney to serche amongest his papers for yt, and to
brynge yt hether to morrowe.

The same copye to be brought which was reade here.

This to be answered to morrowe.

DURESME. Conway to be cleered.

Bristoll at the barre.

L. KEEPER. Whether you wyll undertake to prove that this
lettre was surruptitiously gotten.

R[esponsi]o. He dothe believe yt.

1. The lettre which is the grounde of my charge differs in the All to be croste out.
poynte of my charge.

2. Yf the Secretary have a direccion for a lettre from the K[ing],
and he followes yt not, he may thynke yt surrupticiously.

3. The lettre sayes I yielded to a condicion for the breeding of
the K[ing] of Boh[emia's] sonn in the Emperer's court, whilest the

June 14   K[ing] was in Spayne, wheras the condicion was not agreed to till
after the K[ing] came out of Spayne.

I wyll gyve more reasons when the lettre is brought in.

I wyll not undertake to prove yt. I only beleeve yt uppon theis
reasons.

CONWAY. In the presence of Bristoll denyed the lettre was
surrupticiously gotten, and affirmed that the Kinge himselfe penned
the lettre after he had written yt. Desyred to be cleered.

BRISTOLL. That the parte of the peticion may be reade, whether
yt concernes the L. Conway.

Beinge reade.

All to be   I never knewe that your LL^p sent yt.
croste out.
And I desyre that noatice may be taken that the L. Conway
sayes that he drewe that lettre and sent yt. Then he gave many
reasons why he thought yt surruptitiously gotten, and chiefly that
touching the breedinge of the K[ing] of Bohemia's sonn.

I desyre that the L. Conway be not cleered, but that they may
proceede to examinacion and to tryall, and that I may replye to his
answere, &c.; and that he may not be my judge.

CONWAY. I can produce the originall penned by the King.

I desyre not to be his judge; nor to be at his tryall, but am not
wyllinge this to be the cause.

Withdrawen.

The LL. doe not fynde any cause to believe that this lettre men-
All to be   cioned in his peticion was surruptitiously gotten by the L. Conway
put out.   from the K[ing]: and therfore they doe all cleer his L^p therof for
anything doth as yett apere unto them.

All to be put out touching this.

4.   The 4th parte of the E[arl] of Bristoll's peticion is not to be
Agreed.   entred till their LL^ns have further advysed theron.

Bristoll at the barr agayn.

The L. Keeper related unto him the answeres unto each parte of
his peticion.

Withdrawen.

*   *   *   *

DIE JOVIS, 15ᵗᵒ JUNII, 1626.

[L. J. iii. 681.]

*   *   *   *   *

BUCK[INGHAM].   Hathe retourned the copye of the lettre reade
here 30 Marcii.   Yt was reade by the K[ing]'s comandement; taken
from hence by his comandem[en]t; and now retourned at t[heir]
LL^ps comande.

Reade.

PRESIDENT.   Yt agrees with the originall.

L. KEEPER hathe rec[eived] his Ma^ts comission for dissolucion of
this Parlement, not for any cause gyven by your LL^ps, but proceeding from the Commons.

Maxwell to be sente to the Commons with a message to come and
heare yt reade.

MOUNTAGUE.   That the wholl House move the K[ing] to make
a pawse of this, for that yt may be of a most daungerous consequence.

MULGRAVE ad idem.

Et CLARE.

Et DEVON[SHIRE], and some to be appoynted to sett downe in
wrighting what shalbe presented to his Matie from the wholl House.

SAY et NORWICH.

Generally.

L. President, Chembleyn, Carlile, Hollande, to declare unto the
King that the wholl House desyres to wayte on his Matie with their
humble advyse.

[Committee " appoynted to drawe up the advyse to the Kinge."]

WARWICK.   That eache Erle may gyve the Clerke 40ˢ, each,
Viscount 30ˢ, each B^p and Baron 20ˢ, for his paynes in this and
former Parlements.

Ordered.

June 15.   ST. DAVID.   A message to be sente to the Commons to understande what they wyll doe to joyne their LL.[ps] herin.

To be deferred to sende any message to the Commons before the K[ing]'s aunswere.

Reporte.   DEVON[SHIRE] reported the advyse to the K[ing], and reade yt.

To be fayre wrytten.[a]

PRESIDENT, &c., retourned.   His Ma[t] expressed that his wounde is not from your LL.[ps], but from the Commons.   And therefore that the L. Keeper sende for the Commons, and reade the comission.

CARLILE.   That the K[ing]'s expresse commandement is that nothing of this message to him be recorded.

NORTHE.   That Bristoll's restreynt by this House be taken of.

Aunswered, that the dissolucion dissolves the restreynt.   And soe in all other restreynts, unlesse yt were uppon the censure of the House.

Granted.   MULLGRAVE.   That dyvers beinge sente for for breache of priviledge of Parlement towards the E. of Lincoln his man: that the

_____

* The petition is copied into the book, near the end, amongst a number of blank pages, and is as follows:—

"15[to] Junii, 1626.

"May yt please your most excellent Ma[tie]. We, your Ma[ts] humble and feithefull subjects, the Peeres of this Kingedome, havinge receaved this morning a message from your Ma[tie], intimatinge an intention to dissolve your Parlement, and remembriuge that we are hereditarilye your Ma[ts] greate Councell of this Kingedome, doe conceave that wee cannot deserve your Ma[ts] gracious opynion expressed in this message unto us, nor discharge our duitye to God, your Ma[tie], and our countrey, yf, after the expression of our greate and universall sorrowe, we dyd not humbly offer our feithfull and loyall advyse to contynewe this Parlement, by which those greate and apparent daungers bothe at home and abroade, and signifyed unto us by your Ma[ts] commaunde, may be prevented, and your Ma[tie] made happye in the duitye and love of your people, which wee holde the greatest safetye and treasure of a Kinge; for the effectinge wherof our humble and feithefull endeavours shall never be wantinge.   (Ex[r])   "H. ELSYNGE."

Reade and approved of generally, but not presented to the Kinge, for his Ma[tie] refused to heare of any, &c.   Commaunded that this be not entred.

L. Keeper may free them when they come or punishe them, yf his
L^p shall see cause.

MULLGRAVE. That the subcomittee may peruse and perfecte the Journall booke.

Denyed, after a dissolucion of Parlement.

HERTEFORD, SUFFOLK. Each Earle to gyve the gentl[eman | usher 40^s, and each B^p and Baron 20^s. Agreed.

NORTHE. Each L. to paye the Clerke's man 5^s allso. Ordered.

The Commons came with their Speaker.

The Comission reade, and the Parlement dissolved accordingly.

www.ingramcontent.com/pod-product-compliance
Lightning Source LLC
Chambersburg PA
CBHW020113030726
47498CB00006B/2082